Lonely Planet

Travel with
children

WITHDRAWN

DESTINATION
IDEAS

PRACTICAL
INFORMATION

KIDS'
ACTIVITIES

FAMILY-FRIENDLY TRAVEL WITHOUT THE FUSS

 CONTRIBUTORS

SOPHIE CAUPEIL
Sophie started travelling in the back seat of a car from Paris to Bombay at the tender age of four. Since then, she has been round the world with her husband and children, Gaspard and Elvire, from Africa to Sri Lanka passing by Madagascar, Mexico and Cambodia. She still sets off as often as possible for the other end of the planet (preferably India), but always with the family. From real experience she wrote the practical section of this book, which provides all the tools you need to prepare for departure, have a smooth trip and return home safely. She has also written the pages on camping, the desert and travelling by boat. Sophie would like to thank Claire Lienart, Manuelle and Colette Delaitte, Anne Labretenière, David Lelait, Nadège Tricot, Gérard and Martine Legoubin, Édouard, Gaspard and Elvire.

JEAN-BERNARD CARILLET
Author of dozens of Lonely Planet guides, Jean-Bernard set off for Polynesia with his daughter when she was just a few weeks old. Since then, he has never tired of showing her new horizons, from the Middle East to New Caledonia or the Baltic States. An unrivalled globetrotter, in this guide he makes a sporting or cultural adventure accessible to anyone. He is responsible for the pages on diving with the family and wildlife watching, as well as the introductions for Africa, the Middle East and the Pacific.

SANDRINE GALLOTTA
From Sri Lanka to Mexico, Sandrine criss-crossed the planet before becoming an editor and author of travel books. She has always dreamed of showing the world to her granddaughter. She has compiled many of the pages in the Country by Country section.

JONATHAN TARTOUR
A great traveller who prefers to walk, Jonathan did not wait for his daughter and two sons to reach adolescence before training them up on walking tours abroad. He habitually finds himself out in the wilds with the family, sometimes at the other end of the world. He shares his experience in his writings here on hiking.

MARIE THUREAU
A travel-book editor who has compiled many of the country pages in this book, Marie first began marching round the world weighed down by huge backpacks. She has now learned to travel light. Spurred on by her experience, she is leaving for new adventures, as soon as she can, with her partner and two children, Aimée and Abel.

OTHER CONTRIBUTIONS
This book has also drawn on the knowledge and expertise of a number of Lonely Planet contributors. A big thank you for the help of Marie Barriet-Savev, Cécile Bertolissio, Françoise Blondel, Dominique Bovet, Jean-Bernard Carillet, Sophie Caupeil, Muriel Chalandre, Olivier Cirendini, Christophe Corbel, Régis Couturier, Philippe Cramer, Emmanuel Drogue, Christophe Escudero, Didier Férat, Thomas Fitzsimons, Sandrine Gallotta, Émeline Gontier, Carole Haché, Évelyne Haumesser, Bénédicte Houdré, Carole Huon, Sophie Lajeunesse, Élisabeth Lau, Dominique Lavigne, Julie Marcot, Alice Martin, Dr Ménager (pediatrician at the Pasteur Institute in Paris), Dolorès Mora, Frédérique Sarfati-Romano, Dominique Spaety, Juliette Stephens, Riina Subra, Karine Thuillier, Marie Thureau and Barbara Vernet.

ENGLISH EDITION
This English edition has been translated from the French by **Heather Lima**. It has been updated and revised.

CONTENTS

INTRODUCTION

If you want to spend quality time with your children, help them learn, grow and gain a better understanding of the world and humanity, then travelling abroad is a great way to do it. So take the plunge and set off on an adventure with the family. Whether you're new to backpacking or a seasoned globetrotter, you shouldn't have to put away your passport just because you have started a family.

As a travelling family you'll talk and share experiences, which these days we often struggle to find time for in our busy lives. Babies, toddlers and teenagers may surprise you with their adaptability and affability when the hold of regular routines loosens. Watching your children engage with different surroundings can change your perspective and invigorate you with a renewed sense of wonder. As your children blossom before your eyes in response to new encounters and experiences, it's hard not to share their excitement. Their questions will reveal the depths of their intelligence and the scope of their understanding, which in turn will enrich your appreciation of your children. Their horizons quite literally expand as they realise that the world is bigger than your home town or city, and with it comes an appreciation of cultural diversity, the seeds of tolerance and empathy, which will stay with them for the rest of their lives.

Your trip will also be transformed: you will be given a warmer welcome, people will look on you more kindly, and will have more intimate encounters with locals, as parenting provides a strong common bond with people all over the world.

Anxieties may conspire to place obstacles in your path: which destination to choose and how to get there, what to pack for a change of climate, or fear of strange, 'exotic' diseases. Will the youngest scream all the way through a 24-hour flight? Will the eldest still be able to gorge herself on fruit and avoid a tummy bug? Will you be able to go diving if the kids are in tow? Stop worrying: nothing really stands in your way, even if dragging your brood to the other end of the world does involve a certain amount of know-how. The first part of this book will provide you with basic advice and tips to get to grips with travelling with the family while avoiding disaster.

A big part of getting the planning right comes from choosing a suitable holiday destination for your family. The second part of the book will help you make this decision by looking at a broad range of destinations. Specific activities, points of interest, comfort, health, what to watch out for and the best time to go: every country is carefully scrutinised so that you can be confident about your choice. As several days walking in Morocco is completely different to seeing dolphins in Florida or playing at explorers in the Amazon, this guide gives you a broad idea of where to start. It is then up to you to choose the country that will thrill the small boy who cannot sit still, the little girl who dreams of being a princess or the teenager who is mad about sport. Once you are there, the joy of watching them, wide-eyed in wonder, embarking on this amazing adventure will mean that any misgivings will soon be forgotten. While travelling with children might not be glamorous, relaxing or easy, what will stay with you is the joy of sharing those unforgettable experiences. Better than memories, you will pass on the taste for travel to your children. They will be eternally grateful.

⤳ THE ART OF TRAVELLING WITH CHILDREN

GETTING READY TO GO

CHOOSING THE DESTINATION – TOGETHER

So you want to go abroad! But where exactly? Involve your children in the decision; speak to them about the different countries you are considering, whet their appetites by borrowing a few guidebooks from the library. Think about what they are interested in (see the Destinations by Theme section, p44), and the sort of trips that are possible at their ages (see Holidays with a Difference, p33). Consider how well they might be able to deal with culture shock. Weigh up the length of the trip in relation to the difference in time zones. A difference of four hours or more will mean you will need time to adjust on the way out as well as on the way back, especially children: a week away is too short. Upon your return, you should allow two or three days for the children to recover before starting back at school. The cost of the trip matters as well. Research fares thoroughly: sometimes the air ticket is on the pricey side but the cost of living is so cheap that a change of scenery and the unforgettable memories of 15 days at the other

end of the world will cost you the same as a week's skiing near home. Think about the mountains in summer, the possibilities of camping or farmstays. With a little imagination, it is often possible to match your means and your dreams. Finally, let go of the worry: a trip abroad does not necessarily mean danger. Of course, some precautions are essential, but common sense is the best form of prevention! Your children will be warmly welcomed across the globe. Thanks to them, you will no longer be tourists but a family ready to meet other families. It is one of the most wonderful ways to discover a country. Your children will love it. So will you!

FORMALITIES

Before setting off, make sure your papers are up to date. Many countries now issue biometric **passports** and most insist that all children have their own passports. These usually cost less than an adult one because they are often valid for a shorter period of time. Certain countries demand a passport that

Travelling gives you time and space to reconnect as a family

is still valid six months after the intended date of return. So if yours is due to expire within that time, you will need to renew it even if it is valid for the entire length of the journey.

The introduction of biometric passports is coupled with stricter rules on passport photos (eyes open, mouth closed, no smiling, etc). In some cases, it can be quite difficult to take an acceptable passport photo of a baby or toddler. It is important to read and comply fully with all passport photo instructions and to accept that it may take an afternoon's photography to get the right one.

In the US both parents need to accompany a child under 14 when applying for or renewing their passport. You also need to bring proof of the child's US citizenship, evidence of the child's relationship to yourselves, and parental identification. These rules are in place to protect against international abduction.

Border authorities may demand to see proof that the person accompanying the child is the parent (eg a birth certificate). Any other adult accompanying a child should carry a parental letter of consent authorising them to take the child out of the country.

If the destination requires a **visa**, everybody in the party will need one, which can be costly. Visas mean more form-filling and more photo-taking. Whenever you go away, it is vital that you take out **travel insurance** to cover any medical bills incurred and the cost of repatriation on health grounds, but it is particularly important when travelling with kids. You can do this through a travel agent, an insurance company or bank. Make sure the contract covers the whole family and is valid in the destination country; check what can be claimed back and any exclusion clauses. Check that if you need to curtail or cancel your trip due to one member of the family becoming ill, everyone is covered. Many credit cards include medical travel insurance and repatriation assistance covering all members of the family. However, these guarantees are usually only valid for trips of fewer than 90 days and only if you have paid for your air ticket or holiday with the relevant card. What is more, there is often a ceiling on the amount of money you can claim. Some of the better cards offer insurance for cancellation, luggage, vehicle, snow, theft or loss. Find out from the deal offered by your credit card company and watch out for any restrictions!

If you live in the Economic European Area (EEA) and intend to travel in this region or Switzerland, it is wise for you and your children to apply for a European Health Insurance Card (EHIC) as well as travel insurance. This will entitle most nationalities in this area to reduced-cost or free medical treatment when abroad.

If you need vaccinations for your chosen destination, get an **international vaccination card** stamped when you receive your injections and take it with you.

Check whether your national driver's licence is valid in your intended destination or whether you will need an **international driving permit**. This is usually valid for 12 months and can be obtained through your automobile association or post office.

Before setting off, make copies of any important papers and the main pages of your children's health records and split them between the bags (take a few extra passport-sized photos). You could also scan the documents and attach them to an email sent to your own mailbox or utilise cloud storage options. To avoid taking out your papers every time, you can note the key numbers and references (passport, visa, insurance) in a small notebook that you keep with you.

A HEALTHY START
Get a check-up before you go

One, or even two months before leaving, check whether your child's vaccinations are up to date and whether any others are necessary for your journey (see the table on p11) or if a course of malaria prevention is needed (see 10). Pediatricians or travel clinic specialists will know the best way to protect your child in a particular region and season. They can advise on a first aid kit best suited to your destination and provide information on endemic diseases and the standard of health care available in the country concerned. They may recommend extra vaccinations besides the obligatory ones: these injections may cause discomfort – such as the one for rabies. If kids are going to react to an immunisation, it will usually happen about 48 hours after the injection and can generally be settled with paracetamol (acetaminophen). Children can go on to have further reactions and sometimes develop rashes

Pack a healthy appetite for foods familiar and new

places, who can supply glasses quickly. Teenagers should avoid contact lenses in hot, dry countries. If they refuse to give them up, they must definitely take them out on the flight to avoid damaging their corneas. Carry drops to lubricate the eyes and lenses.

If your child suffers from **allergies** and you are heading to a country where you do not speak the language, stick pictures of the foodstuffs to which they are allergic into a small book. An allergy should not prevent you going away, but make sure you take the usual treatment with you.

If your child breaks a limb or has another **ill-timed accident** shortly before departure, check what you should do with the doctor. There are many things to consider, such as mobility, autonomy, heat, swimming. If the child is in plaster, the doctor could possibly remove it slightly early or replace it with a smaller cast or a temporary splint. Weigh up the pros and cons and see if it is worth changing your itinerary; discuss it with your child. Do not forget to take analgesics (with the prescription), as well as a note from the doctor explaining the injury. If the accident is too much of a hindrance, claim on your insurance and delay your trip.

Required vaccinations

An inoculation against yellow fever is required to enter a number of countries. It can only be administered at a designated vaccination centre. Most children in the West are not vaccinated against TB as babies, however, it is required for travel in areas where tuberculosis is still rife.

Vaccinations against hepatitis A and typhoid are recommended in countries where hygiene can be patchy. Inoculation for meningitis and meningococcal is prescribed in areas where there are currently epidemics.

Preventing malaria

Malaria is the most widespread contagious disease in the world, and children are more susceptible because of their smaller body mass. It occurs mainly in Africa, Asia and Latin America. Antimalarials do not completely guard against infection but do considerably reduce the risk.

Malaria is transmitted to humans by bites from the disease-carrying female anopheles mosquito (which

10 days after the immunisation, so the earlier you get kids immunised, the better.

Watch out as well for **tooth trouble!** A visit to the dentist before your journey will help avoid pain on the road. Make an appointment early: if your child needs a filling, the treatment will take a bit of time. Ask your dentist for a prescription to deal with any potential infection. The flight, altitude and stress can set off pain and discomfort. It's better to deal with it now than wait to see an unknown dentist abroad. If your child wears braces or a dental plate, let your orthodontist know about the trip. Help your child pack what he or she needs (dental elastics etc), and make sure they do not leave them on the edge of a sink!

For children who wear **glasses**, take two pairs packed into toughened cases and a prescription just in case. You will find very good opticians just about anywhere in the world, even in the most unexpected needs blood to produce eggs), mainly at sunset and sunrise. The mosquitoes develop near water but do not survive above 1500m. No mosquito bite, no malaria: so bite avoidance is vital if you are travelling in a malaria zone. Make sure your children cover themselves up even in very hot countries; dress them in light cotton shirts and trousers before nightfall, for example. Use repellent sprays; they exist for children from 24 months. In hot, humid conditions, DEET-based products should be applied once an hour and the more natural repellents containing lemon eucalyptus etc, once every half hour, as all insect repellents will sweat off quickly. Also, children have very sensitive skin and whichever repellent you choose for your child should be trialled on them well before you leave. The best way to do this is to do a 'patch test'. You can also impregnate their clothing and pyjamas before setting off: with one bottle, you can treat 2kg of clothing for two months, allowing for five washes and one ironing. If you take a mosquito net, give it the same treatment (which should last for six months). If you are buying a net abroad, find out if you can get one that is pre-treated or if you will be able to get hold of the product. You need to be extra careful with children under 24 months. Put them to bed early under a mosquito net. Small pop-up beds incorporating a net are ideal. You can also take an anti-mosquito plug-in that slowly vaporises a tablet (you will need an adaptor for certain countries). In the evening, putting citronella oil (available in many places) on clothes is worth doing as well. But be careful, the oils can set off allergies. Remember that air conditioning may keep mosquitoes at bay, unlike fans.

These measures must be carried out in association with an appropriate anti-malaria treatment (chemoprophylaxis). The treatment varies according to the country visited (the disease varies slightly from region to region), the conditions you are staying in, the season, age, previous medical history, etc. Only a doctor can prescribe the right antimalarial for the circumstances. Antimalarials are unfortunately very

VACCINATION INFORMATION

Disease	Age	Administration	Booster
Yellow Fever	From 9 months (6 months in some health cases)	› 1st injection: at least 10 days before departure › Effective: 10 years	2nd injection: effective the same day if administered before 10 years expires
Tick-borne encephalitis	From 1 year	› 2 injections 1 month apart › A 3rd injection 5 to 12 months later › Effective: 5 years	3 years after the last injection, then every 5 years
Meningitis meningococcal	From 2 years	› 1 injection 10 days before departure › Effective: 3 years	
Hepatitis A	From 1 year	› 1 injection 2 to 3 weeks before departure › Effective: 10 years	6 to 12 months later, then every 10 years
Typhoid	From 2 years	› 1 injection 15 days before departure › Effective: 3 years	
Rabies	From walking age	› 1st injection then 2nd injection 7 days later › 3rd injection 21 or 28 days later	A booster 1 year later is no longer always recommended

GETTING READY TO GO

BASIC MEDICATIONS TO PACK

> Children's medicine for pain or fever (paracetamol, ibuprofen, aspirin)
> Saline solution in single doses
> Nappy rash cream
> Cream for burns
> Arnica cream or granules
> Travel sickness prevention (without a prescription – but recommended by your doctor if possible. Homeopathic versions exist.)
> Anti-nausea treatment
> Antibiotics (like amoxicillin), prescribed by your doctor
> Oral rehydration solution
> Diarrhea treatment
> Antibiotic eye drops in single doses
> Insect bite cream
> Malaria treatment and mosquito sprays if heading to a zone at risk

expensive. They come in tablet form, to be swallowed during a meal. Children sometimes find this difficult. You can try crushing them with water, milk, yogurt, honey or jam. You usually start the treatment on the eve of your departure (10 days before for Lariam); it is essential to continue the course after your return (between one and several weeks).

First aid kit

Prevention is better than cure! Do not load yourself down with unnecessary items, but do not skimp on essentials. As well as the medicines specifically prescribed by the doctor for the country you are going to, take medicine for those ailments that often afflict your child. Sure, you are unlikely to be bothered by bronchitis on a tropical beach. Nonetheless, if your child is prone to bronchial problems then take the usual medicine with you. Paracetamol is the best weapon against fever, ibuprofen is useful for inflammation. Aspirin should never be taken in countries where dengue fever (a virus transmitted by certain mosquitoes) is rife because it can lead to hemorrhaging in this instance

(just as ibuprofen is to be avoided for some viruses). If your child has regular medical treatment, do not forget to ask for a **prescription of international non-proprietary name** (INN), indicating the active chemical ingredients and not a commercial name, and keep it with you at all times.

Organise your **medications** well. For simplicity's sake, have two bags – one for adults and one for children – kept them in the same place, then add another bag for items that are frequently needed: eg disinfectant and plasters. You could even pack these into your toilet bag. Maybe take a mini-kit for your handbag of paracetamol, plasters, antiseptic wipes, disinfectant, arnica and tweezers. To save space, remove all the packaging but keep the instructions stapled in a booklet, and bundle items together with an elastic band. If the doctor prescribes syrup, seal the bottle in a freezer bag to avoid spillages, but do not forget to slip in the spoon or pipette and the instructions as well. For creams, it is best to put them into small pots as tubes can get crushed in luggage.

Suppositories are practical for small children with a fever, but not always adapted to warmer climates. Preserve them in a small bag. Five minutes before using, put the suppository, still in its packet, in very cold water. It will then be sufficiently solid to be used.

You can buy tailor-made medical kits containing different items depending on the sort of holiday you are planning. For countries where hospital hygiene is questionable, you can get kits with sterile surgical equipment that you can hand to the medical team.

Climate & environment

The sun, however enjoyable, presents a real danger for children. Do not expose them directly to the sun's rays and avoid the beach between noon and 4pm. Make sure you always carry a high factor sunscreen with you (buy it before you go), as well as a hat and light clothing (preferably cotton) leaving no skin exposed. Buy good-quality sunglasses (even for a baby) – with a protective case and elastic so they stay on your child's nose. If your children swim in strong sunlight get them to wear a t-shirt.

It is the same in the mountains and any region at altitude, where the power of the sun is intense. Children under a year old should not be taken too high (1200m maximum). Do not take a child higher than 2000m before the age of two, 2500m between two and five years, and 3000m between five and 10 years. From the age of 10 a child should be able to follow his parents anywhere (so you can go trekking in Nepal!). Small children should be wrapped up well against the cold for walks in the mountains where the weather can change quickly. In winter you can provide some warmth by slipping small, disposable or reusable hand warmers into their clothing: easy to use, they are really practical for keeping the chill off and helping children get warm again. You can even buy ones for shoes. Liquid-fuel hand warmers are not recommended for children.

Children with special needs

If you are a parent or carer travelling with a child who has special needs, you are the best person to know what destinations, accommodation options and transport choices are suitable for your child. Consult your medical specialist before you go and contact support organisations where people may have already had the same kind of experiences.

Make sure you have adequate travel insurance and that your insurer is fully aware of your child's pre-existing medical condition. Also, ensure that your policy will cover replacement or theft of any medical supplies. If you need any electrical equipment make sure you know the voltage in your destination and take an adaptor.

If you're taking a wheelchair, explain the facilities that will be required when you book your accommodation – easy wheelchair access to the hotel, a ground-floor room or lift access, a room with access to the bathroom and reasonably level surroundings. Also book ahead for hired cars or taxis that can accommodate not only wheelchairs but special equipment and everyone's general luggage. Check with the local tourist office or a special needs organisation in the country you're visiting for details of wheelchair access in the general area. And remember to pack your wheelchair repair kit

When booking a flight, provide all relevant information such as any help your child might need during the flight and special dietary requirements. If your child is in a wheelchair, give the airline as much notice as possible so they can provide assistance.

While travelling, accessible toilets can be hard to come by. To avoid any hassle, take a small plastic potty. If your child is on regular medication, take two copies of the **prescription of international non-proprietary name** (INN). Get your doctor to write a note explaining the contraindications and an emergency plan. In case of a problem, contact your embassy or consulate in the country.

PACKING YOUR BAGS

When you are a new parent, you could fill the entire hold of a jumbo jet with equipment for your one baby. When your child is slightly older, it is still tempting to pack everything but the bunk beds as you plan for every eventuality.

OK, time for a reality check. When travelling with children you need to keep it simple. Take as little as possible and remember that, unless you're going bush, you can buy much of what you need at your destination or you'll be able to improvise or 'make do'.

How many pieces of luggage you take is also crucial. If you've got too many you won't be able to look after the children and keep an eye on all your gear. If you are travelling on public transport, try to fit all but the bulky items in one bag and allow each adult one daypack only.

ESSENTIAL MEDICAL EQUIPMENT

> A shatter-proof medical thermometer
> Sterile compresses
> Adhesive tape
> Adhesive plasters
> Disinfectant
> Dressings for blisters
> Gauze bandages
> Sunscreen (high factor, suitable for children)
> Scissors, nail clippers and tweezers for splinters (do not pack in carry-on luggage); a nail brush
> Antiseptic lotion for cleaning wounds
> Antibacterial hand gel
> Antiseptic mouthwash
> Water purification tablets
> Disposable syringes

GETTING READY TO GO

KIT FOR A FAMILY TRIP

This depends on the age of your children, where you are going, what you are doing and how you're getting there. Following are some guidelines for your checklist:

> A camera
> A torch, small and efficient (maybe a head lamp) with spare batteries
> A sewing kit for quick repairs
> Sheet sleeping bags so your children will always have clean linen (make them yourself by sewing two single sheets or a double together)
> A purse so your child will always have a few coins on him
> Water bottles
> Emergency nibbles for when noses are turned up at everything else on offer
> Plastic bowls and cutlery (for picnics)
> A knife for peeling and cutting fruit (in your checked-in baggage)
> A bag for dirty washing
> Several plastic bags slipped into the bottom of the bag – they are useful for protection or wrapping
> Small hand warmers or a mini hot-water bottle for cold regions
> A small atomiser for hot regions
> Books to read (or audio books for long car journeys) about your destination
> Coloured pencils, notebooks, glue, scissors (packed in the hold baggage) – everything you need to create a travel journal
> Entertainment for younger children: activity books, magnetic drawing boards (where you erase what you draw), some DVDs, a favourite cuddly toy or two
> Entertainment for older children and teenagers: MP3 players, portable electronic games, puzzle books, a pack of cards
> If you're toilet training you may want to take a potty; for preschool children, a waterproof mat is sometimes useful as even older children can have the occasional accident when they're very tired or in new surroundings

Some parents like to give older toddlers or preschool children their own daypacks to carry. This can make them feel involved and help them take early responsibility for some of their own possessions. Other parents, however, find this over-complicated and find these daypacks usually get left behind somewhere, causing anguish or delay.

A good tip to help organise your family packing: you can buy inner pockets made of cotton or polyamide, which stack inside bags and cases and open on the top. They exist in many different sizes and colours and you can assign one to each person. They are thus easy to spot among the medicines, children's clothes and personal effects.

Clothes

If you're travelling in a hot climate you'll need to pack lightweight, loose-fitting clothes. Cotton clothing absorbs sweat and will help keep your young ones cool. Synthetic clothing doesn't get so creased and dries out easily but can make kids feel clammy. Long-sleeved tops and trousers are good because they give vital protection against the sun and biting insects. Comfortable tracksuits for flying, trousers that convert into shorts and some wet weather gear are all recommended. Most important of all is the sun hat, but make sure it protects the back of the neck.

In a colder climate it is best to dress warmly using layers rather than carry around thick, bulky jumpers, which cause you to quickly overheat once you enter a warm room. Woollen tights under trousers are also good for keeping babies warm. Don't forget mittens and a warm hat.

Take note: shoes! Never leave home with a pair your child has never worn before, especially walking boots and sandals. If you plan to do a lot of walking, choose a shoe with a canvas or leather upper for your child (waterproof shoes are essential in wet regions) and which are not too heavy. For the seaside, plastic sandals are great for protecting feet from sharp rocks and sea urchins.

Remember to pack a travel clothes line to give you as many drying options as possible.

For babies

This group will need the most equipment and there'll be very little room left in the luggage for your clothes.

FEEDING

> Baby food: it's wise to pack a few jars of your baby's favourite food, just in case it takes a while to find something similar when you're away
> Bottles and teats: enough for one day's feeds
> Bottle brush: otherwise you'll never get them clean
> Disposable presterilised bottles: although wasteful and environmentally unfriendly, one of two of these might be useful as a back-up; large chemists often stock them
> Formula milk: if you can, take enough for your whole trip, as different brands of formula taste different and your baby might not be so keen. Pack some in premeasured amounts in plastic segmented containers for making up on the go.
> Cloth squares: to use as bibs, adult shoulder protectors and change mats
> Sterilising equipment: tablets, or microwavable sterilising bags that you put all your equipment in (then hope to find a microwave)
> Travel kettle: to boil the water for feeds
> Baby food container, spoons and plastic or disposable bibs and, most importantly, wet wipes
> If you're breastfeeding, bring along a nice big shawl to use in public places or countries where breastfeeding is more of a private affair

Nappies (diapers)

Disposable nappies are easy to use and light to carry, although they are bulky to pack and relatively expensive. Cloth nappies are easy to pack, reusable, relatively inexpensive and environmentally friendly. However, you'll need to carry the soiled ones around with you until you can wash and dry them. If you use cloth you'll need to carry a minimum of a dozen nappies.

As well as nappy cream, biodegradable nappy sacks and wet-wipes, a portable changing mat is invaluable for when you need to change your baby on an airline seat or on the floor of the toilets.

Baby carriers, strollers & car seats

For many parents, a baby carrier and stroller is not an either/or choice: they always take both. Babies and young children love having the option: the baby carrier is good for when your child is alert and interested in the surroundings and it allows you to go anywhere, while the stroller is better when they are sleepy. In addition, a stroller is useful in restaurants where the child can be strapped in an upright position to eat without having to keep them on your knee. A portable baby seat is also an option for dining, but it is one more thing to carry.

Car seats are required by law in many countries, and in these countries they are usually available from car hire companies. Always check in advance if planning to hire a car, because if they are not available (as in some countries in Latin America) you will need to bring your own.

For further discussion of these, see the Transport section (p19).

Cots

Many places you stay in will be able to provide a cot (for a small extra charge) and if they can't, it's easy to improvise with sleeping arrangements. However, take a look at the many lightweight, pop-up travel cots that are on the market; most can be used until babies are eight or nine months old.

DURING THE JOURNEY

There are some tricks to making a journey with children work. Planning for the getting-there stage, setting the right pace and keeping everyone well fed and healthy are vital. Starting out in a positive frame of mind and remaining flexible will save you when your carefully laid plans go off the rails. If you approach the journey with a spirit of adventure, and involve your children in the planning and problem solving, you'll have a better chance of converting setbacks into opportunities.

TRANSPORT

Travelling long hours by plane, train or car is not always easy for little ones. With a few tricks up your sleeve and some careful preparation you can make it more fun for everyone.

By air

Aeroplane is by far the best way to get to far-flung countries. And internal flights can be a practical – sometimes cheaper – way of gaining time between two stages and sparing children a long journey by bus, train or car.

On international flights children under two years pay between 10 and 30% of the standard ticket, as long as the child sits on your lap. Babies six months or under may be offered an in-flight cot (usually attached to the partition in front of the parent's seat). From two to 12 years, children travel for around 80% of the normal fare (there is no reduction with certain low-cost airlines). You can also opt to pay a child's fare to provide a seat for children under two (as a long journey on your lap is not recommended). On some airlines you can take an approved car booster seat. Families with small children often travel towards the front of the aircraft (where there is enough room for the baby's things). Check in early: it is often first come, first served!

Get as much **information** as you can when you buy your tickets (you can also find out a lot on airline websites):

> Will there be a baby cot? Do you need to reserve it immediately or when you check in?

> Can your child use a car booster seat?
> What kind of children's meals are provided? Remind staff of your child's age when you check in so they can supply the right kind of meal (on some low-cost airlines, meals must be reserved in advance).
> Are games and activity packs supplied?
> Are there individual screens on the flight? Some come equipped with a choice of animated films and video games and children find the time just flies past! (Be warned, some children have problems with the headsets provided on board.)

You need plenty of kit in your **hand luggage**: as well as the cuddly toy, the baby bottles, nappies and wipes, you need something to entertain the children at the airport where they can face long delays. Take some snacks (biscuits, juice cartons and puréed fruit in tubes to suck are easy), and some activities (crayons, colouring books, reading books, cards). Put in a jumper for everyone – air conditioning can be chilly – as well as a change of clothes (so that the little ones do not spend the journey sticky with juice when they spill their drinks). Children with a seat have the right to carry a piece of hand luggage. Infants often get no baggage allowance (which is ironic considering how much stuff they need). Your stroller, which you can use right up until the plane door, is not counted towards anyone's baggage allowance and neither is your car seat. Security allowances are usually made for baby foodstuffs: you can take liquids into the cabin such as milk and water needed to prepare food during the flight (but you may be asked to taste them at security). You are also allowed to take any liquid medicine your baby needs (with the appropriate prescription). However, cleansing products and lotions are subject to the rules on international flights. They must be less than 100ml and be placed in a transparent plastic bag measuring 20cm by 20cm.

Almost all airlines will board passengers with children first (unless you prefer to get on later and reduce the time spent waiting to take off). **Once**

Airlines are well prepared for young travellers

on board it is a good idea to let your baby suck a dummy or bottle or breastfeed during take-off and landing: swallowing can help offset any discomfort in the ears caused by changing pressure.

Older children can suck on a sweet or chew gum. In the cabin the air is very dehydrating, so keep a bottle of water to hand.

Children with colds or flu (or any condition that may affect their ears) can suffer badly from the change in cabin pressure at take-off and landing. If your child is unwell the day before you are due to fly, take them to your GP for advice and help.

By rail

There are lots of advantages to travelling by train with children. There is room to move around a carriage, walk up and down the aisles, visit the buffet car and even do some keep-fit exercises in the boarding areas. Unlike when you're in the car, you can concentrate 100% on the children, you don't have to worry how

to get from A to B and trains are often faster with fewer hold-ups. If you've got a child that suffers from motion sickness, a train is often one of the only forms of transport that doesn't make them feel queasy. All in all, travelling by train is a stress-free way to see a region or country and a good opportunity for a family to have quality time together.

A table between two seats of two works especially well as there's room for the youngsters to do their art work and to eat a picnic. Many countries (eg Croatia) still operate the old-fashioned types of trains where you get your own compartment. These are great with children of any age because you don't have to worry about how much noise they make and, if they are younger, they'll happily play 'house' and when they are tired you can pull the seats together for naps. And, if you're travelling overnight, children love the novelty of sleeper trains and sleeper compartments. But be aware that in some countries the sleeping cars are not mixed and families are split up.

Trains can be the best way to see a place

Some countries (eg Germany) are completely set up for travel by train with family carriages and plenty of space to put a stroller. Others will be an interesting challenge. Nonetheless, as long as the windows are not so dirty you can't see out, train travel is an education for your children because it's a good way for them to see a lot of the country you're travelling in.

Of course, rail travel has its disadvantages too. Train stations tend to have more staircases than escalators, which means that competency in weightlifting can be an advantage, especially if you're changing trains and platforms on a tight schedule. Boarding and disembarking can also be an interesting process with lots of luggage and children in tow. Some trains have no smoking restrictions, which can be very unpleasant for children.

But, if you live in northern Europe, one of the fastest and most hassle-free ways of getting around with children is by train. Eurostar (www.eurostar.com) travels to three Continental hubs that can all take you deeper into Europe: from Brussels there are frequent trains to Amsterdam or Vienna; from Lille

the warm climate of the south of France beckons; and from Paris you can pick up trains to Italy or Spain. If you intend to travel by train within one or more European countries, consider an InterRail Pass (www.interrail.eu) or a Eurail Pass (www.eurail.com; for non-European residents).

While airlines worldwide generally define children as being under 12 years of age, there is simply no standardisation among the planet's railways. Under-twos travel free everywhere, but after that discounts vary a lot by age, or in many places by the child's height.

Make sure you take everything you need for the journey, including food. Even if a buffet car is available, they are often not cheap. Get to the train early so you have time to settle in comfortably and stash the suitcases and stroller.

By bus

Long-distance bus journeys are probably the most crowded and uncomfortable form of transport with any child past the baby phase. For crawlers, toddlers and preschoolers, they can be torturous, especially as you often have to hold young children on your lap. Even if you decide to purchase an extra seat for your infant, chances are your space will be eroded by other passengers.

One of the worst things about travelling on buses with children is what to do when they want to go to the toilet. Bus drivers all over the world know what is coming when they see you lurching up the aisle with a youngster in tow, although do this too frequently and you'll quickly make a lot of enemies.

Unless you're in a country where the buses are pretty comfortable and even have on-board toilets, it is wise to avoid long-distance bus journeys with children under the age of 10 or 11 years. If you can't, try to break the trip into smaller sections and if you can't do this, grin and bear it. Take all the food and drink you could possibly need, and if you are travelling overnight make sure you take a blanket or warm clothes.

After a long trip, try to make sure that the next few days are spent somewhere nice and relaxing so your child can get the journey totally out of their system. If you don't space your trips out sufficiently, you may have a mini riot on your hands the next time you approach anything that looks like a long-distance bus station.

In the developing world, another important consideration about bus travel is safety. Check what the road conditions are like and the reputation of the bus company you're planning to travel with.

By car

When travelling as a family, there are advantages to renting a car or taking your own. You can travel when you want and drive for as long as you want, you can stop for the toilet upon request and have breaks along the way at playgrounds and parks. But probably the most attractive reason to travel by car is that you don't have to carry your own luggage and, if you're in your own car, you've got few luggage restrictions.

However, there are disadvantages to car travel with children. Youngsters don't like to be contained and restrained, they will often put up with the car but don't actually look forward to journeying in it. You can't pay them much attention because you're either driving or navigating. Plus, many children suffer from car sickness and this makes every journey, even the smallest, a test of endurance for both you and your child.

If you intend to hire a car overseas it is best to bring your own car seat. You will also need to check that the car you intend to hire has safety belts in the back. Many car companies will allow you to hire car seats but nine times out of 10 you'll find they are not as good as yours or that the message has not got through to the pick-up point.

If you bring your own child seat, think about safety but also comfort: it can be surprising when you actually prod the seats designed to support children's bottoms for several hours at a time! Children must of course wear their seatbelts even on short journeys. Have whatever you may need at hand to deal with minor hiccups or simply improve the journey. Take pillows (you can get blow-up ones) and a large cloth for picnics. Always have a knife and plastic dishes in the car; you could even organise a picnic kit with everything you need and always within easy reach. Do not forget the 12V adapter which connects to the cigarette lighter and allows you to power the baby bottle heater…and, in case it is needed, the games console or DVD player. Try not to sit your children in front a film or video game straight away; save these for the when boredom or irritability start getting out of hand (take music or audio books, make up guessing games to distract them, etc). Take something for

A camper van gives you the ultimate freedom

car sickness. You must never stop on the motorway emergency hard shoulder: even if the child is throwing up, wait until the next lay-by – you can slip a sick bag behind the front seat as on a plane. Think about taking toilet paper for urgent stops, and always carry a large bottle of water. If it is very hot, dampen a towel or cloth and fix it into your child's window to help keep them cool. If you use the air conditioning, do not put it up too high but just enough to freshen the air.

Organise the boot properly so you do not have to empty it out each time. Keep a small bag on top with pyjamas and a change of clothes for everyone. Do not place anything on the rear parcel shelf as it could fall on the children – avoid the temptation to fill the car to the roof!

Think about the best time of day to set off. Ideally it is when the children are most likely to feel sleepy but not hungry, however you also need to think about the most comfortable time for driving to avoid the heat and heavy traffic.Make frequent stops: it is important for the driver but it also allows the children to stretch their legs. In Europe some lay-bys have children's play equipment.

Local transport

You'll find yourself taking local transport with your children not only because you want to get somewhere but because they'll find it interesting and enjoyable.

Children love water taxis, river cruises and gondolas. Some of the best ways to see a new town are on open-topped tourist buses, on a rickshaw or tuk-tuk (although you need to make sure no one falls out of these three options). If your children are old enough, hiring a bicycle is a good way of getting around, as long as the roads are safe and you can find children's safety helmets to rent.

All local public transport, however, will be a challenge with a stroller. Trams, for instance, are sometimes so high off the ground that lifting strollers on and off them is strenuous work. City underground systems are often riddled with stairs and on buses there may not be room for strollers meaning you'll first have to unload the contents of storage baskets then fold them up.

As with long-distance transport, each new destination will have child or family discounts. As soon as you arrive somewhere, make sure you know who you need to pay for and who travels free.

Walking or cycling

When you are travelling, you tend to walk a lot, even with children, and even without planning a major hike. A baby carrier or stroller can be really useful depending on the age of the child and the location.

For babies up to eight months or so, a **baby carrier** or sling (you can use a sarong or shawl) that you strap to your front is a travel must. For toddlers and children up to the age of four years, you'll swap your baby carrier for a backpack. They are rarely comfortable for sleeping (the head lolls) but children love to see the world from up high on your back. Choose one that is comfortable (the quality varies widely), and make a few improvements to it before you leave, such as a piece of sheepskin under the child's bottom.

Just as important (even for four- and five-year-olds) is a folding **stroller** with a well-fitting rain cover. Buy one for newborns that lies flat so your child will always sleep comfortably and you won't have to rush back to your accommodation for naps. One with larger wheels is better for travelling because it can negotiate rougher terrain.

A lightweight stroller is no good if you plan to go trekking on mountain paths, isolated tracks or beaches. But it's really useful for day-to-day excursions to restaurants, shops, hotels and around towns. All-terrain, three-wheeler strollers will get you to more places but they tend to be heavier and bulkier so fitting through the doors of shops or getting onto public transport is more difficult.

Warn your child about **the dangers of traffic** whatever their age: it may be a lot more dangerous crossing a road in Dakar or in Phnom Penh than at home. The street signs and the road rules may be different to home – if they are even respected. In some towns you will have to deal with the hustle and bustle of **crowds**: if you fear you may lose your child, write his or her name on a piece of paper along with your hotel name and number and your mobile phone number (to be placed in a purse or even round a smaller child's neck). This will be useful even for bigger children to help overcome language barriers.

Cycling as a family is adventurous and rewarding

If you are planning to do **bike rides**, children as young as eight are easily capable of cycling a decent distance. Babies and younger children can be taken on a child's seat (up to 22kg) or a bike trailer, but must always wear a helmet (in some countries, like Holland, there are many other clever ways to carry children). Try not to carry a bag when you set off on a major excursion, instead choose handlebar pouches or panniers for the front and rear of the bike. You can place windcheaters, sunscreen, water and snacks in the different compartments.

ROUTINE, PACE & RHYTHM

A long-haul journey or a short break, out-of-the-way places or densely populated towns…the pace of the family holiday may be determined by the location but also by your goals, your mode of transport and your children's ages. By having a few coping strategies up your sleeve, using your common sense and taking a number of precautions, you can keep things running smoothly, whether 500km from home or at the other end of the world.

If the **first few days** prove difficult, be patient! Children can be disturbed by change. Avoid being stressed out on departure day at all cost! If your children are small, start out gently: rest for a day or two when you arrive, then slowly build up the number of activities. Younger children need two to three days to adjust on journeys where the time difference is four hours or more (particularly if travelling west) – this is why a week's stay is nowhere near long enough when there is a significant time difference. Gradually adapt your lifestyle to local time, subtly shifting meal times and afternoon sleeps. After three days you should completely forget about the time in your own country. Encourage afternoon naps during your stay, particularly in hot countries; live like the locals (accept that things are done differently and not as at home) and ensure that everyone has a bed where they can read or rest. Organise times for rest and unstructured play each day where they can catch up with themselves and quietly process some of their experiences.

DURING THE JOURNEY

In a world that has suddenly changed for a young child, nice, safe, familiar routines can reassure your youngster that not everything is suddenly different and hard to understand in his or her new (albeit temporary) life. One of the most crucial routines to try to continue is the one at bedtime. A story or a bedtime read is usually important (or appreciated) for children up to the age of 10 or more or you can tell each other stories about what you've done that day. Having said all of this, bedtimes are usually later when you're on holiday or travelling so watch for the tell-tale signs of children who've not had enough sleep.

Accept that your your schedule will be much slower than if you were travelling alone. You'll need to build in time for them to dawdle and get distracted. And you'll probably need to leave your plans a little looser because sometimes it's really nice, for example, when the children suddenly spot a playground in a nearby park, if you can let them go and play immediately. Or, on the other hand, what you'd planned to do might simply not fit in with your child's mood that day.

Encourage your children to talk about what they are experiencing. You can create a family travel journal to which everyone contributes, whatever their age: drawings, cut-outs and collages from brochures for the young ones, or photo reports by teenagers. Buy disposable cameras for the younger members (they still exist!), or even an underwater camera if you are by the sea; find out what the traditional games are in the region, and do not forget postcards, everybody loves them!

Travel is an enriching experience for people of all ages, and **children do adapt very easily.** The difference in culture and language does not stop them communicating and having fun. After the first few awkward moments, your little dears will be relaxed enough to play with the local children – which, in turn, will help bridge the gap between you and their parents. As for teenagers, deprived of their usual friends and social habits, you may find them transformed. Ensure they are dressing appropriately and remind them of local customs and rituals. Remember when abroad, you are their only source of guidance. It is up to you to help them settle in easily and confidently in this new and inviting world.

EATING & DRINKING

What are they going to eat? Rest assured that almost anywhere in the world you can get hold of basic foodstuffs: rice, potatoes, vegetables, fruit, etc. Food is sold fresh in the most backward, or the least Westernised parts of the world. There are neither freezers nor frozen foods: dishes are prepared as and when required and usually the way you want.

What are the risks?

With boiled or well-cooked dishes you run no risk whatsoever. You can tell when something is not right so there is no need to be paranoid, just careful. Get into the habit of tasting your children's food first on the pretext of telling them what is in it, to check it is not too spicy. In countries where the water is not safe to drink, avoid fruits and raw ingredients in restaurants. On the other hand, there is nothing to stop you buying fresh fruit and vegetables in the market. Washed with mineral or purified water and peeled by your own hand, you run no risk.

Children need to **drink a lot** as they are more prone to dehydration than adults, particularly in hot countries (1 to 1.25L per day for a child weighing 10kg, 2 to 2.5L per day for a child of 20kg). Sugary drinks are ever-present almost everywhere, and very tempting when they taste better than water and are often nicely chilled. Do not let your children get into the habit of drinking them regularly. They should be an occasional treat, preferably outside meal times. Apple tea in Turkey, mint tea in North Africa, chai with cardamom in India…children love these flavoured brews. However, they too should be avoided from the middle of the afternoon onwards (or you could be up all night!) and are not recommended for very young children.

Always keep an emergency snack in your bag for the odd hunger pang, low energy levels or when facing long delays: it is the smallest things sometimes that can maintain morale. Nothing greasy (such as crisps) or chocolate (not good in the heat), but dry biscuits, local fruit or even a favourite snack that you slipped into the luggage before leaving home – they will be delighted with this familiar food early on in the trip, before they forget about it completely!

Mealtimes, a key part of the day

Mealtimes vary from country to country; sometimes people dine early, sometimes late. If your children are old enough, doing as the locals do will help you get the most from your experience. But a child between the ages of three and nine often needs to eat before 6pm or 7pm. This can mean you get your meal over before the main rush of the evening or it can make finding restaurants open that early hard to find. In Spain, for instance, it's hard to find places that will serve you before 8.30pm. If this is the case, consider having your main meal in the middle of the day. This option can be a pleasant and restful way of passing time during the hottest part of the day and a good way of avoiding the problem of evening restaurants opening later than children's bedtimes.

Mornings are often the most productive time for a family and it is essential to get a good start: a good breakfast should be hearty enough to keep the children going for a few hours, but not too heavy. If the children sleep late for the first few days due to the time difference, try to make arrangements with your hotel, as it is not always easy to get breakfast after 9 or 10am.

A stop off in a restaurant for lunch and dinner often provides a welcome break. It is a well-known fact that eating can be soothing! If your children are not very hungry, do not worry: they are probably a little overwhelmed by the change of pace, climate and lifestyle. If it is very hot, watch what they drink and make sure they haven't got a fever.

Choose somewhere where quite a few people are eating. If the locals go there it has to be a good sign! And if there are a lot of customers there is less chance that dishes are yesterday's leftovers. Trust the recommendations of your guidebook too. Before sitting down, find out what on the menu might suit the children. Then be patient: a dish freshly

Meals should be a time for relaxing together

Picnics are easy, affordable and fun

prepared to order takes longer than something that is reheated. Have some distractions on hand, like colouring or a game of cards.

Although you'll probably want to sample a variety of local dishes, chances are that a child under the age of eight might not be so keen. Hence, when you come across a menu that also serves something familiar like spaghetti bolognese, chips or pizza it makes life very easy. At home you might avoid feeding your child from worldwide fast food chains, but allowing your child a meal they recognise can help them feel a little more secure and also reassure them that they won't have to eat 'strange' food forever.

At the end of a busy day, sometimes the last thing you want to do is drag your youngster out to find a suitable restaurant. At times like this, a quiet meal cooked where you're staying or room service can be a terrific alternative. Children of almost any age adore picnics. Another option is the humble street stall. If it's a popular joint where fresh food is cooked in front of you and served piping hot then it's probably a safe and fun mealtime alternative.

The problem with water

Outside first-world countries tap water is often unsafe to drink. This is the case even if it is being consumed by local people who may have built up a tolerance to the bacteria in it. However, all water will be safe to drink as long as it has been boiled thoroughly (approximately five minutes). If your children are very young, you cannot use chemicals for water purification, so boiling or using a nonchemical filter (ceramic filters) are good alternatives. Otherwise, stick to bottled water. However, mineral water that is high in magnesium can cause diarrhoea and mineral water that is high in carbonates can cause constipation. As such, it is best to stick to 'drinking' water, as opposed to 'mineral' water.

Always order drinks without ice, as you don't know where the water came from (in certain regions, unless otherwise requested, ice is always added). If you are worried about clean glasses you can always use your own. In high risk countries, avoid salad or raw vegetables no matter how tempting in the heat. It is the same with fruit that has already been peeled or that is eaten with the skin left on: anything in fact that may have been rinsed in water!

Food to avoid abroad

In many countries, such as in Europe and in North America, food holds no risk. You just need to get used to the local diet – and, once again, you can find chips almost anywhere! It is a little more difficult in very hot countries or in those where hygiene leaves a lot to be desired.

In these destinations, hot or well-cooked **meat** poses no threat (the cleanest meat is lamb, the least is pork). On the other hand you should avoid cold or raw meat. Only eat fish if it is normal fare in the region and only if cooked, and avoid shellfish. You can tuck into large grilled prawns but do not eat cold crustaceans. Also try to avoid dishes containing raw or barely cooked eggs. As for milk, do not let your children drink anything other than boiled milk; refuse fresh cheeses and farmhouse yogurts. Finally, be ready to refuse your children ice lollies and ice creams. Although if somewhere is recommended by your guidebook…go for it! It would be a pity to miss out on some of the best ice cream in the world in Mumbai – it is opposite Chowpatty Beach and you can indulge in anything there quite safely!

Breastfeeding, bottles & baby food

When you are travelling with a baby, breastfeeding is ideal in terms of comfort and hygiene. During the first few days, babies may feed more regularly as a source of reassurance. But everything soon returns to normal once you get into a rhythm. When you breastfeed, be discreet: in some countries it is unheard of to breastfeed a baby in public. Wear clothes that allow you to feed the baby out of sight, such as roomy shirts or a big scarf (some women cloak themselves completely in the wrap used to carry the baby).

If you are not breastfeeding, be sure to take plenty of spare **bottles** as teats and lids get lost all the time. Use plastic ones (lighter and easier to handle), which are wide enough to clean easily. Carefully work out how many boxes of powdered milk you will need. If you are heading for a very humid or hot country, transfer the powder into an airtight container. Prepare a small bag of equipment for making up feeds each day: along with the bottle include a sponge, a small flask filled with washing-up liquid and enough powdered milk for the day (boxes of single servings exist). Bottles of premade milk should be avoided, the tops may not close properly; plus you should not carry an opened bottle in a hot country (opened milk lasts five days but only in the fridge).

If it is hot, it is important that the baby regularly drinks water as well as milk (around 150ml/kg per day). If hygiene is a concern or if the baby is ill then the bottle should be changed or disinfected frequently. Germs spread quickly in the heat – whether in Australia, Italy or Thailand. Bottles and teats can be sterilised by plunging them into a pan of boiling water for five minutes. You can also sterilise in cold water with tablets. If your baby is more than six months old the journey is not the best time to introduce **new foods** into their diet: too much change in one go. Either start experimenting before or wait until afterwards. In most countries you can find jars of baby food in supermarkets in the big towns, even though they are often expensive and heavy to carry. Any restaurant should be able to prepare a plate of vegetables, soup or puréed fruit for your little one. From one year of age, you can order hot milk or chocolate and transfer it to a bottle. Remember you should only use milk that has been boiled or pasteurised. If you take small jars of vegetables, choose ones that may be eaten cold (carrots are good in terms of consistency). If your child is still too young to settle for just any biscuit, take a small supply of your usual kind. Powdered cereals can serve as a supplement to the bottle or as a helping of porridge if you run out of jars. Keep them in a waterproof container: you can also buy them in sachets, which are ideal on a journey. Do not bother to take any homemade meals, which will of course not keep. If your child is quite big (around 18 months old) he can give up the bottle and use a cup. How grown up!

HEALTH & HYGIENE
Basic rules

Good hygiene and general cleanliness will avoid many stomach problems caused by hand-to-mouth contamination either through food and water or from person to person. Tell your children about the risks; they will learn to be careful. With a few simple precautions you can avoid certain inconveniences.

First of all, it is imperative to **wash your hands** as often as possible especially before meals and after going to the toilet. Antibacterial hand gels are easy to carry and use and will kill 99.9% of germs. These lotions bypass the need for water or a towel and are not at all greasy. However, they can cause irritation and are not always suitable for some sensitive skins if used a lot. You can also buy antibacterial wet-wipes, useful to clean hands but also a table or a glass.

In high risk countries, use **bottled water for brushing teeth** and do not hesitate to refuse a glass of water, even from the kindest host, whilst remaining unfailingly polite. Freezing does not kill microbes. In any case, drinks served too cold can spark a stomach ache, especially in children.

Always carry a **small spoon and plate** for younger children. The bigger ones can have a knife and fork.

If you **dry washing outside**, be careful to shake it well before folding.

Use mats rather than towels **on the beach,** as they protect you from insects hidden in the sand.

Do not walk barefoot and wear shoes made from natural materials such as canvas rather than plastic (except to go in the sea); as the latter can cause sweating and lead to fungal infections. Children can wear open sandals where there is no danger of insect or plant stings.

When choosing your hotel, it is not good enough that the hallway or corridors simply look clean: ask to see the room you have been allocated and check out the beds, bedding and bathroom. It is always useful to take a sheet sleeping bag the right size for your child. If your child is prone to night-time accidents, think about protecting the bed for whoever may follow: include a mattress protector in your bag (a plastic bag will do). For babies, take a large piece of cloth for crawling around on. A cotton sarong, easily washed and dried, has multiple

Always protect children from the danger of the sun

uses – pillow, towel, sheet – and also puts a safe layer between you and any questionable seating.

Accidents & Mishaps

Always carry a small first aid kit with basic products (see p14). **Cuts, blisters and burns** often need urgent attention because heat and dust can increase the risk of infection. Clean well with water (purified if need be, depending on where you are) and soap, to remove any dirt or debris; disinfect with antiseptic then protect the wound with a dressing or gauze and a plaster. Repeat every day and seek medical advice if the injury turns nasty.

The tiniest **injury on a foot** can be extremely debilitating and painful. Make sure your children's shoes are not to blame and cut toenails regularly. With a blister, if the skin is still intact, drain it by piercing it with a disinfected needle: it is totally painless. If the blister has burst, you must first cut away the dead skin, disinfect it and cover it with a plaster – if available, a special blister plaster will help heal the wound.

In case of **insect bites and stings**, apply a balm. Also cut your children's fingernails often as scratching may lead to infection.

Do not let young children play with animals. Bites, scratches, fleas and other parasites are not the only dangers – it only needs a lick from a rabid animal on an open wound for the infection to be passed to your child. Explain to your children that animals roaming free are wild and can be dangerous. In case of a **bite, scratch or lick** on an open wound, wash the area with water (purified if necessary) and with soap for 15 minutes, rinse abundantly with water and apply antiseptic. If the animal in question shows signs of rabies (an aggressive cat, dog or wild animal), you must seek treatment even if the child or adult has been vaccinated. Rabies is 100% fatal in humans if not treated. The treatment must be carried out during the incubation period, between two to eight weeks on average. You must seek help urgently from a doctor, hospital, embassy or even your travel insurance firm to find the nearest rabies treatment centre.

Do not ignore the harmful effects of the sun. If, in spite of the recommendations given on p12, your child is seriously **sunburned**, give a simple analgesic (paracetamol) and make sure the child is well hydrated. Use an aloe vera cream or calamine lotion at regular interludes. **Sunstroke and heat stroke** can cause sickness, fever, dehydration, diarrhoea and fatigue. If that happens, place the child in a cool place (but do not have the air conditioning too high), undressed and with damp cloths over their body (a cold bath would be too much of a shock). Make your child drink and let them rest. Heat stroke can cause rapid dehydration: watch out for symptoms in your child. If so, go to a doctor or hospital.

Illnesses

It is important to be able to identify common illnesses. It is not always necessary to go to the doctor; what is more, depending where you are, it is not always easy to get help. Children – especially young children and babies – are more likely than adults to get **diarrhoea** when they are away. Even though usually harmless, you cannot afford to be complacent. The infection can be caused by a virus, bacteria or a parasite and is accompanied by watery stools and sometimes even vomiting, stomach pains and a bit of a temperature. Total recovery normally takes two to three days. It is however more complicated if accompanied by a temperature of 39°C or if the stools contain a discharge or blood. The infection may then be more serious and you should quickly consult a doctor.

Children with prolonged diarrhoea run a serious risk of **dehydration,** which you must try to prevent from the start. Give the baby or young child oral rehydration salts (ORS) prepared with bottled or boiled water in small quantities regularly. If the child throws up, try giving a spoonful every one or two minutes. Then eventually give it to the child each time he or she passes very runny stools. If you are breastfeeding, carry on; if your child is being fed a milk-based formula, you need to replace this with ORS until the diarrhoea is better. As it improves introduce diluted milk feeds then, if your baby is over six months and on solids, reintroduce these too. You can also get the child to drink the water from boiling rice – it's very effective!

Avoid high fibre fruit and vegetables during a bout of diarrhoea. Encourage your recovering child to eat rice, semolina, pasta, carrots, bananas, apple purée, biscuits, bread and crackers; and let them have meat and fish if they want. Choose natural yogurts and cheese. Fizzy drinks are no longer recommended (far too sugary), however if your child fancies a glass then you can allow one on top of the

RECIPES FOR REHYDRATION

Here are two simple and effective recipes to help rehydration.

> Boiled rice water: cook 50 to 60g of rice in a litre of unsalted water. Stir the rice adding ¼ to ½ a teaspoon of kitchen salt and possibly a teaspoon of lemon juice (rich in potassium).

> Rehydration solution recommended by the World Health Organisation: mix a litre of sterilised water, six teaspoons of sugar and one of salt. Respect the quantities; too much sugar or salt can be dangerous for the child.

Basic hygiene is especially important when travelling

other food and drink. Be careful of symptomatic antidiarrhoeal medications ('stoppers'), which are not recommended for children and should be avoided. If your child eats the salt in a restaurant, allow it, it will help with dehydration.

If diarrhoea is accompanied by a temperature then give the child paracetamol (acetaminophen) every six hours. In cases of vomiting, give quite cold water: this will reduce the vomiting and help the rehydration solution to work. If diarrhoea persists longer than 48 hours, or if the child vomits or has blood in their stools, or has a high temperature (39°C), then see a doctor.

If your child shows signs of dehydration you must get to a hospital straight away. It is therefore important to recognise the symptoms; (any one of these may constitute dehydration): hollow eyes, dry mouth, extreme listlessness or abnormal sleepiness, an absence of urine, folds which are slow to disappear when you pinch the stomach skin, and behavioural problems.

Your child may also become **constipated** on the journey. This often occurs as a result of a change of routine or flying. Do not worry, things will quickly return to normal. Just provide plenty of drinks and a diet rich in fibre and fruit. If you treat it with a paraffin-based oil, leave enough time between any doses of antimalarial medicines as it can reduce their efficacy.

For extreme **dental pain**, dose with paracetamol every six hours. If your child starts getting an abscess, pierce it cleanly with a disinfected needle and make them wash their mouth out with an antiseptic mouthwash. If that fails to cure it, seek antibiotics. Instil in your children the importance of good dental hygiene: it may be the moment to brush your teeth together and demonstrate the best method and the length of time needed for effective tooth brushing.

For **ear, nose and throat infections,** flush out the nose and provide paracetamol. Honey is a natural antibiotic. Children are susceptible to conjunctivitis when travelling because of the wind, sand and dust. Clean their eyes with a saline solution and get them to wear sunglasses for some relief. If the child complains, an antiseptic eyewash (in a single dose) can be used. Once opened, eyewash does not last.

Emergencies

In case of an emergency, contact your embassy in the country where you are, it will be able to inform you of the nearest medical centre. Also contact your insurance company: get together all the documents or information you need (passport, social security number, insurance contract number, etc) before you telephone.

COMING HOME

HEALTH CHECK-UP

Just because you have been travelling to far away places does not mean that your children may have picked up dangerous germs. It is, nonetheless, worth a visit to a pediatrician to let him know of anything you have come across during the trip. It may be sensible to worm the family after a seaside holiday because sand contains all sorts of parasites. If your child has a temperature, diarrhoea, dark brown urine or skin problems when you return, visit the doctor at once, especially if you have been in a tropical region. Better still, get an appointment with a specialist in infectious and tropical diseases at the hospital closest to your home. If your children have been taking antimalarial drugs, they must finish the prescribed course, which can continue for one to four weeks after returning home, depending on the treatment. Do not stop earlier, even if the journey seems a long time ago. Do not forget any boosters for injections you had before leaving (see p11) or you may have to start all over again before the next journey. And one other thing – children often grow surprisingly fast while travelling. Their shoes seldom fit them when they get home!

SETTLE THEM BACK IN GRADUALLY

Allow one or two days for your children to adjust, or even two or three when the time zone difference is four hours or more. Make sure you return a few days before school begins.

Even if delighted with the holiday, children are always happy to be back in their bedrooms with their toys and to resume their former lives. They often get back into the swing of things much faster than grown-ups. But coming home can be unsettling for a while, and don't underestimate how much they might miss your company and all the attention you gave them while you were away, being there almost 24 hours a day for them. Take things slowly and try your best to be around as much as possible to ease them back into life at home.

Souvenirs help prolong memories of the trip

To keep the journey alive for them, suggest helping them prepare a project for school on the country you have just visited. Use leaflets and other information you have brought back as well as photographs and travel journals. Teachers often appreciate this kind of initiative: they use the piece to liven up a geography or history lesson. Maybe make some posters together for their bedrooms as another step in the journey. Sort out the photographs, picking out a small selection to put on their walls, and create a beautiful family album together. Let the children choose their own pictures so they really are their memories rather than yours. Take them to the library or let them buy books on the region or countries visited. Try to get them to cook with you, to prepare the dishes they enjoyed – Turkish meze, Indian breads, African sweet-potato chips. Seek out the fruit and vegetables they discovered abroad. Use the enthusiasm of being back home to set aside more family time and plan new adventures! What is more: try not to get sucked back into the unrelenting rhythm of daily life too quickly.

PACKAGE DEALS

Organised holidays, too naff? Not always. Operators have a growing range of packages geared to families; from the most adventurous tour to relaxing holiday clubs. Letting someone else do the legwork for you will ensure your holiday is worry-free – as long as you make the right choice.

ORGANISED TOURS

We are not always willing to battle the logistical constraints involved in planning and mapping out a trip, or to struggle with the language barrier and public transport upon arrival, especially with nagging kids in tow. And some adventure activities, like dog-sledding or a camel safari, are nearly impossible to plan on your own. In these cases it may be tempting to put yourself in the hands of a professional. Typical organised tours are not at all suitable for children (long hours spent on a bus charging from one tourist attraction to another). But you should be able to find just the right thing in the many travel brochures designed especially for family holidays.

Most of the major tour operators propose family packages, which balance cultural visits with fun activities, and unusual means of transport (donkey in Croatia, camel in India, bamboo raft or tuk-tuk in Thailand) with more conventional methods (bus or 4WD). They may focus on the environment, nature and local culture, or on adventure activities like cycling or canoeing, while catering to the needs and interests of children of all ages. Many operators offer customised packages. On a group tour you will enjoy the company of like-minded parents and children. Or you can go in the other direction and have all the fun of travelling independently (no group or guide), but minus the hassle of having to organise everything yourself (the agent arranges the itinerary, reservations and transfers). Whether your children dream of trekking in Nepal or photographing animals in Kenya, or see themselves as explorers in the land of the Mayan Indians or as archaeologists in Pompeii, specialist agencies will help you devise a trip that is safe and comfortable. But beware: peace of mind comes at a price! Discounts are usually limited for children. The smaller the group (for guided tours), the more customised the package, and the more adventurous the activities, the higher the price.

Things to check

When choosing a tour operator, look for one that specialises in family travel, rather than one that's simply willing to allow kids to tag along. You want activities and days planned with children and their abilities and limitations in mind. You should also check that the operator has a good safety record. Glean as much information as you can on the means of transport and the catering, the comfort level of the accommodation, the size of the group and age of other participants, and the precise itinerary, to see whether the trip will suit your particular family. Sometimes the trip depends on the number of participants and is not guaranteed; in this instance the tour operator is obliged to let you know a certain number of days in advance. Find out about any extra costs (for optional activities and visits, etc) and any potential administrative formalities.

RESORTS & HOLIDAY CLUBS

If you are heading to the sun, a stay in a resort may offer a good solution. For certain destinations like the Maldives, it is sometimes better value than if you go it alone. True, you won't get much cultural immersion and it is hardly a big adventure, with little chance of playing at Robinson Crusoe. But you can make the most of being waited on hand and foot, which has a certain appeal when you really need a good, solid chunk of time out.

Make the right choice. From the worst (uncomfortable beds, cloudy water in the pool, kids' club with no real surveillance) to the best (a variety of activities, the latest sports equipment, luxury facilities, good service), in the resort world your accommodation can be a lucky dip. There is any number of very average establishments, which is why it is worth spending time choosing the right

Organised tours provide experiences you can't create alone

one. Study current reviews on the internet to expose any hidden catches or charges. And ask yourself a few pertinent questions:

> Is there suitable equipment for very small children (bath, changing table, high chair, bottle warmer) provided in the bedrooms? In communal areas? Are there strollers available? Do you need to reserve one in advance?
> Does the restaurant cater for little ones (kids' portions, purées)? Some places have a children's restaurant.
> Is there a kids' club (often there are several for different age groups)? Is it open all year or just during the school holidays? During which hours is it open (some operate just in the morning or evening)? Is it included in the price? What are the organised activities (fun, educational)? What qualifications do the staff have?
> Is there a babysitting service? How much does it cost?

Find out, as well, about the resort's clientele. Is it very international? Does it attract many families (important if your children are to make friends and gain a little independence, and if you are to feel you and your offspring are welcome). Find out where the hotel is situated in relation to places of interest and public transport, and if there are is the possibility of booking private excursions or renting a car. A sure-fire way to add a cultural element to your resort experience is to drag your family out of the resort for a wander.

Cost

Costs vary dramatically for resort stays. Brochures help to give you some idea of cost and facilities, but it's worth searching the internet for discounts and last-minute deals.

All-inclusive deals can work well if the variety and quality of food is good. Some resorts include alcohol and snacks, but there's no industry standard. If you're not going the all-inclusive route then you'll probably have more choice about what and where you eat, but resort food is generally expensive.

'Bring the kids for free', or 'kids eat and drink for free' offers pop up frequently. Conditions usually include paying full price for two adults. When kids eat for free you usually need to purchase a (possibly overpriced) meal yourself.

Look out for combined deals offering accommodation and excursions: this is a good way to mix relaxation and exploration.

PACKAGE DEALS

HOLIDAYS WITH A DIFFERENCE

→ CAMPING

If you're feeling the need to get back to basics and the simple life, camping is ideal. It's a cheaper way to travel, relax with the family and really get to know a country.

You can take even the youngest family members on a camping trip, living at their pace with early nights (except in big campsites with organised entertainment) and getting up as the sun rises. Choose a site with the children's age and the type of holiday you're after in mind. A big, busy campsite not far from the beach might not suit very young children. On the other hand, a small site out in the wilds of the countryside might seem boring to teenagers.

Camping can be part of a touring holiday, allowing you to choose a variety of sites. Camping on a farm is possible in some countries, which is a good choice because children love to help with the animals. You can often eat in the farmhouse – a rest for the cook of the family! If you want a campsite near a beach, you will need to book early, especially during school holiday times. Unless you're going to camp in developing nations or obscure regions, you'll find that nearly all parks, government-run campsites and independently owned establishments have websites where you can book or make enquiries. For the first night under canvas, try to arrive early enough to set up the tents and get organised. It is much easier to get set up during daylight. It is important to choose a location that has some shade throughout the day. Make sure it is not sloping or bumpy. Get everyone involved in setting up camp; older children can put up the tents, younger ones can pump up the mattresses and everyone loves trying their hand at camping cuisine! Double check the children's beds so they do not wake you up at night. If they are frightened, spend a little time with them so they fall asleep happy and leave a night light on. Organise your bags so their pyjamas and teddies are easily found. Close your tent when you are out to prevent it getting invaded by insects.

The choice of tent is important. For comfort camping, aim for a tent that is at least 3m by 4m for two adults and two kids. Once the kids reach a certain age (perhaps eight or nine) they could have a separate tent. Look for tents that are simple to put up. Get good quality sleeping bags, nights can be chilly in some areas, even in summer, and a cold kid will make camping a miserable experience. Some children's sleeping bags have an integrated mattress, which is cosy and comfortable. Consider trying a weekend practice run before embarking on longer trips to make sure your equipment is in order and that you've mastered the basics. If you go by car, take stainless steel cutlery; it is a bit heavier, but easy to clean and more hygienic than plastic.

Prepare a kit for the washing up with detergent in a screw-top bottle. A large basin is vital; you will need it for washing clothes, dishes and the baby's bath. During the day you can keep the cooking utensils in it. Take some plastic boxes to store food but don't keep food in your tent as it will attract animals. A small camping gas stove will be enough for cooking. A picnic rug is very useful for outdoor eating. Don't forget a torch and maybe a lamp (there are different types – gas, wind up, solar powered, rechargeable). Also take mosquito repellent for the evening and a potty for small children who might object to going to the toilet outside (or using the campsite toilets) during the night. Remember a 12V power cable that can be plugged into the cigarette lighter in the car to recharge a night light or baby's bottle warmer.

DIVING

Do your children ask to see the fish at the bottom of the sea every summer? For most destinations a mask and snorkel will suffice. But if you've been there, done that, why not take the plunge and go scuba diving – an unforgettable experience!

From the age of eight, children are physiologically capable of diving (not earlier, as their lungs and ears are not developed enough). Some experts recommend a minimum age of 12, to ensure that the child is mentally mature enough as well. Your child must firstly want to dive, must be a competent swimmer who is comfortable in the water, and be able to take instruction and make sound judgements. Check with your doctor that there is no medical impediment, mainly concerning the ears, nose and throat. But children who are ready for this experience are captivated by it – an eel, rainbow-coloured fish, simply being able to breathe under water fascinates them.

The fiirst step is to research destinations that will suit beginners: warm tranquil water, lagoons, little sheltered bays; ideally less than 5m deep, with a rich marine life in a protected area. There is plenty of choice, with islands in the Pacific, the Indian Ocean, the Caribbean and the Mediterranean. Research the best time of year to travel (when there is not too much rain or wind and calm seas) as weather can be unpredictable in tropical destinations (cyclones, sea swells and dangerous currents all occur). Find out if the destination has an area particularly suitable for families. In Polynesia, for example, head for Moorea, an island surrounded by a safe lagoon.

Secondly, research the local dive centres on the internet, in travel guides, specialised magazines and forums. Important points: do the diving centres have special equipment for children (ie four- or six-litre cylinders, small-sized vests and wet suits)? Do they employ English-speaking instructors trained in teaching and dealing with younger children? They should offer a fun approach in a safe environment. Check out the affiliation of the diving centre as well, they should be attached to a teaching body or a federation overseeing the tuition and they must adhere to specific regulations. The best known qualifications include PADI, SSI, and in the French overseas territories, the CMAS (the French Diving Federation). The teaching methods and program do not vary much from one to another.

The first dive usually involves 20 to 40 minutes underwater. On land, the instructor makes sure the diver is properly equipped and explains the basic safety rules and communication signals. Then it is time to take the plunge. The instructor, holding the child by the hand, and watching carefully, takes him or her through the first steps at a depth of 3m to 5m maximum. The child soon falls under the spell of the sea, discovering the feeling of weightlessness and the colourful wildlife darting about. A first dive can cost around US$65-180 depending on the resort, and only parental consent is required. If your children become hooked, there are different courses they can do, but they must be at least 14 to do the Open Water or Level 1 test. These licences allow you to dive in centres worldwide.

THE BEST PLACES FOR A FIRST DIVE

> French Polynesia (p152)
> Fiji (p148)
> The Seychelles (p202)
> Mauritius (p194)
> Malaysia (p170)

> The Maldives (p172)
> Thailand (p182)
> The Philippines (p178)
> Australia (p146)
> Costa Rica (p128)

> Egypt (p188)
> Malta (p90)
> US & British Virgin Islands (p142)

→ BOATING

Tempted by the idea of messing about in boats? Dreaming of taking your children back to some of your old favourite sailing spots? There are plenty of possibilities for a watery trip – it all depends on the age of your children, your preferences and your ideal destination.

For a first expedition by boat, it is best to go for a short trip, perhaps just a week. Discover Luxor and Karnak on board a traditional felucca, coast between Greek islands, take a Turkish *gület* and enjoy the tranquillity of the beautiful coves. With older children you can discover marine life and incredible scenery in the Caribbean or Pacific islands, where you need to allow at least 10 days.

Then there are canal barges in Europe that are great fun for families. Although they can be quite pricey, these trips will give your kids some great memories. After a short training session to get used to dealing with the length of the boat, you are the skipper! It can be tricky to navigate the sometimes frequent locks. Remember to take your bikes so you can visit nearby villages and enjoy cycling along the tow paths.

Generally, you can take a child sailing from an early age, especially if you sail with a crew. The most difficult age is when the child is learning to walk – you cannot take your eyes off a toddler, even when the boat is anchored. You must never leave a child of under six alone. They also need to be kept entertained, although they will love swimming when you drop anchor. To stop kids running around, the best solution is to get them involved in handling the boat. From about seven years of age they will often manage very well. Let them take the helm, use the GPS, or trace your route on the map.

Check in advance that the boat is well secured on all sides, with nets or solid bulwarks, and that there are on-board life jackets and harnesses to fit your child. Make sure the children understand the safety requirements on board – the skipper will frequently remind them. At sea, sunburn can be a problem due to the reflection of the sun's rays off the water. Children must always wear sunscreen, a cap, t-shirts and sunglasses (attached with a cord so the sunglasses do not end up swimming with the fishes).

If you are doing your own cooking, only do so when anchored. You will have to cook what supplies you can get locally; children will love fishing and what a way to try out all the different ways of preparing fish! Keep something to nibble in the cockpit in case anyone has an upset stomach. Avoid going back into the boat if you yourself feel a little queasy

Do not forget to bring a waterproof, boots and warm clothing, even if you are heading for the sun (remember the wind-chill factor and cool nights); if you have young children, remember armbands for swimming. Take crayons, felt tips and lots of pens, paper and colouring books to keep them busy. Bring medication to deal with seasickness: try several brands before the trip, to find the one that best suits your child. Seasickness most often occurs on single hulled boats. Boats are generally cramped and there is a little privacy (though this is less true of barges), so plan breaks on dry land for everyone to let off steam.

HIKING

If your family craves the great outdoors, take them on a hiking adventure for a few days while you are travelling abroad. Rambling is relaxing: time is on your side. You can stop to spot a wildflower or admire an eagle circling, to build a dam on a river bank, or just to chat and share the experience. Kids will learn respect for the environment, independence, mutual support and risk awareness during the hike.

Many national parks maintain well-marked trails with rating levels; start off on the easiest trails to get a feel for how your kids manage. If things get too tough (or steep), turn back. An overnight stay can be part of the adventure: whether a mountain refuge, a cottage or a campsite, it will be a welcome sight at the end of the day. Tailor the adventure to your children's ages.

Between four and eight, a pack animal is a good idea. Depending on your destination, it could be a donkey, mule or camel. Not only can it carry the little one, but it is fun to have the animal around and it can also carry luggage. Between eight and 12, children have much more endurance. They can manage a longer hike and even carry a small bag. To keep it fun, don't walk more than 15km or four hours at a time.

From age 12, children will approach hiking in a more philosophical and mature way. They may wish to go with friends their age or go to an exotic location. The maximum weight of the child's backpack should not exceed 12% of their bodyweight. It is best to aim for about four to seven days for this age group, to get the most out of hiking but to avoid fatigue.

Remember to take altitude into account. Never take a child under five above 2500m or a child under 10 above 3000m. Other than that, children should take the same precautions as adults. If you book with a specialist travel agent (see Package Deals, p30), a good option is to go with a group of walkers of similar abilities on an organised route. If you prefer to go it alone, make some allowance for your fitness levels, the weight of bags, the number of days you are hiking and the distance you walk each day. Always underestimate what you are capable of doing. Check that your travel insurance covers hiking.

The last essential point is the equipment. Check that your children have proper sun protection (sunglasses, cap, sunscreen). Invest in good-quality walking shoes, they will help prevent slipping and sprains, but make sure they are worn in before you leave. Carry a daypack with a map, snacks and plenty of water, and a mini first-aid kit Don't forget the fun stuff – binoculars, compass and (for adults) a penknife. Once you are on your way, be careful to go at the children's pace. And, most importantly, have a great time!

BEST PLACES TO HIKE

> **South Africa:** Tsitsikamma National Park

> **Canada:** the Charlevoix region in Québec

> **Spain:** Parque Natural de Cabo de Gata-Níjar in Andalucía

> **Finland:** Oulanka National Park, on the edge of the Arctic Circle

> **Ireland:** County Kerry

> **Italy:** Casentinesi Forest National Park in the Apennines

> **Morocco:** The Atlas Mountains

> **New Zealand:** Abel Tasman National Park

> **Romania:** The Maramureş region

> **Switzerland:** Val d'Anniviers in the canton of Valais

⤳ THE DESERT

Whether it's North Africa, southwestern USA or the Australian outback, tranquillity, a slow pace, and a sense of being bona fide explorers are all part of the appeal of a family sojourn in the desert.

The desert may not seem like the obvious place to take a family, but in fact deserts offer a huge variety of experiences for all ages. In Tunisia and Morocco kids can hurtle down the dunes, discover troglodyte dwellings, climb arganier trees and listen to the Berbers' tales under canvas. A Bedouin camp at Wadi Rum in Jordan or a trek among the snow-white rock formations of Egypt's White Desert from a local oasis make fascinating adventures. Then there are the cactus-dotted Native American reserves, the red sands and gorges of Central Australia, and the hot springs and salt flats of the Atacama desert in Chile. Wherever you are, desert scenery is magnificent, the sense of space is awesome, and at night, far from the cities, the stars are truly out of this world.

Travel companies have family packages, usually with a minimum age of four, and with discounts for four- to 12-year-olds. Transport may be by 4WD, camel or mule. A cook is provided, who may let children join in the cooking, and introduce you to the local dishes. Tents are supplied and erected for you. They are usually large and comfortable but sometimes everyone sleeps together.

If you wish to travel to the desert independently with a local guide, wait until your children are at least eight and they are used to walking. Start with a night or a weekend in the desert as part of a longer trip. Prepare the route well and take a guide who is recommended and qualified. Plan what to eat, including lots of dried fruits, nutritious foods that keep well (such as sardines) and other precooked foods. Choose cardboard packaging that can be burnt in the fire. Everything should be easy to cook. Cooking can be a problem if it is windy. Take a gas stove. Choose stainless steel dishes, which are easy to clean and hygienic, or paper plates that you can burn. Take away rubbish that cannot be burned. Remember something to sit on (lightweight camping chairs are very handy) as the sand can be very hot at lunchtime. You should plan to take 2L of water per person per day to be carried in water bottles.

Do not pack too much, even if the camels are doing the carrying! Take cotton clothing with long sleeves and full length trousers for sun protection. Remember warm clothing as the evenings are cool and the nights are cold. Don't forget a head torch, water bottles, and sarongs or large cloths to protect you from the sun and sandstorms.

Take eye drops for the children to relieve any discomfort due to the sun, wind or sand. Before you leave, buy suitable shoes and cotton socks. Take special plasters for blisters.

Always check on the safety of travelling to an area before you go. Do not let your children walk barefoot as they may hurt themselves or get bitten. Try not to sleep directly on the sand, and always shake out your sleeping bags and clothes before putting them on. Remember that a scorpion stings only if it is disturbed and that it is only really dangerous when it is more than 5cm long. It is difficult to go to the toilet discreetly in the desert and sometimes you have to walk a long way to be out of sight. Always accompany your children when they need the toilet, even if they protest.

→ WILDLIFE WATCHING

Children are fascinated by animals, especially in their natural environment. But it's not just kids who will thrill at the sight of a whale or giraffe. The ultimate family wildlife-watching destinations are those where you can see the 'Big Five' (lions, elephants, rhinos, leopards and buffaloes) – particularly in the game reserves of Kenya, Tanzania and South Africa. These species, easy to recognise and observe, readily strike a chord with children. But beware of preconceived ideas. Contrary to what we might believe, it is not the lion that impresses children the most. Safari organisers all report that the sight of a reclining lion can be dull after a while, but watching herds of wildebeest, zebra, elephant or buffalo is more exciting, because there is movement, rhythm and action. The best experience is watching large animal migrations, for example wildebeest in Kenya and Tanzania (check for the best time to go with specialised travel agencies). Central and South America also offer fantastic opportunities for tropical safaris. Many operators will tailor safaris to suit all ages.

If your budget does not allow you to go on safari (you need to allow at least a week and costs are invariably high), there are national parks all over the world where you can experience the thrill of seeing animals in the natural landscape. In Canadian national parks, for example, you can observe bears and elk without even getting out of the car. New Zealand, both coasts of North America, Scotland, Italy and many other destinations offer whale watching; depending on where you are, you may also spot porpoises, puffins, sea lions, penguins and dolphins. For open Zodiac tours children generally need to be around eight years old; for larger boats, children of all ages are welcome. While spotting animals in the wild can be a bit hit and miss, you can be sure of a sighting at sanctuaries where wild animals are placed for protection and rehabilitation. In Las Pumas reserve in Cañas, Costa Rica, there are ocelots, jaguars, cougars and jaguarundis (eyra cat) that live in near natural conditions. Sanctuaries may be your only chance of seeing endangered species, such as the Tasmanian devil in Australia. Make a wildlife experience both fun and educational by encouraging your children to create a field journal, taking photographs of the animals, collecting entrance tickets to the parks, using books to identify species, and collecting leaves, bark and stones to keep. Specialist guides offer activities and different ways to experience the animals in most parks and reserves. Make use of their skills. They know the area and can explain, in simple terms, the way animals live, the role of predators in the food chain and the importance of biodiversity. They can also provide a human and social dimension to watching animals, as in Kakadu National Park in Australia, where Aboriginal guides pass on some of their knowledge of the area and also their culture and traditional way of life.

Where children are concerned, health and safety considerations are of course paramount. Where there are wild animals, it is nature in the raw. You should remember that there are often many insects (including mosquitoes) as well as limited medical facilities, especially in tropical and subtropical areas. Read up on the local medical facilities and the possibility of malaria. Take all appropriate medication. And don't forget your binoculars!

WHERE CAN YOU SEE ANIMALS IN THE WILD

> **South Africa:** Kruger National Park (p204)

> **Australia:** Kakadu National Park (p146)

> **Brazil:** Mamirauá Reserve or the Pantanal (p122)

> **Costa Rica:** Parque Nacional Tortuguero (128)

> **Ecuador:** Galápagos Islands (p132)

> **United States (West):** The Rockies (p140)

> **Kenya:** Masai Mara, Tsavo and Amboseli reserves (p190)

> **Sri Lanka:** Minneriya, Uda Walawe, Yala and Kaudulla National Parks (p180)

> **Tanzania:** Ngorongoro Crater and the Serengeti plains (p206)

DESTINATIONS BY THEME

Are you looking for active or more educational activities? Are your children history buffs or animal lovers? Here are some top places to visit arranged by theme to help you find the destination that will both satisfy and delight your children.

CHILDISH DELIGHTS

» Dart amongst the fish in warm waters of Fiji. (p148)

» Meet Father Christmas and visit the cave in Finland where his friends the elves prepare gingerbread. (p72)

» Build sandcastles and snack on *churros* on beaches in Spain. (p110)

» Spend time with the animals on a farmstay in Germany. (p76)

» Admire the windmills from the comfort of a bike trailer in the Netherlands while mum and dad pedal. (p94)

» Take a horse-and-carriage ride around the ramparts of Marrakesh, Morocco. (p196)

ACTIVE ENTERTAINMENT

» Learn to ski or take to the slopes like a champion in the Swiss Alps. (p114)

» Try sailing, water skiing and scuba diving in the Balearic Islands. (p54)

» Enjoy water sports or lounge on some of the most beautiful beaches in the Mediterranean in Tunisia. (p208)

» Speed along Belgium's beaches in a sand yacht. (p58)

» Splash through New Zealand's rivers in a raft, canoe, kayak or jet boat. (p150)

» Learn how to ride the waves in Sri Lanka. (p180)

BEING ROBINSON CRUSOE

» Be a castaway on the islands of Thailand. (p182)

» Become a pirate on the island of Santa Maria, on the east coast of Madagascar. (p192)

» Gather coconuts on the beautiful beaches of the Seychelles. (p202)

» Dip your toes in the sea from a bungalow on stilts in Tahiti. (p152)

» Rent a cottage on a beach in Goa and live with the rise and fall of the sun. (p162)

» Spend the night in a beach hut and wake to the spectacle of flying pelicans in Mexico. (p134)

THE ROAD TO ADVENTURE

» Play at being a *gaucho* in the Pampas before admiring glaciers and icebergs in Argentina. (p118)

» Visit the highest mountains in the world with an easy trek in Nepal. (p176)

» Explore the forest canopy by suspension bridge, zip wire or train in Costa Rica. (p128)

» Traverse the snowy Canadian landscape by dog sledge or snowmobile. (p124)

» Roam the Australian outback as far as stunning Uluru, a sacred Aboriginal site. (p146)

» Climb to the crater of Mt Etna and see the lava flows in Sicily. (p108)

» Go on a camel safari in the dunes of the Thar desert in northern India. (p160)

TALKING TO THE ANIMALS

» Observe orangutans in Malaysia. (p170)

» Watch fish and stingrays from a glass-bottomed boat in Mauritius. (p194)

» Climb into a jeep to see elephants, leopards and monkeys in the nature reserves of Sri Lanka. (p180)

» Spot whales and rorquals in Iceland. (p82)

» Tick off the 'Big Five' in the reserves of Kenya (p190), Tanzania (p206) or South Africa. (p204)

» Track giant turtles, baby sea lions and penguins in the Galápagos. (p132)

» Watch dolphins play around your boat in Tahiti. (p152)

KNIGHTS & PRINCESSES

» Hunt ghosts in the castles of Scotland. (p106)

» Visit the real Dracula's Castle in Romania. (p102)

» Play Sleeping Beauty at Neuschwanstein Castle in Germany. (p76)

» Contemplate the sea from the ramparts of a fort in Oman. (p218)

» Act like a ninja or a samurai in a film studio in Japan. (p166)

» Be a maharaja at the splendidly colourful Mysore Palace in South India. (p162)

TOP THEME PARKS

» Take a tour of the theme parks in Orlando, in the eastern United States, from the not-to-be-missed Walt Disney World® to the Harry Potter Park at Universal. (p138)

» Discover a complete world of Lego in Billund, Denmark. (p68)

» Enjoy the amusement rides of the Prater, the largest park in the Austrian capital. (p52)

» Play at cowboys in Sioux City, a Wild West town reconstructed in the Canaries. (p62)

» Throw yourself down the aqutic slide at Wild Wadi Water Park in Dubai. (p212)

» Relive the South African gold rush of the 1880s at Gold Reef City. (p204)

LOOKING FOR IDOLS

» See the groups of *cosplay-zoku*, crazy looking young people straight out of a manga in Tokyo, Japan. (p166)

» Visit villages and sets used during the filming of *Star Wars - The Phantom Menace* in Tunisia. (p208)

» Follow in the footsteps of cowboys in the old Wild West in the western United States. (p140)

» Wear a Brazilian football shirt and play *keepy uppy* on the beach like Ronaldo in Brazil. (p122)

» Stock up on trendy London t-shirts featuring the likes of the Beatles or Pete Doherty in England. (p70)

GLADIATORS & ANCIENT GODS

» Rub shoulders with the gods of Olympus in Greece and Crete. (p78)

» Explore a Roman library in the ruins of Ephesus in Turkey. (p220)

» Ride a Viking longship out into the fjords of Roskilde in Denmark. (p68)

» Visit the pyramids and temples of Egypt and travel down the Nile on a felucca like the pharaohs did. (p188)

» Walk in the emperors' footsteps at the Colloseum and the Forum in Rome or experience daily life of the ancient city of Pompeii, Italy. (p86)

» Get lost in the maze of alleys in the Diocletian Palace in Split, Croatia. (p64)

IN SOMEONE ELSE'S SHOES

» Take a djembe class on the beach and learn batik in little village in Senegal. (p200)

» Sleep in the middle of the jungle in a lodge run by an Amazonian community in Ecuador. (p132)

» Spend a night in a yurt in Mongolia. (p174)

» Experience the lives of Native American Indians today and join in a powwow in Canada. (p124)

» Meet the Sami people – the reindeer herders of Norway.

(p96)

WONDERS OF THE WORLD

» Take a train up the mountain to Macchu Picchu, the mysterious Inca city in Peru. (p136)

» Walk along the Great Wall of China, the longest man-made structure in the world. (p158)

» Discover the spectacular Taj Mahal and the glittering palaces of Rajasthan in North India. (p160)

» Take a camel ride to the pyramids of Giza, just like one of the majestic pharaohs. (p188)

» Climb the pyramids of the great Mayan and Aztec cities of Mexico and take in the jungle views. (p134)

» Explore Petra, the Rose City, hidden in a canyon in the Jordanian mountains. (p216)

» See the hundreds of temples of Angkor hidden in the Cambodian jungle. (p156)

⤳ COUNTRY BY COUNTRY

Europe

Europe is a great destination for a family holiday. Good hygiene standards, familiar food and quality health services are comforting factors.

In Europe, everyone can get their bearings, including the children. Harry Potter will cast a spell over any trip to England, the Little Mermaid will swim alongside you in Denmark, the von Trapp family will sing you through Austria, and Tintin will transform a stay in Brussels into a breathless adventure. In each country the youngsters will find heroes to follow and will readily soak up the culture. And what could be better than Greco-Roman remains and actual fortified castles to arouse their interest in history!

All the while, beaches equipped with everything you need or mountain resorts with all the creature comforts are never far away, letting you divide your time between cultural visits and outdoor adventure. The distances are short. No need for seven-league boots or endless hours on a bumpy bus to take in new sights. If you're used to driving on the right side of the road, the option of driving yourself makes things a lot easier. However, Europe is not always the easiest place on your wallet and higher prices have put off more than one family. To avoid breaking the bank, use low-cost airlines and try to rent houses or apartments privately. You could also consider an exchange with your own home. Let someone else stay at your place while you discover their quaint Tuscan cottage or Transylvanian log cabin, just for the holidays.The old Continent is a place of adventure – strolling through the Romanian countryside, canoeing on a Finnish lake, or island hopping on a cruise in Croatia – but one of minimal stress for parents.

AUSTRIA

In the land of Mozart and Empress Sisi, Austria's many castles have plenty of appeal for the very young, who will have a lot of fun while discovering the stories they hold. The mountains are as inviting for outdoor pursuits in winter as in summer. The lakes more than make up for the sea when it comes to swimming. The neat villages and homely atmosphere make Austria an ideal starting point for parents taking their first steps as family travellers.

Austria is perfect for family skiing

CHILDREN WILL LOVE...
Memories of emperors, princes and princesses
» In Vienna, the Sisi Museum – particularly for girls! Set inside the Hofburg Palace, it features portraits and clothes of the famous empress.
» The Schönbrunn Palace: this former royal summer residence houses a museum with little ones in mind. It depicts daily life for the royal children (dressing up is possible at the end of the visit!).
» A trip in a horse-drawn carriage through the streets of Vienna.
» The Kaiservilla, another royal summer residence set in a pretty park in the spa town of Bad Ischl in Upper Austria.

A fairy-tale atmosphere
» Painted houses, country villages, baroque churches topped with bells, bulb farms and fertile pastures with grazing cows: this land will transport you into a picture-book past, especially in the Tyrol, home to many Austrian traditions.
» The castles of Salzburg: the Hohensalzburg fortress, which you reach by funicular; and Hellbrunn Palace with its 'trick' fountains.
» Mozart's house, to turn your little angels into budding music lovers.

Custom-made entertainment
» The puppet theatre in Salzburg: classic opera pieces performed by wooden puppets!
» The Prater: home to amusement rides (including the famous big wheel!) and the puppet theatre in this vast park in Vienna.
» Shows at the Spanish Riding School (the world-renowned equestrian centre).

Outdoor activities
» Cross-country and downhill skiing: national pastimes especially in the Tyrol and in the Austrian Alps. The ski resorts of Filzmoos (Salzburg region) and Heiligenblut (Carinthia) are particularly family friendly.
» 50,000km of sign-posted pathways countrywide, ideal for walking, and the superb network of cycle paths.
» Swimming in the lakes when the weather is good. Neusiedl Lake, nicknamed the 'Viennese Sea', is a Unesco World Heritage site.
» The Danube Island in Vienna, with its safe beaches and many recreational pursuits.

Excursions for the adventurous
» The Erzberg iron ore mine: you can explore underground galleries and, for a bit of a thrill, watch a sound and light re-enactment of an explosion. There is also an above-ground tour of the open pit on the back of a huge mining truck.
» The Eisriesenwelt caves, the biggest glacial (in every sense!) caves open to visitors in the world.

BEST TIME TO GO

Winter sports season runs from mid-December to March. The resorts are packed (and more expensive) during the Christmas holidays. The rest of the time you can fully enjoy a rich natural environment, cycle, and swim in the lakes! Most major festivals take place between May and October.

COST

All the grandeur of Austria comes at a cost. It is a fairly pricey place to travel, comparable to neighbouring Italy but not as expensive as Switzerland. Transport is a big expense (along with restaurants), although there are generous discounts for children. Guesthouses in the country are a good option with kids. In summer many hotels and pensions in Vienna offer free bed and breakfast accommodation for up to two children under 12, if sharing their parents' room. Sausage stands are good for a quick, cheap meal.

GETTING AROUND

If you travel by car, you will need to pay a toll to use the motorways and certain highways by buying a windscreen sticker (called a vignette) These are available at the border, service stations, post offices and on the internet. Cycling enthusiasts are well served with thousands of kilometres of bike lanes. Bikes can be hired at one railway station and deposited at another: helpful! During school holidays and on Sundays, children 15 and under can use public transport for free. The rest of the time children under six go free and it is half price for six- to 16-year-olds.

Mealtimes

Your children will love schnitzel – meat or fish in breadcrumbs found on every menu – particularly the famous Wiener schnitzel, the Viennese veal cutlet. They will love the huge range of sausages (*wurst*) available in restaurants and from street stalls. Dishes are often served with potatoes. The Austrians have a well-earned reputation for desserts: tiny food lovers will adore *apfelstrüdel* (flaky pastry with apple and raisins) or *sachertorte* (a Viennese speciality made with chocolate and apricot jam).

🕐 Time difference

→ Time zone UTC+01:00. Daylight saving time observed in northern hemisphere summer.

BOOKS FOR THE YOUNG TRAVELLER
> Teenagers will enjoy Graham Greene's *The Third Man*.

CHILDREN'S SOUVENIRS
> Cuddly marmot toys
> Walking sticks
> Wooden toys, ideal for the very young

BALEARIC ISLANDS

Don't be put off by the crowds of yachts casting anchor in the creeks and at certain packed beaches. In spite of mass tourism, the Spanish islands of Mallorca, Menorca and Formentera have retained their character – unlike Ibiza, which is not at all a family destination. On these three islands, whether it be in hotel kids' clubs, where a range of entertainment is laid on for children, or far from the madding crowd, everyone will find their own thing.

Meandering through Mediterranean villages

CHILDREN WILL LOVE...
Sports and activities

» Long hours swimming in a warm, safe sea. Beaches in Formentera and Menorca are quieter than the rest in summer.
» Walks through scented pine forests along the eastern shores of Formentera or the rocky cliffs of northwest Mallorca.
» Water sports for children aged eight or above: sailing, waterskiing, diving and canoeing.
» Biking along *rutas verdes* (green routes) in Formentera, often old railway lines reclaimed for walkers and cyclists.
» Horse riding round Menorca on the *camino de los caballos* (horse trail).
» Various amusement parks.

Uncovering a long, troubled history
» The prehistoric burial sites of Ca Na Costa (Formentera) and the *taulus* (standing stones) of Menorca, set in place between 1000 and 300 BC.
» The roman theatre of Pollentia (Alcúdia, Mallorca).
» The Moorish ramparts of Alcúdia.
» The medieval feel of Menorcan festivals such as the Festa de Sant Joan in Ciutadella (end of June), marked by a great cavalcade of horses.
» The Formentera towers used by locals to look out for pirates.
» Well-preserved towns like San Francesc (Formentera) and Deià (Mallorca).

Hidden but stunning scenery
» Exploring the five cave systems of the archipelago, such as Drach ('the dragon') and Hams (Mallorca).
» Sublime seascapes, such as at Cap de Formentor (Mallorca) or at Punta des Ras (Formentera).
» An excursion in a glass-bottomed boat at Port Andratx (Mallorca).

Cultural gems in the towns and villages
» The Castell de Bellver in Palma (Mallorca), a fortress that will impress the children.
» The Joan Miró Foundation in Palma (Mallorca) where your children can visit the artist's studio, preserved intact.
» The beautiful port of Mahón (Menorca), best explored by boat.
» Memories of Chopin and George Sand in the Valldemossa Monastry (Mallorca).

BEST TIME TO GO

The Balearic Islands are good to visit at any time but May, June, September and October are the best for children. Summer can be very hot; tourists flood in from all over Europe and invade the beaches in droves (and worse still, hotels raise their rates). Winters are mild and sunny, but do not expect to be on the beach! Menorca, the northernmost of the isles, enjoys much cooler temperatures throughout the year.

COST

While budget airline flights from the UK are cheap and good package deals are available, the islands are a tourist magnet and so accommodation and eating out are notoriously expensive. Prices skyrocket in summer. Menorca is less commercially developed than Mallorca, making it easier to escape the resort prices.

GETTING AROUND

Ferries link Palma in Mallorca with the other islands (frequency varies according to the season). There are also flights connecting the islands but they are far more expensive. Two rail lines cross Mallorca. There are a number of buses on Mallorca and Menorca; in Formentera, a bus service serves the main places. It is possible to rent a car and bicycles are available on all the main islands in the archipelago. There are taxis in every town.

Mealtimes

Paella is fantastic wherever you are. Even better, this dish of saffron rice, fresh vegetables, chicken and seafood, which is nourishing and well balanced, is loved by children. Fish and seafood, along with pork, are basic ingredients in many dishes. In Menorca, the culinary tradition is more surprising: pudding, stuffed turkey and macaroni cheese are widely available, a throwback to the days of English rule.

Warning
→ Protect children well from the heat and sun.

Time difference
→ Time zone UTC+01:00. Daylight saving time observed in northern hemisphere summer.

BOOKS FOR THE YOUNG TRAVELLER
› Two lovely fairy tales are *The Flowers of Mallorca* by Alexander Mehdevi and *The Princess and the Pumpkin: Adapted from a Majorcan Tale* by Maggie Duff.
› For pre-teens, the *Souls of the Sea* trilogy by David J Mason is a combination of mystery, adventure and fantasy in a Spanish island setting.

CHILDREN'S SOUVENIRS
› Treasure boxes carved from olive wood

BALTIC STATES

The most striking feature in Estonia, Latvia and Lithuania? The architecture, a dream come true for would-be princes and princesses! However, children can also discover the joy of outdoor pursuits (canoeing on the lakes and rivers, walking and cycling) in surprisingly unspoilt countryside. Do not forget, as well, the fun to be had in the sea and on the Baltic beaches.

Fairy-tale views of forests and castles

CHILDREN WILL LOVE...

Discovering nature from the water

» Exploring the bogs and marshes of the Soomaa National Park (Estonia), in a canoe or *haabja*, a traditional boat: accompanied by a guide, you may be lucky to see bears, lynx, beavers or elk.
» Canoeing or rafting (without fear for the children's safety, the rivers are calm) on the Gauja, the Salaca or the Abava, in Latvia.
» Rowing on the network of rivers and lakes in the Aukštaitija National Park (Lithuania).

Castles, fortresses & ramparts

» Rakvere Castle (Estonia) has a number of activities geared to younger visitors, such as archery and sword skills.
» The medieval centres of the capitals Tallinn, Riga and Vilnius.
» The film-set like Trakai Island Castle (Lithuania).

» The teutonic castle of Kuressaare, perfectly preserved in the timeless setting of the Saaremaa Island (Estonia).
» The ruins of Cēsis Castle (Latvia), a legacy of the Porte-Glaive knights.
» The Rocca Al Mare (better known as the Estonian Open Air Museum), near Tallinn, where traditional wooden houses and other buildings have been recreated.

The Baltic lifestyle

» Picking berries and mushrooms – almost a national pastime in all three countries. You can even link up with a group of experts for organised foraging.
» Biking on the many cycle lanes; bikes are easy to hire except in Lithuania where you should go through your hotel.
» Sledging, cross-country skiing and horse-drawn sledge rides: all the means necessary for exploring the landscape in the snow!
» Swimming from the Baltic beaches, particularly the small resort of Pärnu (Estonia). Jurmala, in Latvia, and Palanga, in Lithuania, are very accommodating for families.
» Hunting for amber in the Baltic sand. Several mines and museums are dedicated to this fossilised resin: the best is found in the nearby Russian enclave of Kaliningrad.

Activities for all

» Otepää Adventure Park (Estonia) and its tree-top walks, some specially devised for children.
» The mini electric cars at Bernardine Gardens (formerly Sereikiškės Park) in Vilnius (Lithuania), or a tour of the fortified city by horse-drawn carriage or taxi-bike.
» The Tartu Toy Museum (Estonia): its centerpiece is a railway that's almost actual size.

NEED TO KNOW

BEST TIME TO GO

Spring and the start of summer are the best times to visit the Baltic States: the temperatures are kind, nature is in full bloom and the solstice festivals are great fun. Summer is fairly hot, sometimes rainy; forget about swimming if you feel the cold: water temperatures waver between 16 and 21°C. Winter is best avoided as it is really cold – unless you are a fan of skating or cross-country skiing.

COST

The cost of living in the Baltic states is relatively low, but as the tourism industry becomes more upmarket, travel is not necessarily cheap. Food and transport are cheaper than in Western Europe, but petrol is only marginally so, and some goods, like disposable nappies, are more expensive. Higher end hotels and car hire are comparable with Western Europe. Campsite chalets are a very economical form of accommodation, and care hire rates can be more competitive if you go through a small private rental agency. All three countries now have the euro as currency.

HEALTH CHECK

» Tap water is safe to drink. Although in rural areas it is advisable to drink bottled water or use purification tablets.
» Mosquitoes can be unremitting in certain wetter zones. Use repellent and cover up.

GETTING AROUND

Buses are efficient, fast and comfortable in all three countries. They are better than the trains, which are less practical and more costly. In town, public transport is often packed but taxis are very affordable. The roads are in good condition and traffic runs well. You can also rent a car. Flights between the countries are not worth the trouble as journeys are short and prices high.

Mealtimes

Here potatoes reign supreme. In Estonia, they are served with pork, chicken, sausages or smoked fish. In Latvia, children will adore savoury pancakes (*pankukas*) filled with meat or cheese, as well as *piragi* (stuffed bread rolls), delicious with a hard-boiled egg or bacon. The staple dessert is the berry tart of which Latvians are so fond. In Lithuania, the preference is for *cepelinai*, cheesy potato dumplings with meat and mushrooms, and *blyneliai*, blini-like sweet or savoury pancakes.

Time difference

Time zone UTC+02:00. Daylight saving time observed in northern hemisphere summer.

BOOKS FOR THE YOUNG TRAVELLER

› *Between Shades of Gray* by Ruta Sepetys is a moving novel for teens about a Lithuanian girl trying to survive in a Soviet work camp.
› *The Darkest Corner of the World* by Urve Tamberg is a similar young adult novel about a girl trying to keep her family together during WWII, this time in Estonia.

CHILDREN'S SOUVENIRS

› Wooden toys and dolls

BELGIUM

Chocolate, chips and comic books mean Belgium has some serious pluses for the young. With its pleasant towns, trips on the canals, to the seaside and into the country, children and teenagers cannot fail to find something they like.

Belgium abounds in childish delights

CHILDREN WILL LOVE...
Brussels, the capital of comic books
» The Belgian centre of comic books with permanent exhibitions dedicated to the Smurfs and Tintin.
» Explore the city by following the many murals that make up the comic-book trail.
» The futuristic architecture of the Atomium and the Mini-Europe model park stretching beneath it.
» The Mannekin Pis, the statue of a careless kid weeing into a fountain who changes his clothes as often as there are festivals throughout the year.
» Puppet shows at the tiny theatre royal of Toone.

» The Hergé Museum in Louvain-la-Neuve where you can find out all you need to know about Tintin, Captain Haddock and Professor Calculus.

The country of belfries and giants
» The pretty town of Ghent with its turreted castle and belfry.
» Bruges, with its toy-town look: you can ride in a horse-drawn carriage or stroll along the canals dotted with windmills.
» Antwerp: its famous zoo, the oldest in the country; beautiful Het Steen fortress; and model boats at the Museum aan de Stroom.
» Traditional processions of giants. Gigantic figures are paraded round the towns: on 'Crazy Monday' in January in Ronse; during the carnivals in Halle and Stavelot in February; and during the dragon-slaying festivals, the Ducasse of Mons (in June or July) and the Ducasse of Ath (late August).
» The carnival of Binche, one of the most beautiful in Belgium, which takes place in the three days running up to Mardi Gras.

Rivers and canals
» Boat excursions on the canals of Bruges and Ghent.
» A cruise on the Central Canal from Houdeng-Goegnies to the spectacular hydraulic boat lifts.
» Kayaking on the rivers Ourthe, Semois or Lesse.
» A walk in the Sûre River valley and water sports on the lakes.

By the sea
» Long beaches in Ostend and small resorts like Blankenberge or De Panne (with its amusement park, Plopsaland). Sand yachting is a possibility for children aged eight and above.
» Exploring the Mercator, a famous three-masted ship, and Amandine, a former fishing boat, moored at Ostend.

BEST TIME TO GO

True, you have every chance of being caught out by a shower, even in summer, but there are a lot of bright, sunny days. In winter, the cold, dry weather can lead to very pleasant days, perfect for a family day out in one of the country's beautiful towns. The hottest period stretches from April to September. Swimming is best in July and August.

COST

Accommodation and dining will burn the biggest hole in your pocket; though Belgium's exciting fashions, sublime chocolates and speciality beers can all seriously dent the credit card too. Public transport, on the other hand, is cheap – and that, coupled with the diminutive size the country, makes getting around a minor expense. Families can minimise expenses by staying at hostels, B&Bs or self-contained guesthouses. Restaurants often have discounted children's meals, usually costing around €8. Also look out for the occasional restaurant offering complimentary children's meals. Keep in mind too that children under 12 travel for free on Belgian trains.

Mealtimes

If children dislike mussels, they will love the chips that are served with them. Another side dish appreciated by the young, *stoemp* is a sort of puréed potato mixed with other vegetables. In restaurants and brasseries, little ones will find a number of familiar dishes; *waterzooi*, a ragout of fish and chicken cooked with cream, is one they might like. The sweet-toothed will quickly succumb to *speculoos* (cinnamon and brown-sugar biscuits), which pop up in various desserts, and tasty waffles are a surefire bet – they can be bought still warm from the many street sellers.

BOOKS FOR THE YOUNG TRAVELLER

> Invest in a set of Tintin books. Tintin memorabilia abounds in Belgium and most shops stock some of Hergé's books in English.

CHILDREN'S SOUVENIRS

> Countless figurines of comic book heroes

> All kinds of chocolates

GETTING AROUND

The country has a network of motorways, which means travel between towns is easy. The train is also very efficient and painless (InterCity trains are the fastest). Services are free for children under 12. In town, use public transport, particularly in Brussels, which has trams and an underground, and in Antwerp. Bikes are a good option in a country where many roads have cycle lanes. You can also hire boats to travel the canals and rivers.

🕐 Time difference

→ Time zone UTC+01:00. Daylight saving time observed in northern hemisphere summer.

BULGARIA

With its unspoilt scenery, this still little-known corner of Europe is the perfect destination for holidays combining outdoor activities with exploring a rich, cultural heritage. Roman and Thracian ruins can inspire dreams of becoming an archaeologist, while modern beach resorts satisfy any urge to swim.

Bulgaria's beautiful green mountains

CHILDREN WILL LOVE...
Outdoor activities in unspoilt countryside

» Horse riding in the green hills surrounding the museum town of Arbanasi, former summer residence of the aristocracy.
» Bird-watching with a guide around Lake Srebârna, a vast natural reserve, where you can also go out in a caique, a narrow boat used by local fishermen.
» Exploring lakes and rivers by kayak; bigger children can try rafting, accompanied by qualified guides.

Beach resorts on the Black Sea

» The Golden Sands resort (Zlatni Pyasâtsi), which is among the most beautiful in Europe. Situated at the heart of a natural reserve, this family-friendly resort has a wide range of activities aimed at children including an aqua park, Aquapolis, where prices are fixed according to the height of the participant. Under 90cm it's free.

» Varna, 'the pearl of the Black Sea', a coastal town steeped in history. The archaeological museum is the biggest in the country and contains well-preserved Roman thermal baths. The Primorski Park is not short on attractions: a dolphinarium, zoo, planetarium, and open air theatre.
» Nesebâr, a museum town with beautiful, wooden houses and picturesque lanes, on a peninsula with a bewitching charm (especially out of season without the crowds). It is in stark contrast to Sunny Beach (Slânchev Bryag), a popular but soulless resort.

The vestiges of Bulgaria's rich history

» The Roman remains of Plovdiv, and notably the magnificently renovated amphitheatre.
» Veliko Târnovo, the fortified former capital.
» The Rila monastery. The most courageous will head for a hike in the surrounding mountains, with criss-crossing paths peppered with picnic spots.
» Fortresses including Shumen and Kaleto (also known as Belogradchik), evoking battles fought by the Bulgarians against the Thracians, Romans and Ottomans down the centuries.
» The old village of Koprivshtitsa, with its overgrown lanes. Children can roam freely here between the houses, dating from the Bulgarian Revival Period.

Unusual escapades

» A ride in a cable car to the summit of Mt Vitosha, which dominates Sofia at a height of 2290m.
» An expedition into the gorges and caves at Trigrad and Yagodina in the Rodopi Mountains to discover the impressive stalactites and stalagmites.

BEST TIME TO GO

In the spring, the climate is mild and so are the prices. An ideal time to enjoy Sofia!

COST

Since Bulgaria joined the EU in 2007, the dual-pricing system that used to be in force – whereby foreigners were often charged considerably more for hotel rooms and museum admission fees than locals – has been abolished. Inevitably, prices have risen, but travelling around the country remains relatively cheap. All food, drink and forms of transport are surprisingly inexpensive compared with Western European countries, but imported luxury goods, such as international-brand fashion and cosmetics, cost much the same as anywhere else. Many museums and galleries offer free entry on one day of the week. Also, if you fancy staying at a top-class hotel but don't fancy paying the top-class tariff, remember that most offer discounted weekend rates (which usually means Friday to Sunday night). Some top-end hotels in Sofia offer discounts during August, when most tourists have gone to the coast.

Mealtimes

It will be easy to introduce your children to Bulgarian cuisine: meatballs in the shape of *kebabche* and *kyufte* are everywhere and usually served with chips (*pârzheni kartofi*) often coated in local cheese (*sirene*). The little ones will love the very sugary desserts: baklava from neighbouring Turkey, *tulumbichki* (fried pastry dipped in syrup), and Bulgarian yogurt, as tasty as it is famous.

BOOKS FOR THE YOUNG TRAVELLER

> *Folk Tales & Fables from Bulgaria* contains tales of heroes, nymphs and dragons compiled by Roberta Moretti (translated into English by Diana Nikolova).
> Preteens will discover the world of a Bulgarian peasant boy who dreams of being an artist in *Dobry* by Monica Shannon.

CHILDREN'S SOUVENIRS

> *Martenitsi* (embroidered dolls)
> Toys and musical instruments made of wood
> Chess games

GETTING AROUND

Bulgaria is a compact country so it is easy and cheapest to move around by bus. The trains are less comfortable and slower. Cars are useful for reaching out-of-the-way villages, however the roads are in a poor state and you need to buy a windscreen sticker to drive outside the big towns (on sale in service stations, post offices and at borders). Take a decent map; most of the road signs are written in Cyrillic.

🛈 **Warning**
→ At night it is inadvisable to walk around in the big towns beyond the city centres.

🕔 **Time difference**
→ Time zone UTC+02:00. Daylight saving time observed in northern hemisphere summer.

CANARY ISLANDS

Volcanic, lunar landscapes, deserts, white or black sandy beaches, lush pine forests…in the Canaries, there are no end of surprises! This sun-kissed archipelago, a veritable galaxy of islands, has everything laid on for families. Amusement parks, a zoo, water slides: here, holidays last all year round.

Plunging into the Canaries' welcoming water

CHILDREN WILL LOVE...

Beaches, swimming pools and aqua parks

» White or black sandy beaches for swimming or well-organised activities (such as diving and kayaking). Those at Costa Calma and Caleta de Fuste on the island of Fuerteventura are peaceful, as are the ones in southern Tenerife; what is more the waters are shallow.

» Salt-water swimming pools, natural or artificial, all along the Tenerife coast. These are protected from dangerous currents.

» Water slides and other water attractions at Aqualand on Gran Canaria and Baku Water Park on Fuerteventura. A must: César Manrique Maritime Park in Santa Cruz, Tenerife.

Underwater life

» Watching for dolphins, whales and sperm whales on boat tours in the waters between Tenerife and La Gomera.

» Exploring the marine depths on board a submarine with Submarine Safaris, departing from at Puerto Calero (Lanzarote).

Animals with fur, feathers and scales

» Birds of prey, monkeys, caimans, tigers, white lions: they can all be viewed in Jungle Park (Tenerife).

» Giant lizards of El Hierro, an endemic species: see them at the Lagartario centre in the Guinea Ecomuseum.

» The Loro Park (Tenerife): 3000 parrots live here. There is also an underground aquarium and an amazing 'penguinarium'!

» Camel rides organised by Oasis Park, a small zoo in Fuerteventura.

Theme parks and carnivals

» Roller coasters, bouncy castle, ponies… Holiday World in Maspalomas, on Gran Canaria, is the biggest fun park in the archipelago.

» Sioux City, on Gran Canaria: a reconstruction of a Wild West town where budding cowboys can jump on a horse and enjoy the shows.

» Tenerife carnival in February: dancing and singing brings the streets to life over several days, while the floats compete to be the most colourful and outlandish.

Marvellous landscapes

» The lunar landscape of the Timanfaya National Park (Lanzarote), the legacy of earlier volcanic eruptions.

» El Teide volcano, on Tenerife. You can take a cable car to the top, from where the views of the lava columns of Pico Viejo are spectacular.

BEST TIME TO GO

Whatever the time of year, the Canaries enjoy a mild, sunny climate. December to March is considered high season. Numbers of holidaymakers (and the price of flights and hotels) also soar during the Easter and summer holidays (however they remain moderate rates: the Canaries are still very affordable).

COST

Daily living expenses on the Canary Islands are lower than those in most countries of Western Europe. Accommodation, which is plentiful, can be a bargain compared to other popular European holiday destinations. Food, too, is inexpensive for both self-caterers and avid restaurant-goers. Car hire is cheap, taxi transport is good value over short distances and public buses are generally economical. Flying between the islands can be a bit more expensive but time-saving. Theme and amusement parks are all pricey, especially for large family groups.

Mealtimes

Most people dine from 9pm on, except in tourist areas. Children will last if given a solid afternoon tea of local sweet dishes, like *bienmesabe* (a mixture of eggs, honey and almonds) or *quesadillas* from El Hierro (cinnamon cheesecakes). They will love the many fresh fruits (such as dwarf bananas, mangoes and papayas). The restaurants offer a lot of fresh fish. If the children demand chips, let them taste *papas arrugadad*, baked jacket potatoes served with different fillings or sauces, *mojos*. Taste each one first to determine spicyness.

GETTING AROUND

All seven islands in the archipelago have airports: you can fly easily between them, it is not much more than the ferry and a lot faster. Travelling by bike is fun for the children, but beware of drivers who pay scant attention to cyclists. There are no cycle paths in towns, except along the beaches. Buses can be few and far between, especially on the smaller isles. Hiring a car is a good way to get off the beaten track.

! Warning

→ Beware of currents, which can be very strong along the coast, as can the wind at Fuerteventura and Lanzarote. Stick to the most popular beaches where there are lifeguards.

→ The health services may be modern and efficient, but there are few facilities on the smaller islands.

! Time difference

→ Time zone UTC. Daylight saving time observed in northern hemisphere summer.

BOOKS FOR THE YOUNG TRAVELLER

› A family of dolphin researchers visiting the Canaries rescue the endearing animals in *Following the Rainbow* by Ben M. Baglio, part of the preteen *Dolphin Diaries* series.

› Watch the movie of *Pirates of the Caribbean* or read one of the series of junior novelisations – the action takes place around the prime pirate haunts of the Canaries.

CHILDREN'S SOUVENIRS

› A *timple*, a type of local guitar.

CROATIA

With its rugged coastline, shielded by countless sun-soaked isles accessible by boat, its medieval castles steeped in mystery and its many historic sites, Croatia is the ideal destination for the family wishing to combine the beach with a bit of culture.

Enjoying an ice cream in the town of Zadar

CHILDREN WILL LOVE...
Swimming, diving, playing on the beaches
» Six kilometres of pebbly beaches in Brela, near Makarska: not too crowded with ideal temperatures for bathing.
» The picturesque creeks of the Mljet Island National Park, which can be explored by bike with bigger children.
» Brač Island, where water sports enthusiasts can enjoy diving, kayaking, fun boarding and windsurfing.
» *Picigin*, a traditional ballgame played in shallow water: your children can take on their new Croatian friends.

Gifts of nature
» The Sea Organ in Zadar, where waves make music by gushing through a system of pipes and holes. Magic!
» The green labyrinth surrounding the lakes and churning waterfalls of the Plitvice Lakes National Park – where there are fabulous walks.

» The Krka National Park where cascades and lakes fall and flow in turn. Take the children's bathing costumes as swimming is allowed in the lower lake.
» The gaping Pazin Chasm, which inspired Jules Verne's novel *Mathias Sandorf*. The hectic Jules Verne Days festival, including an enactment of the book, among other events, takes place the third week in June.
» A stroll or a bike ride on Cres, an untamed island where you can swim in the creeks, explore the ancient woodlands and visit the old mountain villages.

Cities and castles that transport you back in time
» The spectacular walls and forts that encircle Dubrovnik's medieval old town, which can be explored on foot.
» The imposing Diocletian Palace in Split, a massive Roman fortress which is now a maze of bustling streets dotted with modern shops and ancient temples, where 3000 people still live today.
» Medieval castles like Morosini-Grimani castle, where witchcraft and black magic hang heavy in the air, or the castle of Trakošćan in the north, straight out of a fairy tale.

Dance and puppet shows
» The Rijeka City Puppet Theatre, the International Puppet Theatre Festival of Zagreb or the Vukovar Puppet Spring in March.
» Workshops and theatre shows for children at the magical International Children's Festival in Šibenik in June and July.
» Dances set to the music of violins at the International Folklore Festival in Zagreb in August.

BEST TIME TO GO

High season is from July to August but the Croatian coast is wonderful from spring on. Swimming is generally possible from May, particularly in central Dalmatia and in the south. In September the sea is still around 23°C.

COST

Croatia is still reasonably inexpensive as a Mediterranean destination, but prices soar in July and August, especially for accommodation. Self-catering apartments often cost little more than a hotel room, so can be a great option for families. Privately run rooms are also often a better bet than hotels, which tend to be sterile and unfriendly. If you are not accosted by room owners on arrival, the local tourist office or travel agency will be able to help. There is usually a 30% discount for stays longer than three nights. Tour operators may offer a very reasonable deal on a flight plus car hire.

Mealtimes

If the goulash and ragout – commonly found in the interior, from Hungarian and Viennese influences – do not tempt your children, then they will be more taken with the Italian-style coastal cuisine, where pasta, risotto and crispy pizzas often feature on the menu. They will love *štrukli* (soft cheese pasties), the wide variety of deserts (especially *pala*č*inke*, fine pancakes filled with jam or coated in chocolate), and of course there are the ice creams (*sladoded*) that are as good as any Italian gelati.

BOOKS FOR THE YOUNG TRAVELLER

> *It's Castle Time! A Kid's Guide To Dubrovnik, Croatia* by Penelope Dyan and John D Weigand is a guide to this magical walled city from a kid's perspective, which encourages readers to add their own photographs and observations.

> The folk tales in *Stories of Hope and Spirit* by Dan Keding were told to him by his Croatian grandmother. They originate from many of the countries of Eastern Europe, and reflect the challenges, hope and courage of this embattled region.

> A novel for older children, *Trophy Kid* by Steve Atinsky tells the story of a Croatian war refugee adopted by Hollywood parents who returns to his home country to discover his roots.

CHILDREN'S SOUVENIRS

> Blouses with intricate red embroidery

GETTING AROUND

Croatia is a small country; it only takes a few hours maximum to travel from one region to another. It might be worth staying in one place for the whole holiday and doing day trips. The trains and, even more so, the buses, reach the remotest places. Local ferries link the mainland and the biggest islands: book your tickets and turn up several hours in advance if taking a car.

❗ Warning

↪ Watch out for sea urchins along the Adriatic coast. Plastic sandals are the best protection for little feet.

↪ Tap water is safe to drink but can taste strongly of chlorine, giving children an unpleasant surprise.

🕑 Time difference

↪ Time zone UTC+01:00. Daylight saving time observed in northern hemisphere summer.

CZECH REPUBLIC & SLOVAKIA

Prague looks like something straight out of a picture book, while the rest of the Czech Republic, though less well known, conceals a mass of castles that cannot fail to arouse a child's imagination. As for Slovakia, peppered with caves and mountains, it is ideal terrain for parents to explore and children to have fun in.

Golden Lane in magical Prague Castle

CHILDREN WILL LOVE...
Prague and its theatrical backdrops

» Prague Castle: an enormous fortress within which lie streets and museums, including one dedicated to toys. The changing of the guard is a must see.
» A funicular ride to the top of Petřín Hill for an unrivalled view of the town; the mirror maze found at the top will delight children.
» The astronomical clock in the main square, whose chimes will impress big and small.
» A boat excursion on the Vltava River. On the island of Slovanský Ostrov (also known as Žofín) you can rent boats and pedalos.

Countries of 2000 castles

» Spiš Castle (Slovakia), one of the biggest medieval fortresses in central Europe.
» The fortified castles of Kost, Pernštejn, Karlštejn and Bouzov (Czech Republic) and that of Orava (Slovakia), clinging to its rocky peak.
» The rococo theatre at the Czech castle of Český Krumlov, with its original wooden machinery.

Trips to the past

» The ancient silver mines at Kutná Hora (Czech Republic), an underground visit for children seven and upwards.
» Open-air folk museums, with reconstructed houses, windmills and folkloric entertainment: Wallachian (Valašske) Museum of Rožnov pod Radhoštěm (Czech Republic); Zuberec, Čičmany and Vlkolínec (Slovakia).
» The ossuary of Sedlec at Kutná Hora (Czech Republic) should leave a vivid impression on teenagers, as should the torture chamber at Liptovský Mikuláš (Slovakia).

Caves, lakes and mountains

» Walking along one of the rivers wending through the Šumava National Park (Czech Republic).
» Ascending the Krkonoše Mountains (Czech Republic) in a cable car.
» A peaceful boat excursion through the Kamenice Gorge, in Bohemian Switzerland National Park (Czech Republic).
» The caves and gorges of the Moravian Karst in the Czech Republic (you can take a boat through the subterranean rivers) and of the Slovak Karst (especially Gombasecká, Domica and Ochtinská Caves).
» Swimming in the numerous lakes surrounding the beautiful Slovak town of Banská Štiavnica.

BEST TIME TO GO

May to September is the most popular tourist times; April and October are cooler and could be a cheaper alternative for visiting the two countries. Most Czechs take their holidays in July and August and the hotels and tourist sights are therefore at their busiest. This is even more so in Prague, in the Krkonoše National Park and in the Tatra Mountains. Many sights and hotels, outside ski resorts, close from November to May.

COST

Prague used to be the place Europeans would go for a cheap weekend – unfortunately this is not so anymore. The Czech Republic is still a good bargain though, you get beautiful scenery and that stunning capital city at prices that are cheaper than nearby Austria, Germany and Poland, and there are plenty of low-cost airlines flying to Prague from other European cities. Try accommodation out of the city centre for the best deals. Avoid tourist hot-spots and you will find restaurants very reasonable. Slovakia is cheaper still, commensurate with Eastern European countries. It has not yet suffered from too much tourism, and as a result is an affordable place to travel.

Mealtimes

Czech cuisine has not got much of a reputation, but the usual diet of meat in sauces, potatoes (mashed or puréed, gnocchi or chips) goes down well with children. So does the unbeatable *knedliky* (dumplings). Cabbage and sauerkraut and different sausages should please them too. For dessert, pancakes and big cakes full of cream should leave small tummies feeling full.

BOOKS FOR THE YOUNG TRAVELLER
> Older readers will enjoy James Watson's thriller *Ticket to Prague*.
> *Czech, Moravian and Slovak Fairy Tales* by Parker Fillmore is a noteworthy collection of local tales.

CHILDREN'S SOUVENIRS
> Wooden toys: jigsaw puzzles, logic puzzles and spinning tops
> All kinds of puppets

GETTING AROUND

The best way to get around both countries is by car; otherwise switching from train (for longer journeys) to bus (for short distances) allows you to cross both territories cheaply and easily. Prague is easy to get around either on foot or using the subway and tram.

🕐 Time difference
→ Time zone UTC+01:00. Daylight saving time observed in northern hemisphere summer.

DENMARK

It is one big party for children in the land of Hans Christian Andersen: there are children's sections in the best museums with any number of other attractions elsewhere. The whole family can enjoy a cycle ride anywhere in the country, or you can follow in the wake of the Vikings with boat trips that explore the many fjords and islands.

The chalk cliffs and white sands of the Danish coast

CHILDREN WILL LOVE...
Activities in a kind, natural environment
» Biking the flattest of terrain, crossed by countless cycle paths. The peaceful southern islands (Møn, Falster and Lolland) are perfect for children.
» Swimming off the white, sandy beaches of the Danish coast, particularly in northeast Jutland where the water reaches 20°C in summer. (You will not find warmer!)
» Walking in the hills of the Mols Bjerge National Park.
» Exploring the superb coastline by sailboat or motorboat, readily available for hire in the ports.

Fun for the whole family
» Legoland! The original Legoland is in Billund, where everything is built from those famous Danish bricks.

» Exploring Den Gamle By (the old town) at Aarhus on foot or in a horse-drawn carriage. Wander around this 19th-century village consisting of original buildings (schools, houses, a bakery), which have been dismantled and rebuilt here.
» Andersen's neighbourhood in his native city of Odense, where the cobbled streets are lined with fetching little houses. One of these is occupied by the Hans Christian Andersen Museum.

The Viking legacy
» Trelleborg Viking Fortress, with its market and activities for little ones.
» The former Viking town of Ribe, its exciting museum and its summer fair offering workshops.
» The stunning Viking Ship Museum in Roskilde. It is even possible to get out onto the fjord aboard a Viking longship!
» The Viking Festival in Friederikssund in early summer. The festivities last two weeks with shows in period costumes followed by banquets.

Copenhagen, not only royal, but fun
» The Little Mermaid statue in the city's Inner Harbour, created in homage to the celebrated author Hans Christian Andersen.
» Rosenborg Castle: in summer, picnic in the King's grounds and watch a free puppet show.
» Tivoli Gardens: funfair rides and other attractions are scattered among the flower beds.
» The zoo: get close to seals and the fascinating polar bears (you can even watch them swim as though you were underwater with them), and pet the animals – just the tamer ones!
» Take a boat trip on the canals for a different perspective of the major sites.

BEST TIME TO GO

The best time to visit Denmark is from May to the end of August, when the temperatures are mild, the scenery is at its most tempting and the days are longer. The rest of the year is cold and the nights are never-ending. Many places close from October to May.

COST

Denmark's hardly cheap, but it's less expensive than its Scandinavian neighbours. Hotels, car hire, meals and supplies are subject to the 25% value-added tax, so will all take a toll on your wallet. Car hire is easier to book from abroad through an international agency.

GETTING AROUND

Denmark is ideal cycling territory: there are many cycle lanes, and bikes can be rented almost anywhere and taken on trains, ferries and buses. A substantial network of ferries serves the islands, but you can reach the bigger islands by road bridge – the tolls are costly, as is car hire. Some good news: the motorways are free.

Mealtimes

As in other Nordic countries, herring and salmon take pride of place, but children will probably prefer *frikadeller* (meatballs) or *pølser* (hot dogs), which are available almost everywhere. The *smørrebrød* should also be to their liking: a rye-bread sandwich with a range of fillings including salad, hard-boiled eggs and meat. The *wienerbrød* is the most popular Danish pastry: a flaky exterior filled with almond paste, cream or chocolate, it's a vote winner. Denmark is a pioneer in organic food, which is on the menu in a good many restaurants. Children are made very welcome.

❗ Warning

➔ When you are driving, particularly in towns where the traffic can be heavy, watch out for the many cyclists using the cycle lanes.

🕐 Time difference

➔ Time zone UTC+01:00. Daylight saving time observed in northern hemisphere summer.

BOOKS FOR THE YOUNG TRAVELLER

› Pack a collection of Hans Christian Andersen's fairy tales. To find out more about this famous Dane the kids can read Andrew Langeley's mini-biography *Hans Christian Andersen*.

› Children's historical novelist Henry Treece has written several books set in Viking times, the most popular is *Viking Dawn*, the first in a trilogy.

› The *Eyewitness Guide: Viking* is an excellent beginner's history.

CHILDREN'S SOUVENIRS

› Viking figurines and costumes

› Lego of all shapes and sizes

ENGLAND & WALES

Home to Robin Hood, Paddington Bear and Harry Potter, England strikes a chord with every child. They will love following in the footsteps of their favourite heroes, while delicious scones and crumpets will win them over to the traditional tea time. Bucolic Wales has gorgeous countryside, but the children are more likely to get excited over the unpronounceable town names and the myriad castles.

London's Tower Bridge, one of the world's most famous structures

CHILDREN WILL LOVE...

Iconic London

» London Dungeons: skeletons and fake blood galore. Perfect for children who love being 'scared'.
» The changing of the guard at Buckingham Palace: timeless!
» The classic and ever-popular London Aquarium; Tower of London, with its crown jewels; and Madame Tussauds waxwork museum.
» The London Eye, a 135m-tall Ferris wheel offering spectacular views over the city.
» A musical in London's West End.

The worlds of their favourite heroes

» Following the trail of Harry Potter. Many of the films' scenes at Hogwarts were filmed at Oxford University, while Alnwick Castle, Northumberland, was the setting for Hogwarts in the first movie.
» The magnificent Cardiff Castle, Wales, where every room has a different theme. The splendid nursery is set aside for children's stories.

» Medieval Warwick Castle, Warwickshire, with its historic costume entertainment for fans of the cape and sword.
» The Beatrix Potter gallery, Hawkshead, in the sublime Lake District, where the author's original drawings are on show.
» Sherwood Forest: walk in the hero's footsteps along the Robin Hood Trail and try your hand at archery.

Moors, lakes and Druids

» A stroll over the heathland of Dartmoor National Park to admire the wildlife (buzzards, otters and wild ponies) and to try out canoeing or horse riding.
» The incredible standing stones of Stonehenge and Avebury will transport you into the world of the Druids.
» A cruise on the Norfolk Broads, a labyrinth of lakes and rivers, to take in the rich natural habitat, picturesque villages and windmills from across the water.
» A steam-train trip through the dramatic mountain landscape of Snowdonia, in Wales.
» York's Jorvik Viking festival, held in February, with horned helmets and longboats galore.
» Bath's watery Roman ruins.

Atmospheric beaches

» The east coast of Norfolk and Suffolk, with windswept beaches and quaint towns and villages.
» Brighton's pebbly beaches and sideshows on the Palace Pier.
» Fish and chips by the sandy shore in Cornwall, one of the best places to enjoy a dip.

BEST TIME TO GO

In London there is always something to do and see year-round, whatever the weather. But for the rest of England, November to February is less appealing; the days are short and often cold, particularly in the north. But from April to September it's mild and walking is a real pleasure, though this is peak tourist season on the coast, in the national parks and in London.

COST

England and Wales are expensive when compared with many other countries, particularly car hire, but you can control costs by planning ahead and shopping around. You can also save money by self-catering, camping and choosing activities that are free (such as London's Natural History Museum). Accommodation and meals cost substantially less outside London, and there are often hefty discounts for children at camping grounds, hostels, hotels, museums and historic sites.

Mealtimes

If grown-ups do not always appreciate English cuisine (or at least its reputation), children have no problem with it: fish and chips, sausages and mash, or eggs and bacon for breakfast – the very food they love! They will also like simple, but tasty jacket potatoes with many different fillings. The standard pub ploughman's lunch of bread, cheese and pickles can be fun, while pies and pasties (best in Cornwall) are good for eating on the run. In Wales the classic Welsh rarebit, or toast with a cheese sauce, will probably go down well. Real foodies will appreciate the many different puddings.

BOOKS FOR THE YOUNG TRAVELLER

> Lonely Planet's *Not for Parents: London* and *Not for Parents: Great Britain* will give kids eight and up the inside story – infamous people and dark history included.

> British kids love Terry Deary's series *Horrible Histories* and *Top Ten Tales from Dickens*.

> Susan Cooper's children's fantasy series *The Dark is Rising* combines Welsh folklore and Arthurian legend.

CHILDREN'S SOUVENIRS

> Models of a London taxi or double-decker bus

> A croquet game for the whole family

GETTING AROUND

Driving a car around these compact countries is easy when you are with the family. However cars are a problem in London (you need to pay the congestion charge to enter the centre and parking can be a nightmare) where public transport is efficient and of a high standard. Public transport can be expensive though, as it is in the other cities, despite discounts for children. The United Kingdom has good, if pricey, rail links; the buses are cheaper but slower.

❶ Warning

> In small towns it can be difficult to find a place to eat after 7pm.

> Certain pubs do not accept children, even in big towns.

🕑 Time difference

> Time zone UTC. Daylight saving time observed in northern hemisphere summer.

FINLAND

Children will be captivated by the land of Father Christmas, a land where nature rules. Creature comforts combine with great outdoor family pursuits, topped by a tourism industry catering for the very young.

The Northern Lights above Lemmenjoki National Park

CHILDREN WILL LOVE...

The scenery, come sunshine or snow

» Living like a real Finnish family. There is nothing like renting a cabin on the edge of a lake. On the agenda: canoeing, picking blueberries and a sauna.
» The islands of Åland: the virtually flat ground and the many cycle lanes are great for biking.
» The hills of Koli National Park: take a stroll to take in one of the best panoramas in the country…at a mere 347m!
» Skating on the frozen sea, *pulkka* (tobogganing) or cross-country skiing in Paloheinä in winter. Or charter a team of dogs, a posse of reindeer, or a snowmobile for a trek across the snowy expanses, lit by a beautiful, pale sun.
» Visiting the seaside resort of Hanko, which is as charming as any on the Mediterranean.

Helsinki, just the right size

» The maritime fortress of Suomenlinna, which stretches over several islands outside the city. Explore the fortifications and even the tunnels (with a torch).
» Helsinki Zoo on Korkeasaari island, perfect for finding out about Finnish wildlife and plants.
» Helsinki Icepark at Railway Sq, for the thrill of ice skating outdoors.
» The Linnanmäki amusement park, with its roller coasters, big wheel and labyrinthine aquarium with sharks.
» The Helsinki Festival in August, which has a program of events just for children. It is a chance to dance with the entire city.
» Numerous small islands to visit for a day on the beach, very geared to families.

The magic of Lapland

» The impressive SnowCastle of Kemi. Rebuilt every winter, it has a hotel and restaurant.
» Santa Claus Village at Napapiiri, with its post office and cave where the elves prepare gingerbread.
» Panning for gold in Tankavaara or in the Lemmenjoki National Park.
» An envigorating dog-sleigh ride across the snowy landscapes.

Unusual sights

» The Spy Museum in Tampere: gadgets that will fascinate junior James Bonds.
» An outing to the town of Naantali and its nearby theme park, Moomin World, dedicated to Tove Jansson's trolls, the Moomins.
» Taking a cruise from Finland to Sweden with much on-board entertainment for children.
» Discovering the biggest sand castle in Scandinavia at Lappeenranta in summer.

BEST TIME TO GO?

Summer is perfect for visiting most of Finland: temperatures are pleasant and ferries and steamboats operate on lakes and rivers. It is also when many organised cultural events take place. Avoid summer though if you are heading north, particularly to Lapland, due to the invasions of mosquitoes; it's better to go in October or from February to April and catch the famous Northern Lights. And, of course, there is no better time to visit Father Christmas than the December holidays.

COST

Finland is an expensive country, but it's not quite as bad as its reputation would suggest. Summer can offer exceptional value, with hotel prices slashed and seasonal restaurants open. With a bit of planning, you can have a great time here on almost any budget. Helsinki is substantially pricier than the rest of Finland, particularly on the accommodation front. As bus and train travel is expensive, budgets would not be inflated hugely by hiring a car, particularly if you can nab a decent deal over the internet. There are numerous ways to reduce the amount you spend on holiday in Finland. Nearly all hotels and hostels will put extra beds in a room for little extra charge. There's a discount on buses for groups of four or more when booking tickets together, and most attractions offer a good-value family ticket. Campsites nearly always have some sort of cabin accommodation sleeping four or more. These range from simple huts with bunks to luxurious wooden houses, and are always excellent value. It's much cheaper to eat in restaurants at lunchtime, when there are daily specials and often a groaning buffet table.

HEALTH CHECK

» The central and northern parts of the country are infested with mosquitoes in summer from June. Provide protection for children.

BOOKS FOR THE YOUNG TRAVELLER
› Pack the classic *Tales from Moominvalley*, by Tove Jansson, for under-10s.

CHILDREN'S SOUVENIRS
› All kinds of wooden toys for children big and small
› A snow scooter or sledge, though you will need snow to have a wild time with your mates!
› Moomin figurines and toys

GETTING AROUND

Finland is flat and cycling is fun, especially on the many cycle lanes. Summer is ideal for boat journeys, which allow you to explore the country via its waterways; the bus is better for longer journeys the rest of the year. It is more expensive than the train but covers more of the country. Hiring cars is easy but not very cheap, plus the distances are long and petrol is expensive.

Mealtimes

Most restaurants offer children's menus, even free meals. If your children seldom eat salmon or herring, the mainstay of the local diet, they may enjoy meatballs (often reindeer meat). Those with an 'allergy' to soup can choose potatoes, served mashed or boiled. Youngsters will love the desserts, sugary and filling, including *pulla* (sweet bread roll with cardamom seeds), *munkki* (donuts) and cakes with berries.

🕐 Time difference

→ Time zone UTC+02:00. Daylight saving time observed in northern hemisphere summer.

FRANCE

Travelling *en famille* in France means you'll probably have to abandon dreams of eating five-course meals and savouring the Louvre. But it hardly matters when there's so much you can all enjoy together, whether it's running through fields of lavender, picnicking on baguettes and brie, or paddling on the Atlantic coast.

Paris' parks and gardens are made for strolling

CHILDREN WILL LOVE...
Paris for *petits*
» Taking the lift or climbing to the top of the Eiffel Tower.
» Disneyland Resort, just outside Paris, where all those well-known characters speak French.
» The Jardin du Luxembourg, with crêpes, pony rides, miniature boats and carousel all part of an enduring tradition.
» The Cité des Sciences et de L'Industrie, in Paris, a science museum with 20 themed exhibits, hands-on installations and a real submarine, and the adjacent Parc de la Villette.

The great outdoors
» Pottering on the lovely beaches of scenic Île de Ré, on the Atlantic coast.
» Learning to ski at a *jardin de neige* in the Alps.
» Canoeing in the Dordogne through delightful flower-filled villages.
» A boat trip along an underground river, the Gouffre de Padirac, southeast of Carennac. Nearby, in Quercy, you can rent houseboats on the River Lot.

Nods to history
» The eye-opening prehistoric cave paintings (and accompanying theme parks and museums) in the Vézère Valley and at Lascaux, both in the Dordogne.
» The medieval walled town of Carcassonne, in Languedoc, whose conical-topped buildings send children's imaginations into overdrive.
» The chateaux of the Loire (most notably Chambord and islandlike Azay-le-Rideau), with twisting staircases to turrets and crenellated towers overlooking patterned formal gardens.
» The Roman ruins among the lavender fields of Provence.

Pure *joie de vivre*
» The state-of-the-art aquarium in sunny, family-friendly La Rochelle.
» The green parks and puppet theatres of Lyon's Parc de la Tête d'Or.
» The enchanting Christmas markets, decorations and celebrations of Alsace.
» Parc Astérix, a theme park 30km north of Paris, which despite its Gaullish comic-book name, covers the whole gambit of history, with adrenelin-pumping attractions and shows suitable for all ages.

BEST TIME TO GO

Spring has some of the best weather and it's usually warm enough for the beach in May. Autumn isn't necessarily cold, but short days mean limited sunlight, even along the Côte d'Azur. Winter is snow season in France's Alps and Pyrenees, reaching a crowdy peak over the Christmas school holidays. Most city dwellers take their annual vacation to the coasts and mountains from mid-July to the end of August, and the emptied-out cities tend to shut down at the same time.

Mealtimes

French regional dishes that really appeal to children include Brittany's crêpes and galettes, Provençal pizza and cheesy fondue and raclette from the Alps. But eating out can pose a few challenges. Highchairs, children's menus and half-portions are thin on the ground. *Cafétérias* usually have simple dishes like *croque monsieur* (toasted cheese and ham sandwiches) and ready-made food you can see before ordering, something that works for many kids. Picnicking and self-catering are probably the best ways to keep the family fed, however. Grab a baguette, some cheese, a bunch of grapes *et voilà*!

If you are eating out, having the main meal at lunchtime can work well for families. Dinner can often take hours, and many restaurants, especially in the south, don't open for dinner until 8pm. Also, French children have immaculate table manners and know how to behave – if yours don't, avoid classy restaurants.

BOOKS FOR THE YOUNG TRAVELLER
> Lonely Planet's *Not for Parents: Paris* will give kids eight and up the inside story on one of the world's most famous cities.
> Pack the adventures of *Madeline*, by Ludwig Bemelmans, for the under-eights.
> Asterix comics give a good insight into French culture, especially *Asterix in Corsica*.

CHILDREN'S SOUVENIRS
> Mini Eiffel towers, available everywhere in Paris – kids particularly love glowing fiber-optic ones
> Cute ceramic or glass jars which hold yogurt and dairy products from the supermarket (great for storing shell collections or pencils)

COSTS

Accommodation and restaurant meals are usually expensive in France, even from a European perspective. But self-catering and camper-vanning are enjoyable ways to rough it and save money, and long-term rentals can also work out quite cheaply.

GETTING AROUND

France has an efficient and far-reaching rail network with superfast TGVs travelling in all directions. Reduced fares are available for adults travelling with a child aged four to 11, in addition to child discounts. Within Paris, the metro is fast, efficient and easy to navigate (though not with a stroller). Arranging car rental from abroad can be less expensive than doing it once you arrive. If you're going to be in France for between two weeks and six months, and you're not an EU resident, purchase-repurchase plans from Peugeot and Renault are much cheaper than renting.

Time difference
→ Time zone UTC+01:00. Daylight saving time observed in northern hemisphere summer.

GERMANY

Prepare for feasts, treats and temptations as you take in Hansel-and-Gretel forests, romantic palaces and half-timbered towns where streets were laid out long before Columbus set sail. From big cities to sky-scraping Alps, there's plenty to see and do in Germany.

The crowd-pleasing dinosaurs of the Berlin Natural History Museum

CHILDREN WILL LOVE...
Fun-filled Berlin
» A boat excursion on the Spree to see the town and its historic sites in a laid-back way.
» A show at the Firlefanz Puppet Theatre.
» The Berlin Zoological Garden. One of the biggest zoos in the world with some of the rarest species, it also includes an aquarium.
» The dinosaurs of the Natural History Museum. The giant skeletons and the meteorites from Mars will also impress.
» A swim in one of the many covered or open-air pools.

Fairy-tale castles
» The fortified castles of the upper middle Rhine, known for good reason as the 'Romantic Rhine'.
» The Neuschwanstein Castle in Bavaria. The most popular castle in Germany may look familiar; it was used as the model for Disney's *Sleeping Beauty* and serves as a backdrop in *Chitty Chitty Bang Bang*.
» Linderhof Castle: smaller, less well known and with fewer visitors, the parks and whimsical follies are ideal for games of hide-and-seek.

Historic towns and villages
» The ramparts and old houses of towns along the so-called Romantic Road, such as Rothenburg ob der Tauber and Dinkelsbühl, which are virtually medieval museums.
» Nuremberg and its many timber-framed houses, an absolute must-visit at the end of the year when the Christmas market is held.

The joy of the great outdoors
» Farmhouse holidays, which are very popular and easy. Great for smaller citizens.
» Excursions in the Black Forest, on the German side of Lake Constance, and on the islands of Hiddensee (where cars are banned) and Rügen.
» Discovering the East Frisian Islands: at low tide you can walk there, picnic at high tide and wait for low tide to walk back again.

Theme parks
» Cinema and television studios, particularly the Bavaria Filmstadt in Munich, the Filmpark Babelsberg in Potsdam and the Movie Park Germany in the Ruhr region. All open to visitors for tours and shows.
» Phantasialand near Cologne, one of Europe's first amusement parks, built on reclaimed industrial land in the Ruhr.

BEST TIME TO GO

May to October is the most pleasant time to visit Germany. The weather is gentler than the rest of the year and ideal for walks in the countryside. February is carnival month; let your hair down in Mainz, Cologne and Munich.

COST

For a European country, Germany is very good value. Accommodation is much cheaper than in other European countries, and the best deals are found at guesthouses and hotels that include breakfast. Food in general is also cheap, especially if you tuck into the street-stall sausages. High-speed trains are the exception to the rule, being quite expensive, but good discounts are available for tickets booked well in advance. Free sightseeing buses in the major cities are a great way to get an overview of the sights for no cost. Car-hire rates are reasonable, with good deals for longer hire periods.

Mealtimes

In German cafes breakfast can be a hearty affair (including cold meats, cheese, eggs and muesli), even at midday! Your children will be in heaven. Generally speaking, cold meats are served at every meal. Side dishes are no longer limited to the traditional cabbage and potatoes, and there are many different kinds of tasty bread. For dessert, those with a sweet tooth will be spoilt for choice with many cakes and tarts, such as *Schwarzwälder Kirschtorte* (the famous Black Forest gateau).

GETTING AROUND

The train is a good way to get around in Germany, thanks to an extensive, reliable rail network, even if it is a little pricey. Buses are slower but are a good way to reach more isolated, rural destinations not served by the railways. The road network is excellent, comprising 11,000km of motorway. Bicycles are a good way to see the countryside or get across town. There are cycle routes stretching thousands of kilometres and many places from which to hire bikes, especially at railway stations. Children's seats and trailers are easily available. Bikes can be taken on trains and on some regional buses.

Time difference

→ Time zone UTC+01:00. Daylight saving time observed in northern hemisphere summer.

BOOKS FOR THE YOUNG TRAVELLER

› If it's Christmas, pack a retelling of *The Nutcracker*.

› Follow little Emil's adventures in Berlin in Erich Kastner's classic *Emil and the Detectives*.

› Judith Kerr's story *When Hitler Stole Pink Rabbit* is a good introduction to the period for 10-year-olds.

CHILDREN'S SOUVENIRS

› A teddy bear: Germany is the toy's birthplace

› Beautifully made wooden toys – cranes, doll's houses, farms and animals

GREECE

Warm sparkling seas and ancient ruins where the imagination runs riot, scrumptious food, whitewashed villages and reasonable prices: Greece is a top destination, where children are treated like gods.

Exploring the rock pools in glorious Greece

CHILDREN WILL LOVE...
Archaeological sites and myths
» The theatre of Epidavros in the Peloponnese with perfect acoustics; and that of Dodoni, in the Epiros region, less busy but equally impressive.
» Olympia and the remains of its stadium, a dream for aspiring athletes. Also Delphi, with its temples and stadium.
» The ruins of the palace at Knossos (Crete), on the trail of the Minotaur, imprisoned inside its labyrinth.

Child-friendly Athens
» The Hellenic Children's Museum, inside a historic house in the heart of Plaka: dressing-up games, cooking classes, hands-on science exhibits and the like aimed at under-12s make this a great option for a rainy day.
» The hourly changing of the guard at the Tomb of the Unknown Soldier. The *evzones* (presidential guards) wear their white kilts and red pom-pom shoes on Sundays.
» The iconic Acropolis, perched on its rock for 2600 years.

A constellation of islands
» The island of Aegina, close to Athens, where an impressive temple dominates the sea.
» Naxos, swimming heaven for small children with good facilities and safe beaches. They will also love a visit to the medieval clifftop citadel of Kastro.
» The island of Kos, really flat and easy to cover on a bike with very accessible beaches.
» Rhodes with its aquarium and castles.
» The Ionian Islands, greener than the Cyclades in summer.

Natural curiosities
» The strange, rock-tower monasteries of Meteora, which fire the imagination.
» Santorini and its steaming fumaroles, and Milos with its multicoloured cliffs: two islands for apprentice volcanologists.
» Sub-aqua diving in the sheltered bays of Karpathos, Milos or Kythira.
» Watching for dolphins on a boat trip, for example at Paleohora, and monk seals in the Alonnisos Marine Park.
» The extraordinary Diros Caves in the Mani region.

BEST TIME TO GO

The best time to visit Greece extends from Easter to mid-June, when the climate is mild, and also from the end of August to mid-October. In July and August you have to factor in busy beaches and crowded archaeological sites, while inland and in Athens temperatures are very high. Most tourist attractions close from mid-October to early April.

COST

Prices in Greece have been creeping up and it's no longer really a budget destination. Food can be cheap – even seafood if you choose carefully – but room rates are now often higher than those in Italy or France. Rooms in private homes can be an economic option, and are very well appointed; some are even luxurious. Many hotels let small children stay for free and will squeeze an extra bed in the room.

Mealtimes

In Greece everyone (including the kids) shares whatever is on the table. This isn't limited to *mezedhes* (small dishes for sharing), but these do offer a fun way to sample lots of different things. Dips, feta, calamari, salads, meatballs, roast chicken (often one of the cheapest things on the menu) and even grilled sardines will usually go down well. If you have a fusspot on your hands there are always potatoes. Taverns are popular, good value and welcome children. Dinner starts around 9pm – tavernas are often open from 7pm, but you may find yourselves dining alone.

BOOKS FOR YOUNG TRAVELLERS

> Robin Lister's retelling of *The Odyssey* is aimed at children aged 10 to 12, but makes compelling listening for younger children when read aloud.

> The Greek publisher Malliaris-Paedia puts out a good series on the myths, retold in English for young readers by Aristides Kesopoulos.

> If it's too hot to think, opt for Terry Deary's light-hearted approach in *The Groovy Greeks* or *Top Ten Greek Legends*.

CHILDREN'S SOUVENIRS

> A *komboloï* (worry beads)

> A *tavli* set, the national Greek game which is something like backgammon

GETTING AROUND

As is often the case, the easiest solution with young travellers is to hire a car. If you plan to hire a car in country, it's wise to bring your own car seat or booster seat as many of the local agencies won't have these. For travel between the islands, fast boats will get you to your destination twice as fast as a regular ferry, but their 'stay seated at all times' requirement means they're not great for young children. Ferry hopping between various islands can be a lot of fun, but remember this sometimes involves catching a boat at 2am. For long journeys, a cabin can be well worthwhile. If the train is slow and a bit behind the times, buses are very efficient. The bus network covers the whole country, including the islands.

ⓘ Warning

→ Avoid long walks with the children: the sun beats down, and the paths are often stony and steep.

→ Keep children covered up in the sun and well hydrated.

ⓛ Time difference

→ Time zone UTC+02:00. Daylight saving time observed in northern hemisphere summer.

HUNGARY

In Hungary children will be enchanted with Budapest, one of the most beautiful cities in Europe. They will relish the many castles that have witnessed the country's glorious past, and get active in the perfectly preserved landscapes, from the great plains and the Hungarian steppe, to the wooded mountains and the still waters of its lakes.

Beautiful Budapest on the blue Danube

CHILDREN WILL LOVE...
A bit of fun in Budapest

» The Széchenyi and Gellért thermal baths, where the whole family can splash around in the indoor and outdoor pools. There is also a wave pool.
» The children's train: operated by children from 10 to 14 years of age (the driver is an adult!), it climbs a hill close to the capital to an area perfect for picnics and walks.
» A cruise on the Danube to see the city strung out along the banks.
» The Vidámpark, an amusement park with exciting fairground rides and wooden roller coasters.

Outdoor Pursuits

» Taking a horse-drawn carriage ride in Hortobágy National Park to watch buffalo and the skilled horseback acrobatics of the Csikós (Hungarian cowboys and herdsmen for generations).
» Canoeing on Lake Tisza.
» Swimming and water sports on the enormous Lake Balaton (the shallow waters on the south side are better for young children), then enjoying a mini cruise to the strains of gypsy music.
» A walk in the stunning Matrá mountains, which rise gently to their highest point, Mt Kékes, at 1014m, along well-signposted paths.
» Exploring the spectacular Baradla-Dominica cave system, near Aggtelek. Less dramatic but more relaxing, a boat trip in the Lake Cave of Tapolca (Tavasbarlang).

Stunning Castles

» Baroque-style Esterházy Palace at Fertőd. In July concerts, firework displays and puppet shows follow in quick succession.
» Sümeg Castle, where young visitors can learn archery.
» The Gödöllő Royal Palace, the favourite residence of Empress Sissi.
» The castle of Diósgyőr, in Miskolc, which hosts a medieval fete at the end of May.
» A night-time visit to the labyrinth at Buda Castle by the light of torches. Spine-tingling shivers guaranteed!

BEST TIME TO GO

Hungary is pleasant in spring and in autumn until November (the rainy season). In summer Budapest is dead while the lakeside resorts are jam-packed, especially at the end of July and in August.

COST

This is a good-value destination, especially when compared with expensive neighbouring Austria. This is especially true when it comes to dining, with all-you-can-eat buffets, delicious coffee and cakes all quite cheap. Food is even cheaper if purchased at the markets. Accommodation is also inexpensive: standards may be a bit lower than you expect, so it is worth going a little upmarket. While Budapest has many of the cultural attractions of Prague, it hasn't yet succumbed to the price hikes that accompany increased tourism. Many attractions are free or low cost.

GETTING AROUND

Hungary has a substantial and efficient bus network. You can easily hire a car on arrival, but be warned that the secondary roads are often mediocre. The trains are reliable but quite slow. You can take a trip on a steam train around Lake Balaton. In the cities and towns, there are plenty of inexpensive taxis.

Mealtimes

Hungarian cooking is not particularly light: vegetables (usually marinated) are rare, unlike hearty soups and ragouts. Children will generally prefer meat cooked in breadcrumbs than goulash. Despite the generous use of paprika, the dishes are not too spicy for tender young palates. Good news for food lovers: Hungarians love puddings and desserts, particularly covered in cream. Success is guaranteed with chocolate *somlói galuska* (rich trifle) and *palacsinta*, pancakes filled with cream, chocolate or dried fruit.

Time difference

Time zone UTC+01:00. Daylight saving time observed in northern hemisphere summer.

BOOKS FOR THE YOUNG TRAVELLER

> Pre-teens will be inspired by rural Hungarian life and traditions in Kate Seredy's novel *The Good Master* and its sequel *The Singing Tree*.

> A favourite Hungarian folk tale about a red rooster and a diamond button exists in several picture-book versions: one worth checking out is *The Valiant Red Rooster*, by Eric A Kimmel.

CHILDREN'S SOUVENIRS

> Hand-painted Easter eggs, for a brightly coloured egg hunt

ICELAND

Iceland is first and foremost a fantastic reminder of how planet Earth was formed. Confronted by the forces of nature, children will feel they are exploring an almost magical land. And it's all the more exciting because the Vikings strode across the country in ages past and signs of their presence are everywhere.

Clowning around in a geothermal spa

CHILDREN WILL LOVE...
Reykjavík and surrounds: Vikings to mink

» Visiting the excellent museums including the open-air folk museum at Árbæjarsafn; the Saga Museum, where waxworks scenes retell the history of the island; and the National Museum, where you can dress up as a Viking!

» The international Viking festival at Hafnarfjördur, not far from the capital. It takes place in June but you can visit and stay at the Viking village any time of year.

» The little zoo, where you can discover the country's wildlife – reindeer, mink, seals, horses. There are rides and activities for children including electric mini-cars and mini-bulldozers.

Fire and ice adventures

» Trekking on an Icelandic horse, almost anywhere on the island. This small, gentle horse is perfect for young riders, even beginners.

» Strokkur, a geyser that explodes up to 30m in the air every five to 10 minutes.

» A hike of several hours or days to Lake Mývatn, an accessible site abounding in geological phenomena.

» Walking, with care, on glaciers with impossible-sounding names such as Sólheimajökull et Vatnajökull (from eight years, accompanied by a guide).

» Seeing the unforgettable aurora borealis (Northern Lights). The glowing red and green night skies can be seen from October to February, without travelling far from the capital.

Seagoing adventures

» A boat excursion to see finback whales, seals and dolphins – and also the cliffs where cute puffins and guillemots perch in their thousands – from Reykjavík, Húsavík, Keflavík or Ólafsvík.

» A cruise between the luminous blue icebergs floating in the waters of the glacial lagoon of Jökulsárlón.

Swimming without the beach

» Swimming in the Blue Lagoon, in Keflavík, a mineral-rich natural spa where the water is milky and warm even in freezing weather.

» Reykjavík's geothermal swimming complexes of Laugardalslaug or Árbæjarlaug, with children's pools and water slides.

» The most amazing natural pools, in the Landmannalaugar region, with views over the glowing red hills of rhyolite.

BEST TIME TO GO

The weather is variable, whatever the season. Between May and July the midnight sun holds sway over the island, but it is in July and August that Iceland is the most pleasant: the thermometer easily reaches 15°C, even higher in the south of the island. However a trip to Reykjavík and the surrounding area is totally feasible in winter, as long as you wrap up well.

COST

Iceland is one of the world's priciest destinations, especially if you want to engage in activities such as whale watching or guided glacier walks. Restaurants are expensive and accommodation often doesn't include breakfast; self-catering is a far more economical option. In the off season (late autumn through to early spring) prices drop considerably.

HEALTH CHECK

» The water is safe to drink all over the country, despite of the smell of sulphur, which is sometimes extremely strong.

» Watch out for aggressive Icelandic midges, which resemble mosquitoes, and are found near fresh water. They move around in groups forming clouds that can leave you with several hundred bites. Use insect repellent and cover up.

Mealtimes

Children will no doubt prefer lamb, widely available, to the traditional delicacy of puffin meat, and will more likely choose salmon, fresh or smoked, rather than haddock. Dairy lovers can choose from around 80 different sorts of cheeses; they will also appreciate *skyr*, a sort of yogurt prepared from skimmed, pasteurised milk, delicious with sugar or blueberry jam.

BOOKS FOR YOUNG TRAVELLERS

› Younger readers should enjoy the adventures of a sheepdog in *Sebastian Goes to Iceland* by Jacqueline Ann Gibson.

› For a taste of the great Icelandic sagas, try *Thorkill of Iceland* by Isabel Wyatt.

CHILDREN'S SOUVENIRS

› The strategy game of *ad elta stelpur*, thought to be a precursor to backgammon

› An Icelandic horse figurine

GETTING AROUND

Car hire is available in all of the major towns but it is costly. Inland, a 4WD is essential and the children can expect to be shaken around. Alternatively you can hire taxis for excursions, and it is also perfectly possible to see much of the country via organised tours. Long-distance buses cover the country between June and September. On the coast, a number of ferries provide links between the different ports. Flying is an option, thanks to several internal flights provided by Air Iceland, which the locals use much as we would a bus service, but the prices are quite high in summer.

❗ Warning

→ Hot-water springs can reach high temperatures. Except in areas designated for bathing, do not let your children get too close.

→ There are easy walks all around the periphery of the island. Inland you need to be in good physical shape; in addition, fords may make paths inaccessible for children under 1.5m tall.

❗ Time difference

→ Time zone UTC.

IRELAND

Green, green and more green…nothing beats a trip to Ireland if you wish to teach your children about nature in its purest form. It is the place where water and land collide – waterfalls, streams running across meadows, oystercatchers pacing the sand. Explore by boat, bike, on horseback or in a horse-drawn caravan.

A sense of fun is one of Ireland's great attractions

CHILDREN WILL LOVE…
Living in the midst of nature
» Pony riding in Connemara.
» Taking off in a horse-drawn caravan (sleeping up to five) on the stunning Dingle Peninsula (March to September).
» Travelling by water on a rented canal boat. Leave the rest of the world behind and live at one with nature on the Shannon-Erne Waterway, which is interlaced with canals, rivers and lakes.
» Walking, cycling or taking a boat out in the Killarney National Park (Ring of Kerry), where deer, birds, trout and salmon thrive in its mountains and lakes.

Studies brought to life
» Exploring botany: exotic plants on Garinish Island (Cork); the National Botanical Gardens (Dublin); the gardens of Powerscourt Estate (Wicklow); fuchsia and rhododendron hedges lining the roads.
» Delving into geology: the Giant's Causeway with its organ pipes of basalt plunging seaward; the Burren plateau with its fascinating limestone scenery carved by the sea.
» Studying zoology: sheep gambolling across the heath (to get a closer look, take your children to the Sheep and Wool Centre at Leenane, Connemara); dolphins in the Shannon estuary (at Carrigaholt, near Kilkee); the seals of Inishmór (Isles of Aran).
» Uncovering history: the Ulster American Folk Park, an open-air, living museum dedicated to the history of Irish emigration to the United States.

Celtic legends and culture
» The mystical fortress of the Rock of Cashel, perched dramatically on a cliff.
» Prehistoric remains such as the tumulus at Newgrange (Meath) and the Poulnabrone dolmen (in the Burren).
» Circular forts and celtic crosses including Dún Aengus (a prehistoric fort on Inishmór) and the medieval crosses in the cemetery of Glendalough (Wicklow).
» Celtic music shows and *ceili* (Irish dances).
» Medieval banquets at Bunratty Castle, following a visit to the folk park where curious, but friendly, hens, pigs and donkeys play about.

BEST TIME TO GO

The climate is extremely changeable and you can live four seasons in one day. From June to August the temperatures are mild and the days are long; this is high season and prices soar.

COST

Ireland can be expensive, particularly when it comes to petrol, food and alcohol, and prices in Dublin are higher than those in the rest of the country. You can save on food by filling up on a hearty Irish breakfast and stocking up on supermarket snacks for picnics during the day.

GETTING AROUND

Car hire is ideal for crossing the country with the family. Otherwise, Bus Éireann provides an excellent service, unless you prefer the romance of a horse-drawn caravan, horse or boat. On the Aran Islands, exploring by bike is a great option.

Mealtimes

Most children will happily feed on potatoes, shepherds pie, toasted sandwiches and other pub grub in the warm, friendly pubs (open until 9pm for those under 16), and fish and chips eaten on the go. For teatime, the sweet-toothed will savour apple or rhubarb pies topped with fresh cream – seemingly straight from the cow! – or ice cream. Irish breakfasts (including egg, sausage and bacon) are delicious and essential before a bracing walk in the fresh air.

❗ Warning

↦ Do not forget wet-weather gear and a change of clothes. The weather is unpredictable and you will need layers of clothing like an onion.

↦ The ferry crossing to Ireland is often choppy. It can be stomach churning for all ages.

🕔 Time difference

↦ Time zone UTC. Daylight saving time observed in northern hemisphere summer.

BOOKS FOR THE YOUNG TRAVELLER

› Curl up in bed with *Tales from Old Ireland*, by Malachy Doyle and Niamh Sharkey.

› Ann Pilling's *Black Harvest* is a classic set in the Irish Potato Famine.

› For older readers, pack Joan Lingard's series of stories about a young couple trying to overcome the religious divide: the first book is called *The Twelfth Day of July*.

› Younger children will love Michael Mullen's *Magus the Lollipop Man*, while parents will delight in the fun illustrations.

CHILDREN'S SOUVENIRS

› Wild flower seeds for budding gardeners

› A toy lamb or leprechaun (cheeky little fairy folk dressed in green)

› Marble and silver jewellery

ITALY

Italy is one big open-air museum, a treasure trove of ancient ruins, gardens and Renaissance palaces dotted across plains and mountains. But beware of cultural overload: for a truly child-friendly visit to Italy, it pays to keep the focus on gelato and the lakes and beaches, a welcome respite in summer when the scorching sun beats down on the country.

Italy's cities are full of surprises

CHILDREN WILL LOVE...
Roman Italy
» The Colosseum, where gladiator duels and wild animal hunts were held, and the nearby Forum (which has somewhat less of the grisly appeal).
» The ruins of Herculaneum, which are as impressive as those of Pompeii, but being more compact, are better suited to children.
» Villa Adriana, the home of Emperor Hadrian, at the gates of Rome; and the ancient harbour of Ostia (Ostia Antica), which kept the capital supplied.

Beaches, islands and lakes
» Canoeing or windsurfing on Lombardy's enchanting alpine lakes: Maggiore, Como and Garda. Close to the latter are two giant amusement parks – Gardaland, the largest in Italy, and CanevaWorld, with an aqua park and movie studios.

» Swimming on the Adriatic Coast, where the beaches slope into shallow waters, perfect for young children, particularly around Ferrara.
» The beaches of the south in Puglia (Apulia), Basilicata, Calabria, particularly those of Otranto in Porto Cesareo, the islands of Tremiti and Gallipoli.
» The island of Elba, edged with beaches lapped by blue water.
» Exploring the Amalfi coast by boat, although the beaches are not very practical with children.
» The islands of Sardinia and Sicily, with fascinating history, captivating towns and spectacular beaches.

Venice, home to explorer Marco Polo and comic-book hero Corto Maltese
» Exploring the city of canals (and no cars) on foot, by gondola or *vaporetto* (water taxi).
» Piazza San Marco, where they can chase the pigeons before climbing the Campanile (bell tower) for a panoramic view of the city.
» The islands of Murano, to see glass blowers at work, and Burano, with its colourful buildings that look like doll's houses.

Strange towns and extraordinary gardens
» Bizarre displays at the Specola Natural History Museum in Florence, and a visit to Palazzo Vecchio with actors in period costume.
» Walking, cycling or rollerblading round the ramparts of Lucca.
» The Tower of Pisa – the 'lean' is still impressive.
» The water features in the Villa d'Este in Tivoli.
» The monsters lurking in the gardens of Bomarzo (Parco dei Mostri), near Viterbo.
» The *trulli* villages of Puglia, with their curious, conical houses.

BEST TIME TO GO

While Italy is a place you can visit year-round, it is during spring and autumn that you will reap the most from its charms. The tourist sites are less crowded and the temperatures more comfortable. In summer (and often in spring) swimming is as exquisite off the Tyrrhenian shore as in the Adriatic.

COST

Italy is one of the most expensive destinations in Europe. If you're coming from northern Europe, prices won't come as such a shock but be prepared to pay top euro – particularly for accommodation – in Venice and Rome. In Tuscany choose *agriturismo* (accommodation on a farm) rather than a hotel in the town.

GETTING AROUND

There is no problem getting around Italy where the roads are in a good state of repair. Car rental is expensive (as are petrol and tolls), and is best arranged before leaving home. The motorways are tolled; buy a pre-paid card to avoid the long queues, especially in summer. Avoid driving in Naples where anarchy rules. Trains on certain lines are short on comfort and somewhat tatty looking; the bus network is fairly extensive. Large car ferries travel between the mainland and Sicily and Sardinia, while smaller ferries and hydrofoils run to other islands. There are also ferries between Sardinia and Corsica. Many ferries travel overnight, in which case a cabin is worthwhile.

Mealtimes

The advantage of pasta is children are pretty much guaranteed to like it. Lasagna, cannelloni and bolognese sauce with tagliatelle are always winners. And then there's pizza! Veal Milanese (schnitzel in breadcrumbs) is also much appreciated. In the land of gelato, ice cream tastes heavenly and there is no end to the different flavours you can try.

! Warning

→ Leave the stroller behind when visiting Venice: between the many bridges and the narrow streets you will be hard-pressed to get around.

→ Book trains well in advance to avoid the family standing all the way.

🕐 Time difference

→ Time zone UTC+01:00. Daylight saving time observed in northern hemisphere summer.

BOOKS FOR THE YOUNG TRAVELLER

> Lonely Planet's *Not for Parents: Rome* will give kids eight and up the inside story on the secrets of Rome.

> Peter Connolly's *Ancient Rome* is an excellent first history with fantastic illustrations that will bring the ancient sites to life.

> For under-10s pack Geraldine McCaughreans's *Roman Myths*.

> To get them interested in the Renaissance, pack *The Genius of Leonardo,* by Visconti and Landmann. Or for something a bit lighter try *The Lost Diary of Leonardo's Paint Mixer,* found by Alex Parsons.

CHILDREN'S SOUVENIRS

> Carnival masks from Venice

> A wooden Pinocchio

> Model cars from the Fiat 500 to the latest Ferrari

MADEIRA

A small Portuguese island lost in the ocean off Morocco, Madeira is a lush, peaceful haven where the whole family can relax. Short walks, swimming in natural pools and discovering the fauna and flora are more than enough to keep the children happy.

The Flower Festival children's parade is a highlight

CHILDREN WILL LOVE...
Swimming year-round
» The small beach of Praínha, in the far east.
» The fine sandy beach at Porto Santo, a neighbouring island. (Beware, it is a much sought-after destination.)
» Natural pools carved out of the rock and filled with sea water at small resorts such as Porto da Cruz and Porto Moniz.

A floral paradise
» Flowers along the roads and on the mountainsides: hibiscus, bougainvillea, fuchsias, hydrangeas…all that is needed to become a botanical know-it-all.

» Exotic gardens in Funchal, including the botanical gardens, the Jardim Orquídea (orchid garden), the tropical garden of Monte Palace and the manor garden of Quinta das Cruzes, scattered with archaeological sculptures.
» The Queimadas Forest Park near Santana.
» The Flower Festival in Funchal, held in April or May, with its eye-catching children's parade.
» Flowers in the sky during the world-class fireworks display on New Year's Eve – an absolutely stunning pyrotechnic show!

Excursions on land and sea
» A cable-car ride from Funchal up to Monte, and the fun descent over 2km on a two-seater wicker sledge!
» A walk with a picnic along the *levadas* (former irrigation canals) that weave across the island. Almost everywhere there are signposted routes suitable for children.
» A mini cruise from Funchal aboard a catamaran or a replica of Christopher Columbus' caravel, the *Santa Maria*. With a bit of luck, whales and dolphins may cross your path.

Journeys in pursuit of the island's history
» The pretty capital, Funchal, with its bleached white houses clinging to the slopes, its cathedral dating from the age of chivalry and the distinctive atmosphere of the old town.
» The odd little triangular cottages in the village of Santana.
» The Whale Museum in Caniçal, which explores the village's dependence on hunting these mammals, right up until 1981.
» Christopher Columbus' house at Vila Baleira, on Porto Santo, where the explorer lived before voyaging around the world.

BEST TIME TO GO

It is mild year-round (6°C in January on average, 22°C in July), though fog may spoil your view of the scenery from October to February, especially in the central and northern parts of the island. Flowers cover the island from April. The temperatures steadily climb to their hottest in July and August (the busiest time for tourists). The off-season is also very pleasant.

COST

Prices in Madeira are considerably lower than you might expect for a small island, commensurate with Portugal, which is one of the cheapest European destinations. Food is good value, especially in restaurants aimed at locals rather than tourists, with large portions served. Accommodation and other costs are higher in Funchal than elsewhere on the island.

Mealtimes

Look out for *bolo do caco*. This small round bread made with sweet potato accompanies every meal but is so delicious children will forget to eat everything else. Young carnivores will love the *l'espetada* (skewers of marinated beef) that abound, but fish is the main feature of any menu. Even if they rarely eat fish, children should enjoy *pastéis de bacalhau* (cod in breadcrumbs). There should be no problem with the usual rice and chips on the side. For desert, *bolo de mel* (honey cake) is hard to beat as is a tropical-fruit salad with banana, mango and papaya.

GETTING AROUND

Other than hiring a car, there are few transport options that allow you to go anywhere on the island. The roads are quite good, but winding: cruising speed is limited to 40 to 50km/h. A daily ferry links Funchal with Porto Santo: in the high season, book the crossing in advance as it is oversubscribed.

ⓘ Warning
- The island rises to 1800m and is steep in many places with cobbled paths in the towns. For walking, take a sweater and waterproof clothing as the climate changes at altitude.
- Most of the *levadas* are on the edge of the mountain with no barrier between walker and thin air. Make sure you use the well-maintained sections with children.

🕐 Time difference
- Time zone UTC. Daylight saving time observed in northern hemisphere summer.

BOOKS FOR THE YOUNG TRAVELLER
› Whet the children's appetite with the photograph-laden *Globetrotter Islands Madeira* travel guide.
› Older teens may enjoy Ann Bridge's *The Malady in Madeira*, a high-adventure spy novel which beautifully evokes the island's lush and mountainous setting.

CHILDREN'S SOUVENIRS
› A wicker basket to play shopping games
› Flower bulbs, on sale in all the markets

MALTA

The Maltese archipelago is a great family destination simply for a seaside holiday among fossil-studded cliffs and glittering hidden coves. However, its rich heritage – from the megalithic temples to the many buildings left by the Knights of the Order of Malta – will doubtless awaken the junior Indiana Jones within every small traveller.

Valletta, home to knights in shining armour

CHILDREN WILL LOVE...
The underwater colours
» Admiring the marine depths, some of the richest in the Mediterranean, equipped with mask and snorkel: wonderment guaranteed around the islands of Comino and Gozo.
» Learning to dive (from eight years) in a number of centres on the archipelago.
» Gazing at the seas below from a *dghajsa* (traditional boat) or a glass-bottomed boat, departing from one of the many ports.

Sites that transport you back to pre-history
» The impressive megalithic temples of Ħaġar Qim, Mnajdra and Tarxien, constructed between 3600 and 2200 BC.
» The Hypogeum of Hal Saflieni, a subterranean network of caves and tunnels cut into the rock 2500 years ago.
» The St Paul's Catacombs (Mdina) and those of St Agatha in Rabat.

Quirky attractions
» Popeye's village, a film set from the 1981 film made on the island at Anchor Bay: you can stroll around the intact sets and enjoy the family attractions celebrating the spinach-eating sailor.
» Valletta's carnival, celebrated in great style in February with floats and fireworks. Children take pride of place: they perform the sabre dance that kicks off the festival.

The knights remembered
» St John's Co-Cathedral in Valletta, the resting place of the Knights of the Order of Malta.
» Fort St Elmo, Valletta, built by the Knights and recently reopened as a military museum, with tour guides wearing period costume.
» The great fortifications protecting and enclosing the 'three cities': Vittoriosa, Senglea and Cospicua. Older children may shiver in the Inquisitor's Palace in Vittoriosa.
» The fortified city on Gozo, Gran Castello, built by the Knights in the 15th century to defend the island from pirates and Saracens.
» The many audio-visual events on offer in Valletta and Mdina recreating the age of chivalry.
» Dining while watching a firework show at Siġġiewi.

BEST TIME TO GO

Spring and autumn are the best seasons to visit Malta (the latter is wetter): the beaches are less packed than in July and August, the sun is shining but not overwhelming, and the water temperature is pleasant and inviting. Winter holidays are also pleasantly mild (14°C on average), but do not expect to swim from November onwards.

COST

With many low-cost airlines flying to the country from Europe, and package deals readily available, Malta makes for an inexpensive holiday. Transport and food are very reasonably priced in Malta. Car hire is cheaper than elsewhere in Europe, especially if you pre-book online.

GETTING AROUND

Cycling is not recommended on the island: the roads are narrow and in a poor state and car drivers pay little heed to cyclists. On the other hand, buses are very convenient as Malta has an extensive network. Plus children will be thrilled with Maltese buses painted in yellow, orange and white. However these picturesque survivors of the 1950s, '60s and '70s are not very comfortable. You can always hire a car: the rates are some of the lowest in Europe. Cars drive on the left here.

Mealtimes

Maltese gastronomy has the tastes and aromas of nearby Italy with the pizzas and pasta that children dote on. Let them taste the *ravjuls* (local ravioli) or a *timpana* (macaroni gratin). However youngsters will probably not appreciate the local specialty, *stuffat tal fenek* (rabbit stew). They have their pick of desserts though, notably the irresistible *kannolis* (cake filled with ricotta and preserved fruits). Restaurants are generally very child-friendly.

❗ **Warning**

↪ For a chance to see the Hypogeum of Hal Saflieni, you must book ahead: to preserve the site, only 80 visitors are permitted a day.

🕐 **Time difference**

↪ Time zone UTC+01:00. Daylight saving time observed in northern hemisphere summer.

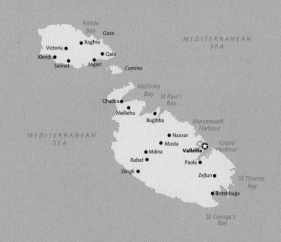

BOOKS FOR THE YOUNG TRAVELLER

› Children and adults will delight in *Cat Tails from Malta*, by J Elizabeth Roche, a story in verse of two cats travelling through Malta and Gozo, accompanied by beautiful photographs of the islands.

› Pre-teens will meet the Knights of St John in *The Time Travels of Arabella and Tom: The Great Siege of Malta*, by Sue Huband.

CHILDREN'S SOUVENIRS

› Models of *luzzi* (colourful Malteste fishing boats)

› Models of Maltese Knights and their accessories

MONTENEGRO

A small, mountainous country with the Adriatic lapping its shores, Montenegro offers a mass of outdoor activities. Just an hour's drive transports you from the family beach resorts on the coast, up into the mountains into magical, timeless places.

Sveti Stefan is one of many safe swimming beaches

CHILDREN WILL LOVE...
Diving in the waves or riding on the water
» Games on the long, sandy beach of Velika Plaža, near Ulcinj. This gently sloping strip is ideal for children to swim from.
» The beaches facing the picturesque island of Sveti Stefan, those on the Luštica peninsula or the coast of Petrovac, and those of the popular, but more commercial, Budva resort.
» Windsurfing, principally near Ulcinj.
» Rafting in the Tara canyon (the deepest in Europe); the calmer sections are open to beginners.
» Kayaking in the superb Bay of Kotor, ringed by mountains.

Small peaceful towns
» Podgorica, the capital, dotted with a number of parks and an old quarter edged with low houses overshadowed by the Ottoman clock tower.
» The ramparts of the medieval city of Kotor, set between mountain and sea.
» Verdant Cetinje, whose curiosities include a relief map of the whole country.

Mysterious monuments
» The churches and monasteries strewn across the islands of Lake Skadar and those in the Bay of Kotor, such as the tiny isle of Our Lady of the Rock, entirely taken up by its church.
» The orthodox monastery of Ostrog, lodged in a steep cliff.
» The Njegoš Mausoleum, on Mt Lovćen (Black Mountain), housing the remains of prince-bishop Petar II Petrović Njegoš in gilded glory. It is situated at 1700m altitude with an incomparable view – watch out though, there are 461 steps for little legs to climb!
» The atmospheric ruins of Stari Bar, which stand guard from on high over the new town built on the coast.

BEST TIME TO GO

Spring and autumn are the best times to visit the country but every season has its advantages. In the north and central mountains of the country, abundant snow means skiing is possible in the family-friendly ski resorts. The heat can render the capital and surrounding area suffocating in summer, but the coast remains more pleasant because the high temperatures (up to 38°C some years!) are offset by the cooling sea air.

COST

Montenegro is one of the most expensive countries in the Balkan region (with the exception of Croatia), but it's cheap by European standards. Self-contained villa accommodation is better value than hotels, and restaurant portions are generous. The glittering beach resorts of Budva and the Bay of Kotor are becoming luxury destinations, but there is still budget-friendly accommodation and food to be found, and Ulcinj is a cheaper alternative.

Mealtimes

While the Balkan influence is discernable on your plate, the Montenegrin cuisine is also imbued with the flavours of Italy: the children will be pleased to find pizza and pasta on the menu. In coastal regions, fish and seafood should be a hit. Inland they can have their fill of dairy produce (yoghurts, and cheese from cows or sheep) but also sausages, grilled lamb and various skewers of meat accompanied by potatoes, polenta or cabbage. For desert, there is baklava and also pancakes with filled with rich treats.

BOOKS FOR THE YOUNG TRAVELLER
> Older teens might enjoy the historical romance *Montenegro*, by Starling Lawrence, set on the eve of World War I, which strongly evokes Balkan politics and the landscape and atmosphere of the country.

CHILDREN'S SOUVENIRS
> Small carved wooden boxes
> A decorated water bottle for scaling the mountains
> A doll in traditional costume

GETTING AROUND

Buses and minibuses serve every town. They are an efficient and easy way to get around, but the twisting mountain roads may cause motion sickness, particularly in children. If you wish to explore the country at will, then hiring a car is ideal. Police checks are frequent: remember to put your headlights on, even in daylight. The railway is restricted to a line linking Bar-Podgorica-Bijelo Polje (in the northeast) and Belgrade, in Serbia. It is also a tourist attraction, as the train, which is fairly slow, crosses the most amazing landscapes. There are plenty of taxis for hire in towns.

ⓘ **Warning**
→ The country is mountainous so plan your journeys by time rather than distance.

🕐 **Time difference**
→ Time zone UTC+01:00. Daylight saving time observed in northern hemisphere summer.

NETHERLANDS

The Netherlands is one of those countries where the well-being of children is a priority. Children are welcome everywhere. With them at your side, you can cycle, ice skate, take a boat on the canals or enjoy a fun trip to a museum, while they will relax quickly into the local way of life.

The quintessential Netherlands experience at Zaanse Schans

CHILDREN WILL LOVE...
Special trips for children in Amsterdam
» A teatime cruise on the 'pancake boat', a great way to plough up and down the canals.
» A visit to the replica 18th-century sailing ship moored in front of the Maritime Museum, which has a pirate-led welcoming committee!
» The Rijksmuseum (don't miss the incredible doll's houses), the Tropenmuseum (Tropics Museum), the New Metropolis (NEMO) interactive science museum and dozens of other museums with dedicated children's corners and fun educational activities.

Trips on the water
» A cruise on the Delft or Utrecht canals, a means of exploring cities much appreciated by children.
» A pedalo on the Amsterdam canals.
» Exploring the Frisian Islands, peaceful havens for a stroll along the beaches and collecting all kinds of shells in the dunes.
» Ice skating on the frozen canals during bitter winters, just like the locals!
» A stay on a barge. Barges can be rented at Loosdrecht for a family expedition along the canals.
» The traditional, tranquil fishing village of the Marken peninsula, from where you can set off on a cruise on the inland sea.

Hunting for windmills and tulips
» A visit to Zaanse Schans open-air museum, northeast of Amsterdam. Experience life as the region's population did 150 years ago, visit a clog maker and see inside the working windmills.
» Taking in all the sights of the entire country in just a few hours at Madurodam in The Hague: Amsterdam, Rotterdam, windmills, canals and fields of tulips are reproduced in miniature.
» Exploring the country by bike, tandem, or from a bike trailer. The terrain is flat enough for even little legs to cover some distance on two wheels.
» The tulip fields around Haarlem or in the grounds of the Keukenhof Castle (near Lisse).
» A day at Efteling, the 'Dutch Disneyland', at Kaatsheuvel. It is one of the oldest and most prestigious parks in Europe, famous for its fairy-tale scenery.

BEST TIME TO GO

The Netherlands can be visited year-round. Of course summer (always mild) and spring are the most suitable times for taking a break on a terrace overlooking a canal. Winter is cold, but not too extreme, and you are less hassled in the museums (in summer you may well have to elbow your way around, the crowds are so dense). And if it is really freezing, the children may get the chance to skate on the canals.

COST

The Netherlands really isn't a budget destination, but neither is it the most expensive European country. Groceries are quite cheap, while transport can be expensive. There are a lot of free activities to stretch your budget, especially in Amsterdam in summer, and discount passes such as the Museumkaart and the Amsterdam Pass can save loads on admission. The first Sunday of the month is free at many museums, the Concertgebouw holds lunchtime concerts for free and some restaurants have cheaper children's meals.

Mealtimes

Chips! Children may even get sick of them here, where they are served everywhere and with everything, usually topped with mayonnaise. They will no doubt appreciate them as a side dish with mussels (from September to April) or *kroketten*, croquettes of meat or fish. For dessert, they can feast on *pannekoeke*, thick pancakes, or fruit tarts with Dutch custard (*vla*) and ice cream. Just before the dessert they might help themselves to a piece of Edam or Gouda.

BOOKS FOR THE YOUNG TRAVELLER
> Pack a copy of *The Diary of Anne Frank* or Carol Ann Lee's *Anne Frank's Story*.
> Older kids will enjoy Aidan Chambers' *Postcards from No Man's Land*, which tells the tale of a young boy's first trip alone to Amsterdam and his father's experiences on the battlefields of Arnhem.

CHILDREN'S SOUVENIRS
> Tulip bulbs
> Miniature windmills
> A wooden *sjoelen* game (a game of sliding discs) for the whole family
> Clogs decorated with windmills

GETTING AROUND

Welcome to a country where cyclists rule! Cycle lanes abound and it is easy to take your bike on the train. On the other side of the coin, pedestrians, especially the young, need to watch out for bikes in the cities. There is a substantial and efficient rail network; the trains are comfortable and the prices very low for children under 11 years. Buses are also very convenient. Travelling by car can prove expensive: parking is dear in town and spaces are few and far between.

❗ **Warning**
→ Many believe it is still possible to leave your bike in the street without a lock in the Netherlands: this is a myth. Do as the Dutch do, lock it up!

🕐 **Time difference**
→ Time zone UTC+01:00. Daylight saving time observed in northern hemisphere summer.

NORWAY

From the expanse of the far north to sea-going explorations of the isles and glaciers that dominate the fjords, Norway has everything it takes to entrance children, summer or winter. Even better, it is the land of Vikings, trolls and reindeer, whose presence in the museums and shops serves as a constant reminder to the young.

The mesmerising beauty of the fjords

CHILDREN WILL LOVE…

Spectacular natural surroundings

» Staying in a chalet at the water's edge or in a *hytte* (basic but comfortable campsite cabin).
» Canoeing on the lakes or learning to fish in the rivers.
» Taking a boat out to tour bankside villages, follow the canals or reach the islands – or to watch whales (from Andenes).
» The fjords, whose glaciers scatter blocks of ice onto the deep blue waters.
» The supernatural beauty of the Lofoten Islands with their high cliffs, small fishing villages and seabird colonies.
» Spotting some of the highest waterfalls on the planet! See a number of them from the train departing from the beautiful village of Flåm.

The mystical far north

» A dog sledge across the snow in the Øvre Dividal National Park and at Karasjok.
» Cross-country skiing, even in summer, at Stryn and Folgefonna.
» Meeting the Sami people, reindeer herders proud of their traditions.
» Seeing the midnight sun from mid-May to the end of July from the North Cape (Nordkapp), a 307m-high cliff that symbolically marks the most northern point of Western Europe.
» The Norwegian Glacier Museum at Fjærland, with a panoramic cinema, an interactive glacier tunnel and a walk-through climate change experience.

Vikings and explorers

» The museums of Oslo's Bygdøy Peninsula, particularly the Norwegian Folk Museum, with traditional buildings and craft demonstrations; the Viking Ship Museum; and the Kon-Tiki Museum, commemorating the expeditions of Norwegian explorer Thor Heyerdahl.
» The Lofotr Viking Museum near Vestvågøy (Lofoten archipelago), where artisans in period costume re-create village life.

Norwegian theme parks

» The Kristiansand Zoo and Amusement Park, the top destination for young Norwegians. The zoo has a section dedicated to Norwegian wildlife and there is a reproduction of the imaginary town featured in the classic Norwegian children's book *When the Robbers Came to Cardamom Town*.
» The Hunderfossen Familiepark, near Lillehammer. There's no Mickey here to shake your hand, but there are plenty of trolls, some more frightening than others.

BEST TIME TO GO

Between May and September the weather is at its best for exploring the country, even if some paths and refuges are only open from the end of June. The thermometer often exceeds 30°C in summer and -30°C in winter, when the days are darkest. In the north, the sun disappears completely from the end of November until around the 10th of January. On the other hand, from the end of May to mid-August it never really gets dark.

COST

Norway is one of the most expensive countries in the world. This is particularly true when it comes to transport. Car hire is costly and there are many road tolls in the south. When travelling by train, look for discounted 'minipris' tickets, available from ticket machines and on the internet. Fortunately, admission to sights is usually free for under-sixes and half-price for under-16s. Self-catering chalets rented by the week are the most economical form of accommodation.

HEALTH CHECK

» Take plenty of insect repellent and cover up against the many flies and mosquitoes prevalent in the north in summer.

GETTING AROUND

The road network is excellent but the journeys are often expensive, and can be taxing due to the mountains. Public transport is extensive: there are trains and buses (punctual and comfortable) and ferries. The coastal ferries run by Hurtigruten, serving all the ports between Bergen and Kirkenes, are a practical and enjoyable alternative to the car. Car ferries are often the only way to reach villages higher up the fjords. Flying is another option, especially with children: it is no dearer than the train if booked in advance.

Mealtimes

Most places cater for children and offer special menus. Smoked, roasted or stewed, the meat is always delicious. Salmon, smoked or grilled, is on every menu (and quite affordable); potatoes are served at almost every meal. The children will be keen to try breakfast 'in a tube': conveniently packaged cheese spread, caviar and even bacon. That's not to say they will repeat the experience!

Time difference

→ Time zone UTC+01:00. Daylight saving time observed in northern hemisphere summer.

BOOKS FOR THE YOUNG TRAVELLER

› For older kids pack Henrietta Branford's powerful novel about one young girl's fight for survival in Viking Norway, *The Fated Sky*.

› There's plenty of drama and action in Barbara Leonie Picard's *Tales of the Norse Gods* which should whet younger appetites for Norse sightseeing.

CHILDREN'S SOUVENIRS

› Trolls in every shape and size

› Christmas decorations

POLAND

Young travellers will enjoy visiting the many castles dotted around the country. They can discover the real Poland by staying on a farm, or roaming hospitable landscapes on foot, horseback or by bike. The warm-blooded may even appreciate a dip along the Baltic coastline.

The Wawel Dragon, part of enticing Polish folklore

CHILDREN WILL LOVE...
Fun, historic trips

» A ride in a horse-drawn carriage to admire the beautiful monuments of Kraków and reach the splendid royal castle on Wawel Hill.
» The historic centres of Wroclaw and Gniezno, whose colourful houses are among the oldest in the country.
» Promenading the Royal Way in Warsaw, lined with palaces and churches, and stopping in Łazienki Park for a boat trip on the lake.
» A cruise between Gdańsk, the 'pearl of the Baltic', and the Hel Peninsula.

The joys of life in the open air

» A stay at an agritourism farm, for example in the Beskid Mountains.
» The Baltic coast beaches: the waters are shallow, the sand is fine and white, and there are often children's play areas. Be warned though, the water rarely gets above 21°C and there is sometimes a strong wind.

The land of Slavs, Vikings and Teutonic knights

» Immersing themselves in the daily routine of an earlier age at one of the many open-air folk museums scattered across the country. In Sanok Park, there are reconstructions of 17th- and 18th-century villages.
» The archaeological site of Biskupin, in which part of a fortified Iron Age village has been rebuilt.
» The splendid, fortified Malbork Castle, which features a thrilling sound-and-light show from mid-April to mid-September.
» The castles of Niedzica, Bytów, Gniew and Golub-Dobrzyń. At some, international knights' tournaments are held in summer.
» The August Slavs and Vikings Festival on the Pomeranian island of Wolin.

Exploring natural wonders

» Travelling down the Dunajec Gorge on traditional wooden rafts piloted by boatmen in the Pieniny National Park.
» Meandering through a fantastic natural labyrinth in the Stołowe Mountains National Park.
» Canoeing down the Biebrza River in the heart of the biggest area of marshland in Central Europe.
» Sailing or kayaking on the Great Masurian Lakes.
» Taking an easy stroll to the shifting sand dunes in the Słowiński National Park.
» Visiting the underground salt mine of Bochnia: you descend a wooden slide, 140m long, before taking a little train to complete the visit!

BEST TIME TO GO

From spring to autumn the temperatures are very pleasant. Winter, however, is bitter and snowy, and the sun sets early. For a seaside holiday on the Baltic in July and August, book early as the resorts get very crowded.

COST

Children enjoy discounts on local transport, accommodation and entertainment, but don't assume Poland is a cheap option for a family holiday. Restaurants in Warsaw are surprisingly pricey and to get the facilities and services you need with children, you'll be better off heading for the best hotel you can afford. It is possible to find good-value family-oriented guesthouses in Zakopone.

GETTING AROUND

You can get across the country by train (fast and cheap) and reach more out-of-the-way locations by bus. Hiring a car is a convenient way to travel. Watch out however, as secondary roads are often in a poor state and can even be dangerous. The risks on the road are increased by the growing number of lorries crossing the country at great speed on narrow lanes. Cycling in the countryside is a pleasure in this mainly flat country; cycles lanes are rare in cities and towns where it is best avoided.

Mealtimes

Meatballs are likely to find favour with your children, while the many soups, such as *barszcz* (beet soup), are less likely to appeal. But who knows? On the other hand, there should be no problem with *kotlet schabowy* (breaded cutlets of meat) or sausages, which are eaten a lot here. Same for the *pierogi* (ravioli stuffed with all sorts of ingredients, savoury and sweet), which are found on almost every menu. Children will be tempted by desserts such as *naleśniki serem* (pancakes filled with soft cheese) and *makowiec* (traditional poppy-seed pastry or cake).

⚠ Warning
→ It's best to park your car in car parks with surveillance. Foreign cars are the preferred targets of thieves.

🕐 Time difference
→ Time zone UTC+01:00. Daylight saving time observed in northern hemisphere summer.

BOOKS FOR THE YOUNG TRAVELLER
› *The Silver Sword*, by Ian Serraillier, tells the tale of four starving children's escape form Poland during WWII.

CHILDREN'S SOUVENIRS
› Typical Polish toys made of wood, such as chess sets with traditional folk characters

PORTUGAL

It was from Portugal's Atlantic shore that Christopher Columbus and Vasco de Gama set sail for distant lands. Today, its 800km of coastline attracts families, especially to the south where the water is warmer. But you can also play explorers and go into the interior in search of medieval castles, mountains and charming villages. It's difficult to find a country where children are more warmly welcomed than Portugal.

Belém is as welcoming as the rest of Portugal

CHILDREN WILL LOVE...

Lisbon, the city of seafaring explorers

» Taking the No 28 tram, a roller-coaster ride through the medieval district of Alfama to the Castelo, or a ride in a funicular up the city's steepest hills for a superb view.
» The Belém area, where you follow in the footsteps of the great explorers: the Maritime Museum and the Discoveries Monument (to be clambered upon) will fascinate children.
» A day trip to Sintra, the spectacular mountain retreat brimming with multicoloured palaces and castles, which you can explore by horse and carriage.
» The Iberian Wolf Recovery Centre, where you have a good chance of meeting a wolf on your walk.

The joys of the seaside

» The warm, calm Algarve beaches, the best for swimming or snorkelling.
» The prized resorts of Cascais (the liveliest) and Estoril (more family-orientated), and the family beaches of the Costa da Caparica (Praia do Norte and Praia do São Sebastião) – where you can even learn to surf.

» Boat excursions to watch the dolphins from Lagos, Albufeira or Setúbal.

Ready-made activities

» Oceanário, the biggest aquarium in Europe, where children can see sharks and otters among hundreds of other species. It's part of the Parque das Nações in Lisbon, a large, modern park set on the banks of the Tagus.
» The Puppet Museum (Museu da Marioneta) in Lisbon, for its collections and shows.
» Portugal dos Pequenitos (Portugal for Little People) in Coimbra, where castles and villages from across the country are reproduced in miniature.

Dungeons, dragons, temples and dinosaurs

» The medieval castle of Vide, with its small museum dedicated to the kings who once lived there.
» The red ramparts of Silves Castle, constructed when the city was the Moorish capital of the Algarve.
» The city of Mértola, a genuine open-air museum where children can discover medieval Portugal.
» The Templar Commandery of Tomar, prickling with spires, which will plunge you into the world of the Knights Templar.
» The ruins of Conímbriga, bringing to life the daily routine of a Roman town.
» The Roman temple of Évora, a superb fortified town.
» The prehistoric open-air paintings at the Côa Valley: horses, aurochs and ibex have gambolled across the rock walls here for 20,000 years.
» Dinosaur footprints in the Serras de Aire e Candeeiros Natural Park.

BEST TIME TO GO

In spring and autumn temperatures are hot without being suffocating. If you are travelling in the summer avoid the Algarve, Alentjo and the upper valley of Duoro where the mercury can exceed 45°C. What is more, holidaymakers lay siege to the Algarve in August.

COST

Portugal remains one of the most affordable destinations in Europe, and meals especially are great value (with one portion often being enough to feed two). Preschool-aged children usually get into museums and other sights free, and museums are often free to all on Sundays. Car rental is usually cheaper if booked from abroad, though small Portuguese firms can offer good rates. If you need to keep costs down, camping grounds are widespread and cheap, and great places to meet other kids. But if you can splash out a little, Portugal has an amazing array of *pousadas* (mansions and palaces that have been converted into upmarket places to stay), many of which cater to families.

Mealtimes

A country where the bread is delicious, green vegetables are hard to find, cured meats are everywhere and the desserts are spectacular (including the unbeatable *pastel de nata* – custard tarts) – Portugal is a paradise for tender tastebuds! But watch out for indigestion, as Portuguese portions are gargantuan: happily you can usually order a *meia dose* (half portion). Fans of television (and those who are not), should know that tvs are found in most establishments.

BOOKS FOR THE YOUNG TRAVELLER

> Older readers will enjoy reading the adventures of the explorer Vasco da Gama in Joan Elizabeth Goodman's beautifully illustrated book *A Long and Uncertain Journey: The 27,000 Mile Voyage of Vasco da Gama.*

CHILDREN'S SOUVENIRS

> All kinds of wooden toys: models, articulated puppets, small cars

GETTING AROUND

Portugal is a compact, compelling country to explore, especially if you've got your own wheels. Thanks to its rectangular shape, it's not too difficult to cover all corners – and the middle – either. In towns the buses will save little legs; in a number of seaside resorts you can climb aboard a small train taking tourists to the beach. For long distances, the *expresso* buses are fast and comfortable. The train is the best value (half price for children aged five to 12), but slower.

Warning
> The coastline has many sandy beaches and superb creeks. However they are on the Atlantic coast where the water can be cold. Some shores are not safe for bathing due to the waves and undertow.

Time difference
> Time zone UTC+01:00. Daylight saving time observed in northern hemisphere summer.

ROMANIA

Forget the clichés! With its colourful villages, rich folklore and magnificent countryside peppered with ancient fortresses, Romania offers families a safe, easy trip. Even while hunting down the infamous ancestor of the *Twilight* gang, Count Dracula.

The magical forested Apuseni Mountains

CHILDREN WILL LOVE...
Tracking down Count Dracula

» Bran Castle, nicknamed 'Dracula's Castle', where Prince Vlad Țepeș, the inspiration for the famous vampire, once stayed.
» The impressive fortified town of Poienari, the real castle of Vlad Țepeș.
» Count Dracula Club in Bucharest: the Prince of Night appears while one enjoys a bloody steak in a decor more kitsch than frightening.
» The beautiful, medieval city of Sighișoara, the birthplace of Vlad Țepeș.

Mountains, seas and mysterious caves

» Swimming and games on the Black Sea beaches. Try those of Doi Mai and Vama Veche to avoid the crowds in summer.
» Family walks in the Carpathian Mountains or in the Maramureș region.
» The caves of the Apuseni Mountains or the Bear Cave near Chișcău, with its fantastic natural formations.
» The Praid salt mine. In this subterranean world, swings and slides await the young. Back on the surface, dive into the salt pool.

The countryside of yesteryear

» Transylvania, where farms, horses, herds of geese and carts will plunge children into a rural existence that has disappeared elsewhere in Europe.
» Saxon villages with colourful houses, such as those found near Brașov and Sibiu, two superb towns. In the latter there is a folk museum containing 120 houses and a small zoo.
» The monasteries of Bucovina, with frescoes as bright and colourful as a comic book, all set in picturesque countryside.
» Maramureș, a rural region hidden away, where the many wooden churches and grindstones will transport you to an earlier age.

BEST TIME TO GO

Each season has its own appeal in Romania. Summer is the best time to enjoy the beach; Bucharest, on the other hand, is best avoided at this time because the heat can prove to be suffocating, with temperatures rising above 40°C. If the countryside is beautiful and ideal for walking in summer, it is just as pleasant in spring after the snow melts. Make a date from December to March if you want to ski in some of the cheapest resorts in Europe.

COST

Cheaper than much of Europe, Romania has nevertheless graduated from the dirt-cheap-trip category in recent years. Car-hire rates tend to be high, but bus and train tickets are quite cheap. Those looking to save can enjoy the abundant fast-food stands selling burgers, kebabs and pizza, and take advantage of the economical *agroturism* B&B network, which can provide lunch and dinner upon request as well as breakfast.

Mealtimes

This is country fare with little variety and nothing to scare the children. Pork and potatoes are the staples in Romanian cuisine. If the children wrinkle their noses at the *ciorbă* (soup) or cabbage, they will enjoy the local specialty, *mămăligă* (polenta sprinkled with salty goats cheese), served as a main course or side dish. For dessert, you cannot beat *kuros kalacs* (donuts with sugar or chocolate), *clătite* (pancakes) or *saraillie* (delicious almond cake).

HEALTH CHECK

» Try to use hospitals in the bigger towns, if necessary, as elsewhere the sterilisation of medical equipment may leave something to be desired.

GETTING AROUND

The rail network is extensive and travelling through the countryside by train has its charms. The Maramureş steam train has become an attraction in itself. Avoid the *personal* trains, slow and crowded, and choose instead the slightly more expensive *accelerat*, *rapid* or *expres*. Buses are fairly cheap but slow and the timetables, like the stops, are erratic; the *maxitaxis* (or *microbus*) are the fastest. Be careful when driving: many roads are not sealed and there are carts as well as other vehicles to watch out for. Some remote areas – such as Maramureş, Transylvania's Saxon churches, and Moldavia's painted churches – are far easier to see with a guide or a hired car.

ⓘ Warning

↳ Be careful during walks: the Romanian mountains shelter a sizeable population of bears.
↳ Most accommodations do not provide cots for very young children.
↳ The Danube Delta is best avoided in summer due to the mosquitoes.

◑ Time difference

↳ Time zone UTC+02:00. Daylight saving time observed in northern hemisphere summer.

BOOKS FOR THE YOUNG TRAVELLER

› Pack a retelling of Bram Stoker's *Dracula*, such as the abridged Dover Children's Thrift Classics version.
› *Dracula: The Real Story*, by Ken Derby, is an enjoyable biography for pre-teens about the country's most famous character.
› For younger children, read *Old Romanian Fairytales*, by Mirela Roznoveanu.

CHILDREN'S SOUVENIRS

› Traditional wooden toys
› Beautifully decorated Easter eggs

RUSSIA

Your little angels will not be short of things to enthrall them in Moscow and St Petersburg, which, incidentally, offer every amenity in terms of accommodation. The situation is completely different, however, in more isolated areas, which you might wish to avoid with children. Between the two extremes there are endless towns, palaces, landscapes and sights to behold.

Russia is perfect for snowball fights

CHILDREN WILL LOVE...
The star attractions of Moscow
» The enormous Red Square with the incredible St Basil's Cathedral, Lenin's Mausoleum and the Kremlin, the latter bristling with golden domes.
» Gorky Park, where they will enjoy the fairground rides in summer and the ice rinks in winter.
» Viewing the seven Stalinist skyscrapers dominating the Moscow skyline from Vorobyovy Gory Nature Preserve (Sparrow Hills).
» Admiring the famed Russian acrobats of the Nikulin Circus or the Moscow Great State Circus.
» The All-Russia Exhibition Centre, with its gargantuan statues, flamboyant fountains and grandiose pavilions spread throughout a vast park. Just in front is the obelisk of the Cosmonautics Museum, which space-mad kids will enjoy.

The fairy-tale city of St Petersburg
» The Peter and Paul Fortress, whose ramparts dominate the Nava River.
» The colourful domes of the Church of Our Saviour on the Spilled Blood, the pretty blue Smolny Cathedral and St Isaac's Cathedral.

» The zoo and the Central Rail Museum: sure winners for kids.
» A trip to Pavlovsk Palace park with its squirrels that are no longer really wild.
» Letting off steam on a bike or rollerblades on Krestovsky Island and trying the rides at the island's amusement park, Divo Ostrov.
» A cruise on the canals to admire the palaces and cathedrals.
» The splendid Peterhof, a 'Russian Versailles' with its beautiful park on the edge of the Baltic dotted with waterfalls and fairy fountains.

Lake Baikal and surrounds
» A cruise on Lake Baikal, the oldest and deepest lake in the world, to the isles and the small wooden villages built on its banks.
» Discovering the region's wooden buildings at the open-air museums of architecture and ethnography at Taltsy and Ulan-Ude; the latter is a pleasant town with a mix of Russian, Soviet and Mongolian cultures.
» An excursion into Buryatiya to see herds of wild horses and get an insight into Mongolian culture.

Russia's special places
» The seaside resorts of Anapa, Gelendzhik and especially Sochin, in the Russian Riviera on the edge of the Black Sea. They have everything you need to keep the children happy.
» Camping, rafting and canoeing in the beautiful countryside of Karelia, speckled with lakes. Kizhi island is worth a visit for its Transfiguration Church made entirely of wood, even the 30 bubbling domes.
» Veliky Ustyug, an achingly beautiful little town in the northwest – and the official home of Ded Moroz (Father Frost), the Russian Father Christmas.

BEST TIME TO GO

If you wish to miss the crowds and the heat then avoid July and August; choose May to June or September to October instead. The winters are harsh, but the towns and scenery look superb in the snow. The climate is pleasant in spring but the melting snow often leaves the roads thick with mud.

COST

Flights into Russia can be found quite cheaply, but be aware that complicated tourist visas can cost up to a couple of hundred dollars. Prices are markedly higher in Moscow and St Petersburg than elsewhere in the country. Decent hotels in cities and tourist areas, especially Moscow, can be extremely expensive, so try short-term rental accommodation instead, or boutique 'minihotels'. On the other hand, transportation, attractions and restaurants aimed at locals rather than tourists are very affordable.

GETTING AROUND

Internal flights are not recommended as aircraft are often old and safety regulations are not always respected. Luckily the rail network is extensive with trains reasonably priced and comfortable; though as they are fairly slow, consider travelling at night. Buses operate between the smaller towns. Driving in Russia is not easy: opt for a car with a driver (often you have no choice outside Moscow and St Petersburg). Rivers provide a means of transport for long journeys in summer (from Moscow to St Petersburg, along the Volga and the Don). In the cities public transport is packed during the rush hour.

Mealtimes

In Moscow and St Petersburg the menu is global, but your children might also enjoy the flavours of Russia. The many types of starters should satisfy small tummies if the main courses – fairly heavy stews – are less appetising for them. *Pelmeni* (meat ravioli) and *kotlety* (grilled meats) are certain to please. You will find snacks such as *pirozhki* (pasties) in the many street stalls. And do not miss the traditional vanilla ice cream.

❶ Warning

→ It is inadvisable to travel to North Caucasus and Ukrainian border regions due to ongoing conflicts in these regions.

🌓 Time difference

→ Most of European Russia falls in the UTC+03:00 time zone, but other areas fall between UTC+02:00 and UTC+12:00.

BOOKS FOR THE YOUNG TRAVELLER

› Older children will enjoy the story of *Natasha's Will* by Joan Lingard, which is set in both modern-day and revolutionary St Petersburg.

CHILDREN'S SOUVENIRS

› *Matryoshkas* (Russian nesting dolls)

› *Bogorodskoye*, a traditional paddle toy with pecking chickens

› A nutcracker doll, from the eponymous fairy tale and ballet

SCOTLAND

A land of haunted castles where monsters splash in the lochs, children will be spellbound by the magic of Scotland. They will be entranced by the mystery of the moors and cliffs and the raw beauty of a natural landscape given to all kinds of outdoor activities.

Exploring castles and searching for monsters

CHILDREN WILL LOVE...
Ghost hunts
» A walk through the old streets and maze of underground passages that is Mary King's Close, in Edinburgh, accompanied by a guide dressed in 17th-century costume.
» Haunted castles, notably Culzean Castle (with its ghostly bagpipe player), Glamis (home of the Grey Lady) and Fyvie (the Green Lady).
» Sandwood Bay, one of the most beautiful beaches in Scotland. Lost sailors are said to roam its shores come nightfall.

Edinburgh and Glasgow on show
» Street entertainment during the Imaginate Festival, held every May in Edinburgh. While the famous Edinburgh Festival held in August also offers plenty for kids, this international performing arts festival is specifically for children and young people.
» A visit to the Sharmanka Kinetic Theatre in Glasgow where mechanical sculptures perform to haunting music.
» Edinburgh Zoo, one of the biggest in the world.

The untamed beauty of the Highlands and Islands
» A cruise from Inverness along the Moray Firth to watch bottlenose dolphins and admire the scenery.
» An outing on Loch Ness to spot the famous monster; or for those lacking sea legs, a date at Urquhart Castle, a huge 12th-century fortress overshadowing the lake.
» A day tour of the Isle of Mull in a 4WD to encounter the wildlife, including red stags, golden eagles, otters and porpoises. And a seagoing excursion to possibly see whales.

Outdoor pursuits
» Fishing lessons at various locations, for example Orchill Loch Trout Fishery (near Auchterarder) or Inverawe Smokehouse and Fisheries (at Taynuilt) – find out the secret of smoking fish straight afterwards.
» Kayaking or canoeing on the lakes (Loch Lomond, Loch Morlich) or on the open sea at Oban or the Isle of Skye.
» Horse riding across Scottish moorland; there are riding centres everywhere.

BEST TIME TO GO

Spring and summer (although wet) are the best seasons for visiting Scotland. In summer the sun sets late (not until 11pm in Shetland), so you can make the most of the long days. In winter the days are short and many visitor sites are closed outside the big towns. What is more, bad weather can affect the ferries connecting the islands.

COST

The strength of the pound sterling makes Scotland an expensive destination for non-Europeans. Food, accommodation and transport are all fairly pricey, more so in Edinburgh, Glasgow and Aberdeen than in the rest of the country. The only real bargains are the many excellent museums and galleries that you can visit for free. The price of food and fuel rises quite steeply in remote parts of the Highlands and islands where delivery costs are higher. Petrol can cost 10% to 15% more in the Outer Hebrides than in the Central Lowlands.

Mealtimes

It's not very likely that children will appreciate the national dish, haggis (offal stuffed inside a sheep's stomach). They will no doubt prefer shepherd's pie (minced beef topped with mashed potatoes), delicious locally smoked salmon, or fish and chips. For puddings they will be spoiled for choice; be careful though, as some are flavoured with whisky. You are safe with clootie dumpling (rich fruit pudding) and shortbread, the famous butter biscuits. Children are not always warmly welcomed in restaurants, especially outside the big towns. Children are allowed into so-called 'family' pubs but only from age 14 and between 11am and 8pm.

BOOKS FOR THE YOUNG TRAVELLER

> Allan Burnett's series of biographies of famous Scottish characters such as William Wallace, Robert the Bruce and Mary Queen of Scots are illustrated, humorous looks at history.

> *The Water Horse*, by Dick King-Smith, is a charming chapter book for young readers about how the Loch Ness monster found its home.

CHILDREN'S SOUVENIRS

> Child's set of bagpipes (if you're prepared for the noise)

> A Loch Ness monster cuddly toy

GETTING AROUND

Trains only connect the big towns, but there is a substantial network of comfortable buses. The roads are in a good state and car hire is affordable. Two wheels are a good way to visit the islands, which are best reached by ferry, as internal flights are expensive overall.

❶ **Warning**

→ Certain hotels and B&Bs refuse to take very young children, so make sure you check before booking.

→ In the Highlands and Islands blood-sucking midges are prevalent at dusk, particularly between mid-June and mid-August. Cover your children well in the evening and get them to wear light colours (the insects are attracted to darker colours). Watch out for horseflies as well, which are rife in the same regions, especially in summer.

❶ **Time difference**

→ Time zone UTC. Daylight saving time observed in northern hemisphere summer.

SICILY

Volcanoes and temples for inquisitive little scholars, a crystal-blue sea for novice divers, Homer's *Odyssey* for young dreamers…Sicily lends itself remarkably well to travelling with children, who will be captivated in an instant by Cyclops and other ancient myths.

Kicking back in Cefalù

CHILDREN WILL LOVE…

Beaches, islands and marine life

» The sandy beaches at Castellammare del Golfo (west), those bathed in light around Avola (southeast), cliff-lined Scala dei Turchi (south), and the big beach at Cefalù, a superb medieval city.

» The Aeolian and Egadis Islands, where a mask and snorkel are all that is needed to study the underwater landscape.

» Boat excursions to explore caves along the coastline, notably near Taormina.

Volcanoes

» Climbing Mt Etna – at 3350m, this is no mean feat. Children will manage well enough by first taking the bus, then the cable car and finally a 4WD to the crater's edge. The sight of the lava flows is quite something.

» Etnaland, the island's theme park, with a zoo, cable car, Prehistoric Park and, let us not forget, the water slides and Crocodile Rapids!

» The Aeolian Islands, a volcanic archipelago – a true-life geography lesson under the open sky.

Palermo, something for everyone

» The International Puppet Museum where the children can make their own *puppi* (puppets) and watch a show.

» A ride in a horse-drawn carriage in the historic centre.

» The Regional Archaeological Museum, a fascinating introduction to antiquity.

» The mummified bodies at the Catacombs of the Capuchins. A macabre spectacle that may intrigue teenagers, but perhaps not for sensitive little souls.

Greek gods, heroes and knights

» Some of the best-preserved Greek ruins in Europe, including the ancient theatre in the beautiful town of Taormina, the theatre at Syracuse, and the temples of Agrigento, Segesta and Selinunte.

» The mesmerising medieval town of Erice, reached by funicular from Trapani.

» The impressive Lombardy Castle at Enna, built by the Moors.

BEST TIME TO GO

Sicily is blessed with a mild climate year-round on the coast and you can swim from mid-April until October, if you are not too susceptible to the cold. In the height of summer temperatures reach 30°C, the beach resorts are often packed, and prices are higher, as it is one of the major holiday destinations for continental Italians.

COST

Generally speaking, travelling in Sicily is cheaper than in mainland Italy, although resort towns such as Taormina are more expensive than elsewhere. Under-18s benefit from a range of sizeable discounts, including free entry to museums. Public transport is quite cheap, but accommodation will be the greatest expense. Avoid eating near tourist sites, and take advantage of the delicious, cheap pizza sold at bakeries.

Mealtimes

Few Sicilian restaurants are equipped with high chairs or children's menus but you can easily order a *mezzo piato* (half portion). Youngsters rarely sulk over their plates when they find them filled with delicious pasta (spicy sauces aside). They will also enjoy *lasagna cacate* (with minced beef and sausages) and nibbling at the *antipasti* (cured meats, cheese, marinated vegetables). When hot, nothing beats an ice cream. Not so light but just as tasty are the famous *cannoli* (cakes stuffed with ricotta and preserved fruits).

GETTING AROUND

The easiest option is to hire a car. There are extensive public-transport networks, mainly serving the most popular destinations. The trains are slower than the bus, but are less expensive. While it is easy to visit Palermo and other major towns on foot, it can be tiring for little legs. It is better to use public transport than taxis, which are quite expensive, not to mention subject to dangerous driving. Ferries (*traghetti*) and hydrofoils (*aliscafi*) connect the islands around Sicily with Palermo and Trapani.

❗ Warning

→ Reserve train tickets well ahead to avoid having to stand.

→ In Sicily, as in the rest of Italy, pickpocketing is commonplace. Cars with foreign plates attract unwanted attention.

→ For walks in the countryside, ensure children have boots that come up over the ankles and they wear trousers to reduce the chance of viper bites. If bitten, most chemists sell antidotes.

🕑 Time difference

→ Time zone: UTC+01:00. Daylight saving time observed in northern hemisphere summer.

BOOKS FOR THE YOUNG TRAVELLER

› *Cartwheel to the Moon: My Sicilian Childhood*, by Emanuel di Pasquale, is a lovely, nostalgic collection of poems evoking the sights, sounds and smells of old Sicily.

› *Beautiful Angiola: The Lost Sicilian Folk and Fairy Tales of Laura Gonzenbach*, translated by Jack Zipes, is a collection of classic tales with a very Sicilian slant.

CHILDREN'S SOUVENIRS

› Puppets

› Reproductions of traditional wooden carts

SPAIN

Spain conjures up many familiar images for children, with bulls and flamenco heading the list. However there are also endless beaches, generous sunshine (sometimes too much, be careful in Andalucía and Madrid), and an infinite number of sights and activities. To top it all, there is the kind of dream-inspired architecture that fires the imagination.

The Alhambra inspires the imagination

CHILDREN WILL LOVE...

Catalonia the colourful

» A visit to Barcelona's stunning Sagrada Família cathedral by Gaudí and a stroll in the peaceful Park Güell, some of the most entertaining works by the master.
» A walk through the pedestrian lanes of Barcelona's medieval quarter, Barri Gòtic, and along La Rambla, a lively pedestrianised road.
» A visit to the wonderful aquarium in Port Vell.
» The Dalí Theatre-Museum in Figueras. The building alone will delight children, while the artist's castle at Púbol and the Port Lligat Casa Museu Dalí near Cadaqués will interest them as well.
» The many beaches on the Costa Brava, principally those within reach of Palafrugell, which are the least busy.

Andalucía, a Moorish tale

» The Mezquita, the giant Mosque-Cathedral of Córdoba, which cannot fail to impress.
» Visiting the desert cinema studios northeast of Almería, where a number of westerns were made.

» Exploring the white towns of Cádiz and Seville from a horse-drawn carriage.
» The Alhambra Palace and Generalife Gardens in Granada.
» A visit to the Royal Andalucían School of Equestrian Art in Jerez de la Frontera, where you can watch the riders training.
» The largely unspoilt beaches on the Costa del Sol around the small white town of Mijas.

Madrid and Don Quixote country

» The Spanish capital, with its attractions to suit every taste including the Casa de Campo Park with its zoo, fairground rides and swimming pools; the Parque del Buen Retiro for renting a pedalo; the Parque Secreto and its bouncy castles; and Faunia, the nature park.
» The fortified town of Toledo with its medieval streets.
» The windmills dominating the plain around the Consuegra Castle and at Campo de Criptana.

Coastal wanderings

» Valencia's City of Arts and Sciences, an immense futuristic complex where scientific experiments and marine life are on the agenda.
» The Mediterranean resorts of the Costa del Azahar and the beautiful beaches along the Costa Blanca.
» San Sebastián, with its long beaches, impressive aquarium and Naval Museum commemorating the whaling era.
» The lovely seaside resorts of Asturias and long stretches of sand.
» The cliffs and creeks in the verdant region of Galicia, perfect for walking.
» The small fishing villages and the whaling ship *Aita Guria*, in Bermeo.
» The pretty medieval village of Santillana del Mar and the fortified town of Olite, bristling with turrets.

BEST TIME TO GO

Spain is a country you can visit year-round, although spring is the best time because the heat is less suffocating than in summer. This is also the time to avoid Andalucía, when the mercury can hit 45°C. However you can always escape the excessive heat by visiting the beaches in the north and along the Atlantic coast, or by heading to the mountains.

COST

Spain is, as locals will quickly tell you, not as cheap as it once was. What you spend on accommodation (probably your single greatest expense) will depend on various factors such as location (Madrid is pricier than Murcia), season (August along the coast is packed and expensive), the degree of comfort you require and a little dumb luck. Most sights are fairly cheap. Keep an eye out for free days (especially on Sunday and set days for EU citizens). Public transport is reasonably priced, although high-speed trains are pricey. Casual eateries and self-catering are inexpensive but tasty ways to fill up.

Mealtimes

In the land of tapas, everyone will find something they like: tortillas and small *croquetas de queso* (cheese deep-fried in breadcrumbs) are dishes that work for children. They generally have nothing against paella either and many will even tuck into gazpacho (cold tomato soup). Food lovers will relish *turron*, a local nougat of which there are many varieties, and churros (a sort of donut, very sugary and delicious). Dinner is served late here and you will be hard pushed to find a restaurant serving before 9.30pm. Rest assured, the extremely convivial tapas bars offer a wide range of tasty dishes.

BOOKS FOR YOUNG TRAVELLERS
> Pack a children's version of the tales of Don Quixote.
> Teenagers will enjoy Laurie Lee's tales of '30s Spain in *As I Walked Out One Midsummer Morning*.

CHILDREN'S SOUVENIRS
> Castanets
> A ball and wickerwork racket for playing traditional Basque *pelota*

GETTING AROUND

The bus and rail networks are extensive and provide a decent service between the big towns and cities. Sometimes it is cheaper to take an internal flight than to take the train (which is quite expensive). The roads are also good and there are a number of motorways.

🛈 **Warning**
> Avoid going out between midday and 4pm, especially with very young children. The sun can be scorching, even by the sea. A siesta at this time can be helpful, especially if your children are living like locals and staying up late.
> Mediterranean or Atlantic, there are no end of beaches. However, on the Atlantic the water is cooler. Look out for the blue flag, which identifies the cleanest beaches.

🕑 **Time difference**
> Time zone UTC+01:00. Daylight saving time observed in northern hemisphere summer.

SWEDEN

Sweden is a place that lends itself well to family travel: a superb natural landscape lures you out of doors and even younger children find a welcome at the numerous amusement parks. Everywhere – in hotels, museums, shops and restaurants – there are special play areas for children.

Nothing beats the excitement of dog sledding

CHILDREN WILL LOVE...
Stockholm, a child's paradise

» An outing to the island of Djurgården where there is an amusement park, Gröna Lund, as well as the Junibacken, in Galarparken, a museum dedicated to the fictional children's heroine Pippi Longstocking. Not far away is the Skansen, an open-air museum depicting Sweden in the 'olden days'. Children can also see the *Vasa*, an almost perfectly preserved 17th-century ship in a museum of the same name.
» The Historiska Museet (Swedish History Museum) at Östermalm, which has numerous Viking artifacts and an enormous model of the fortified town of Birka.
» Birka, on the isle of Björkö, with its small Viking village where the children can dress up and pretend to be famous Scandinavian explorers.

Parks and museums designed for kids

» Finding Father Christmas! He is living near the picturesque village of Mora, which is like something out of a fairy tale. Children will also bump into trolls and elves before shaking hands with the great man.
» Astrid Lindgrens Värld at Vimmerby, a theme park inspired by author Astrid Lindgren's character Pippi Longstocking.
» The Universeum at Göteborg: a temple to science on seven floors where children can go up in a spaceship, ride in a funicular and try out all kinds of experiments.
» The Toy Museum (Leksaksmuseum) in Malmö: it has a play area and even a haunted room for the more courageous!
» Liseberg, the biggest amusement park in Scandinavia, situated in Göteborg.
» Kolmården Zoo, the biggest in Scandinavia, which will enchant young visitors with its bus safari.

Adventures in the wild

» Bike rides on well-marked paths, notably in the regions of Skåne and Gotland.
» Horseback rides, which are possible throughout the Swedish countryside, and especially recommended on the island of Gotland, birthplace of the pony of the same name which is an ideal mount for little ones.
» A memorable dog-sledge ride across the deserted landscapes of Jämtland, from the lively town of Åre.
» Pedalling a *dressin*, a unique family-sized cycle that runs along disused railway tracks in Värmland.

BEST TIME TO GO

It is in autumn and summer that the climate is the most agreeable, but if you are looking for sunshine then head here between the end of May and the end of July (August is often rainy). Stockholm is pleasant from April. Sweden is the camping kingdom, even though most of the sites are only open in summer. Winters can be harsh; life slows down except in the ski resorts and big towns.

COST

There's no getting away from the fact that Sweden is expensive, although it is cheaper than elsewhere in Scandinavia. There are ways to mitigate costs. Hotels usually have family rooms for little more than the price of a regular double and there are plenty of family-friendly camping grounds and hostels. Most attractions allow free admission for under-sevens and half-price for under-16s. Transport is the biggest expense, but in Stockholm, public transport is free for children under seven. Petrol prices are high, but you can hire cars fairly cheaply from some petrol stations.

Mealtimes

Restaurants often provide children's menus and high chairs. For breakfast, starving youngsters will be happy to devour cakes and cereals. Herring, along with salmon, are staples in Swedish cuisine. If they dislike fish, children will make up for it with *köttbulla* (meatballs), usually served with mash and *lingonsylt* (cranberry sauce). They should like *pytt i panna*, a dish with potatoes, diced sausage and meat. They will undoubtedly melt at the sight of the cakes, especially the popular *kanelbullar* (delicious cinnamon-flavoured bread).

BOOKS FOR THE YOUNG TRAVELLER

> *The Wonderful Adventures of Nils*, by Selma Lagerlövis, Sweden's best-loved children's writer, is the story of a little boy who flies across the county on the back of a magic goose.

> Enjoy together the classic *Pippi Longstocking* series by Astrid Lindgren.

CHILDREN'S SOUVENIRS

> Wooden toys, a Swedish specialty

> Troll figurines

GETTING AROUND

An interesting way to visit the country is by boat: there are a number of cruises on the waterways linking the lakes, and ferries let you hop round the islands scattered along the coast. The train is ultra-comfortable: second class on the X2000, the high-speed train, is almost as good as first class elsewhere. The only hitch is the high prices. In a car, moose and reindeer can pose real hazards, especially in the north. Be extra vigilant at sunrise and nightfall.

🕐 **Time difference**
→ Time zone UTC+01:00. Daylight saving time observed in northern hemisphere summer.

SWITZERLAND

Watch out for upset tummies! In this famously peaceful country there is a real danger of overdoing the chocolate. Best drag your children quickly up a mountain, summer or winter, to make them forget this sweet temptation.

Mountains and tree-top parks: bring a head for heights

CHILDREN WILL LOVE...
Family-friendly hikes
» Climbing Mt Pilatus (near Lucerne) by the rack-and-pinion train, a real curiosity for little ones. From there, the trail to the top of Tomlishorn is easy (even with a stroller). A cable car takes you to a tree-top suspension rope park (Seilpark).
» The adventure stations along the Dwarf Trail, suitable for four- to 10-year-olds, or the Marmot Trail, both accessible from Hasliberg or Meiringen (canton of Bern).
» Looking for marmots and edelweiss in the Swiss National Park (Graubünden, in the Engadine Valley), which has a children's discovery trail and a multimedia centre.

Summer activities
» Summer toboggan runs, found in practically all the mountain resorts.

» Cruising and swimming in the lakes of Geneva (Geneve-Plage, with lawns, bouncy castles, pools and slides); Zurich (swimming in the River Limmat); Neuchâtel or Biel.
» Exploring caves, such as the ice palace at the Aletsch Glacier (near Interlaken), the Rhone ice cave (Gletsch, Valais), and the caves at Vallorbe (Vaud) with their magnificent collections of minerals.
» Panoramic trains, funiculars and cable cars, especially the Glacier Express from Zermatt to St Moritz, and the spine-tingling ride up to Niesen (the 'Swiss Pyramid') near Spiez!

Fun in the snow
» Outstanding toboggan runs. Among the longest are Pizol (7km), near Wangs, and Faulhorn (15km – a record in Europe), near Grindelwald.
» A carriage or sledge ride in Zermatt, a car-free ski resort.

The land of Heidi, chocolate and cheese
» Exploring *Heidi* country. The bucolic region near Maienfeld on the Austrian border is a patchwork of meadows dotted with chalets, where the author, Johanna Spyri, set the adventures of the little orphan girl.
» The Swiss Museum of Rural Habitat near Brienz (canton of Bern), with dozens of traditional houses in a large park and demonstrations of ancient crafts.
» The vast Toy Worlds Museum and the Museum of Carriages in Basel, with every type of conveyance from dog carts to landaus.
» Uncovering the secrets of the master cheese makers on the cheese trail near Gruyères.
» The chocolate factory of Maison Cailler at Broc, a chocolate-covered universe.
» The other-worldly HR Giger Museum in Gruyères, dedicated to the artist best known for the special effects on the film *Alien*.

BEST TIME TO GO

The summer period from June to September is the most pleasant for outdoor activities. However the prices are higher, accommodation is hard to come by and the main tourist attractions are crammed. It's much better to visit from April to May or from the end of September to October (swimming is still possible). For winter sports, the season stretches from the end of November to April, with Christmas being the busiest time.

COST

Let's get this over and done with quickly: Switzerland is an expensive place. One very good piece of news is that petrol in Switzerland is often cheaper than in its neighbouring countries, particularly Italy. Local agencies are your best bet for competitive car-hire rates. Your biggest expenses are likely to be long-distance public transport, accommodation and eating out. However accommodation is clean and of a high standard, making it a good place to travel with babies, and camping is a more affordable option. Travel passes almost invariably provide big savings for families on trains, boats and buses – it is essential to check these out and see which might suit you.

GETTING AROUND

Fast and well-maintained, the motorways shorten the distances. Be careful though: you need to buy a *vignette* (toll sticker), which costs 40 Swiss francs for the year, and is on sale at the border, in post offices and service stations. The train is very practical and affordable, particularly for holders of the Swiss Travel System's Swiss Family Card (free), available online or at stations. It allows under-16s to travel free if accompanied by a parent. The Swiss Pass, available for different durations, offers unlimited travel on the rail network, buses and boats, as well as free access to almost all the museums, mountain trains and cable cars.

Mealtimes

Raclette, *rösti* (fried, grated potato patties), cured meats, cheese…children will find Swiss specialities slide down easily, apart from the many bones in the lake fish. As well as chocolate bars, children will appreciate Gruyère double cream with meringues. Be careful, alcohol in the fondue may not always go down well with younger diners.

⏱ Time difference

→ Time zone UTC+01:00. Daylight saving time observed in northern hemisphere summer.

BOOKS FOR THE YOUNG TRAVELLER

› Don't leave home without a copy of *Heidi*, by Johana Spyri, or an audio version for the car.

› Older readers should get their teeth into Gaye Hicylmaz' novel about how a young Turkish girl adjusts to a new life in Switzerland, *The Frozen Waterfall*.

CHILDREN'S SOUVENIRS

› A Swiss army knife

› A cuckoo clock to wake you up in the morning

› A cow bell to wake the parents!

The Americas and the Caribbean

Cowboy or Indian? Parents and children must pick their corner according to their preference for the North or South continent. Whatever the choice, the vast open spaces and the legendary roads will be sure to provide unforgettable memories.

In the United States and Canada, ranches and the great plains offer a reassuring setting. Countless movies, basketball stars, Disneyland and Tom Sawyer have undoubtedly inspired your coyote pups. Hygiene, comfort and safety make travelling easy here with your brood. At the end of the day, you can explore a whole new world of high-rise cities, Texan hats and theme parks, without a care in the world.

For a more tropical version of the trans-Atlantic dream, set sail for the Caribbean. Guadeloupe and Martinique provide worry-free destinations. By not overdoing the trips and combining the pleasures of the beach and mountains, you will secure the complicity of your young pirates.

Latin America and its main entry point, Mexico, suggest a more colourful, adventurous journey. Playing at being a gaucho on a ranch, rubbing shoulders with indigenous culture, rafting through tropical forests or consorting with the countless animals in Costa Rica: so many astounding experiences can be had on any budget. For sure, strolling round the colonial cities, ambling over ice fields and, and surveying the sand or salt deserts does come with a price: no guarantee of comfort, altitude that is prohibitive for younger children, often long and exhausting distances, and that is before you even consider the mosquitoes eyeing up your legs. However, by the end of the adventure, you will have lived many rare and exotic moments, helped by convenient domestic flights and a minimum of preparation.

So then, will it be North or South?

ARGENTINA

Colourful cities, breathtaking scenery, kid-friendly cuisine…sublime Argentina has yet another advantage: it is a very easy place to take the family. So you need only decide, La Pampa, Tierra del Fuego or both?

Los Glaciares National Park will astound young and old

CHILDREN WILL LOVE...
Buenos Aires, familiar and exotic
» A bike or boat outing in the Parque Tres de Febrero. The children can also amuse themselves in the planetarium or zoo in the same sector.
» Puppet shows at the Museo Argentino del Titere.
» Multicoloured birds in the Reserva Ecológica Costanera Sur.
» Dwarf hippopotamuses, pumas and white tigers living in the beautiful, natural enclosures in the Parque Temaikén.
» An excursion to the small town of Tigre to tour the delta by boat or in canoes.

Experiences to send shivers down your spine
» Playing gauchos while staying on an *estancia* (cattle ranch) typical of the plains of La Pampa.
» Tandem paragliding in La Cumbre in Córdoba or in Bariloche.
» A dog-sled ride in Tierra del Fuego in the winter.
» Skiing in Las Leñas, in the superb powder of the Andes.

Scenery carved out by giants
» Glaciers and icebergs in the Los Glaciares National Park.
» The endless pampas plains.
» The jaw-dropping Iguazú Falls in the heart of the northern subtropical forest: 80m high and 2km wide!

Wild animals
» Mischievous penguins on the Patagonian coast.
» Capybaras in the northeastern swamps. (They're the biggest rodent in the world – like something out of a cartoon!)
» Sea lions in the Península Valdés wildlife reserve, and from June to December, southern right whales.
» Domesticated or wild llamas posted along the Andean trails.

On the trail of the dinosaurs
» Discovering the huge skeletons and dinosaur footprints in Neuquén.
» Joining the dig at the Centro Paleontológico Lago Barreales, under the watchful eye of a paleontologist.
» Joining the team of 'explorers in pyjamas' in the Museo Paleontológico Egidio Feruglio, in Trelew. They have a night-time visit to the museum by lamp light especially for children.

BEST TIME TO GO

The period from September to November (spring) is the best season to travel in the north. For Patagonia, the Argentinian summer (December to February) is better. On the other hand, if you are banking on skiing it is better to visit from mid-June to mid-October.

COST

Argentina is still a cheap destination by world standards, and about average for South America. However actual costs can fluctuate wildly. Due to galloping inflation, prices are constantly being driven up, but the instability of the peso means exchange rates can be good. There are two exchange rates, the official one and the 'blue' one – an illegal black market for US dollars which is very common and can be up to twice the official rate. Prices are generally higher in Patagonia, due to the isolation of the area. Save money by staying at guesthouses rather than chain hotels and eating at local restaurants rather than those aimed at tourists.

Mealtimes

The famous Argentinian beef will undoubtedly be a revelation for young meat lovers. But fresh pasta and pizza appears on menus everywhere, as do paellas and empanadas (pastry filled with meat or cheese). Argentinian cooking is heavily influenced by Spanish and Italian cuisine. Adult portions are usually generous enough to feed a young child as well, as long as the waiters do not begrudge bringing extra plates and cutlery (sometimes there is a small charge). Other good news for young foodies: tons of sweets made with *dulce de leche* (very sweet caramel condensed milk) are sold in street stalls, which, along with the delicious ice cream, show that Argentinians are rather partial to sugar.

BOOKS FOR THE YOUNG TRAVELLER

> For young readers, *On the Pampas*, by Maria Cristina Brusca, paints a colourful picture of gaucho life.

> *Tierra Del Fuego: A Journey to the End of the Earth*, by Peter Lourie, is an adventure-packed look at the history and geography of this amazing land.

CHILDREN'S SOUVENIRS

> A poncho or *bombachas* (gaucho riding trousers)

> A pinquillo (small Andean recorder)

HEALTH CHECK

» Malaria is present in rural areas along the borders with Bolivia and Paraguay. The risk is marginal and it is not worth taking an antimalarial treatment for holidays of less than seven days. Protect yourselves from mosquitoes as there is also a risk of dengue fever.

GETTING AROUND

Fast and comfortable – sometimes even luxurious – Argentine buses provide a vast network covering the country even to the tiniest backwater, and are practical with the family. You can save money by taking small children on your lap for short journeys. For long-haul trips, the '*cama* suite' (first-class) option is strongly recommended – full reclining luxury. The rail network is minimal, connecting some major cities, and certainly inferior to bus travel. Hiring a car is a real measure of freedom outside the crowded cities. Be careful though, as on some routes service stations can be few and far between. Finally, domestic flights are expensive but will save you quite a lot of time, as the country is huge. Book well in advance for the best deals.

❗ **Warning**

⇢ Distances can be long and journeys may seem interminable for small children. Be sure to have a supply of entertainment on hand: MP3 players, games, books and colouring pencils.

🕐 **Time difference**

⇢ Time zone UTC–03:00

BOLIVIA

Children will be dazzled by the striking native dress of Bolivia, as well as its lunar landscapes and Amazonian forest. And locals will be similarly taken with them, especially if they have fair hair. This is a great destination for adventurous families and apprentice explorers but it is not suitable for very young children due to the very high altitude.

Copacabana, the gateway to Lake Titicaca

CHILDREN WILL LOVE...

Towns clinging to mountainsides
» Potosí, perched at more than 4000m altitude, with its 33 churches and convents and colonial houses.
» La Paz, the highest capital city in the world, stepped up the side of the mountain. Children will be thrilled by its colourful markets, particularly the Mercado de Hechiceria (the Witches' Market).
» Sucre, a fabulous city with whitewashed buildings and lively markets.

The search for lost civilisations
» The pre-Inca fortress of El Fuerte de Samaipata.
» The archaeological site of Tiwanaku (Tiahuanaco, in Spanish), of the eponymous civilisation, which disappeared in the 12th century.

Colourful indigenous traditions
» Cholas, Aymara and Quechua women in traditional dress – bowler hat, shawl and big, brightly coloured skirts with petticoats – virtually a national symbol.
» The Valle Alto villages, with their brightly coloured markets, the most beautiful in the country.

Lunar landscapes and jungles
» Salar de Uyuni, the totally magical salt flats where flamingoes can sometimes be seen overhead.
» An excursion in a reed boat on Lake Titicaca, a national jewel that has inspired many a legend.
» The Torotoro National Park to seek out dinosaur footprints, take a dip in the waterfalls and go caving.
» An easy hike in the Cordillera de los Frailes to view cave paintings and villages nestling on the sides of the Maragua crater.
» The Cañon de Palca, with its stunning rock formations.
» A boating expedition from Trinidad on the Bolivian Amazon, the best-preserved part of the river.
» Spotting monkeys, jaguars, tapirs and peccaries in the Amboró National Park on an organised trip from Santa Cruz.

BEST TIME TO GO

The dry season is ideal for the traveller (mid-March to mid-November). At altitude (pretty much everywhere!) the nights are cold, even when the days are hot and sunny.

COST

Bolivia is one of the cheapest countries in South America, indeed the world, and food, transport and accommodation are all very affordable, if not quite up to the standards you may be used to. Foreigners are often charged more than locals, but it is possible to bargain for accommodation. Family-run guesthouses (*hostals* or *alojamientos*) are the best value.

Mealtimes

Potatoes, often fried, rice, corn and chicken (grilled, roasted or fried) are usually on the menu. *Sopa* (soup), the starter for every meal, might not appeal to little ones although it is always delicious. Dishes are always a little spicy due to a chilli sauce called *llajua* that you will soon learn to avoid. Stuffed meat pasties (empanadas, *salteñas* and *tucumanas*) are more likely to hit the mark as are tamales (made with corn flour): avoid the ones sold in the streets and buy them in the *confiterías* and the *pastelerías*.

HEALTH CHECK

» Watch out for *soroche* (altitude sickness). Learn to recognise the symptoms (nausea, headaches, fatigue) and how to prevent it (sleep below the altitude reached during the day, descend another 500m in case of illness).

GETTING AROUND

Despite a rudimentary road network and a lack of asphalt, car (preferably a 4WD) and bus are the best way to get around. On roads that are considered dangerous, use minibuses instead of regular buses and travel by day. Trains are often late; it is a good idea to book tickets through a travel agency. Domestic flights are usually an effective way to save time and to reach more out-of-the-way destinations. For getting about town, micros and *trufis* (collective taxis or minibuses), pick up and put down passengers along a set route.

ⓘ **Warning**

→ Both children and adults need to acclimatise gradually to the altitude. Ease into your trip by flying into Santa Cruz and visiting the plains first. Then go somewhere like Samaipata (1650m) to explore the fort before climbing up to the mountains or Altiplano.

ⓘ **Time difference**

→ Time zone UTC−04:00.

BOOKS FOR THE YOUNG TRAVELLER

> *Bolivia (Children of the World)*, by Yoshiyuki Ikuhara, gives young readers an insight into the life of an Aymara Indian boy living on a Lake Titicaca island, as well as the history and geography of Bolivia.

> *Yara's Amazing Nose*, published by Dot-to-Dot Children's Books, is a picture book about a tapir and other animals in the Bolivian Amazon. It concludes with facts about tapirs and the country in general, and profits from the sale of the book go to help Bolivian charities.

CHILDREN'S SOUVENIRS

> Pretty dolls made of wool or cotton dressed in traditional costume

> Musical instruments: *sicus* (pan pipes), *quena* (recorder) or *charango* (a small guitar with 10 strings)

BRAZIL

In Brazil the happiness is contagious. The carefree way of life fires the imagination and kindles a taste for adventure. Toddlers and teenagers will love the vast beaches where, in between dives in the sea, everyone plays the national sport, football. However, there is also the Amazonian jungle where the flora and fauna will amaze the whole family.

In Brazil, partying is an art form in which children play a huge part

CHILDREN WILL LOVE...
Rio, the carnival city

» A trip in the cable car up to Sugar Loaf Mountain and the rack-and-pinion train up to Cristo Redentor from where the views are absolutely stunning.
» Swimming on lifeguard-covered beaches at Ipanema or family-friendly Leblon (a dedicated children's area exists between posts 11 and 12), before a game of football.
» The zoological gardens for a foretaste of Brazilian wildlife. The pavilion for nocturnal animals houses sloths and bats.
» The animated displays at the Museu de Folclore Edison Carneiro, dedicated to Brazilian folk art, where rodeo and samba top the bill.

Salvador the festive

» Numerous open-air concerts that make you want to dance.

» Demonstrations and lessons in capoeira, a blend of martial art and acrobatic dance.
» Attending a show by the Olodum school, particularly its impressive *batucada* (type of samba).

Playing at explorers

» A trip on the famous Maria-Fumaça steam train between the colonial cities of São João and Tiradentes (Minas Gerais).
» An expedition into the Amazonian jungle leaving from Manaus. Comfortable lodges allow you to experience the astounding jungle nights.
» Sledging on the sand dunes at Jericoacoara, in the northeast.
» The magnificent Iguazú Falls (Paraná), on the Argentine border.
» The Mamirauá Reserve (Amazonas). In June and July you can paddle a canoe in this incredible flooded forest to see sloths, caiman, parrots, toucans and monkeys.

Encounters with rare animals

» Turtles on the beach of Parque Estadual de Itaunas between September and March.
» The maned wolves in the Parque Natural do Caraça (Minas Gerais), particularly close to the monastery (Santuário do Caraça) where they are fed every evening.
» A safari in Alta Floresta (Mato Grosso) to observe the birds and the rare mammals such as the white-nosed saki, the giant otter or the titi monkey.
» An outing on the Transpantaneira, an elevated road, which runs from Cuiabá and crosses the Pantanal, to observe the wildlife.
» An excursion to see the southern right whales along the coast of the state of Santa Catarina, leaving from Imbituba or Itapirubá (June to October).

BEST TIME TO GO

In this vast country, the climate varies from one region to another. From December to March it is summer, with crowds of tourists and higher prices. From May to September visitor numbers thin out, the exception being July, during the school holidays. In Rio during this period the humidity diminishes and the heat is more bearable (23°C); in the south it is cool, even cold. The northeast coast from Bahia to Maranhão enjoys a milder climate year-round due to the tropical wind and less humidity. From December to May, heavy rains make travel in Amazonia difficult.

COST

Prices have increased considerably in recent years and Brazil is no longer a cheap destination, with São Paulo and Rio ranking as the first and second most-expensive cities in South America. But the cost of travel here still compares favourably with Europe and the US. Food (both in restaurants and groceries), accommodation (except in Rio) and bus travel are all reasonably priced. Many hotels let children stay free, although the age limit for this varies. Family-run B&Bs, apartment rentals or *pousadas* (inns which include breakfast) are alternative economical options. Many of the best attractions – such as the beaches – are free, but expeditions such as an Amazon River cruise can be hundreds of dollars. Prices in Rio soar during Carnival.

HEALTH CHECK

» Tap water is not safe to drink.

GETTING AROUND

A network of comfortable buses operates throughout the country, but the journeys can seem interminable. Sometimes it is better, and not necessarily more expensive, to fly. The train service is limited. If driving in town, windows should be kept closed and doors locked. Avoid going out at night (by car, on public transport or on foot).

Mealtimes

Meat is the centrepiece in Brazilian cuisine. Children love *churrascarias*, not just for the meat (grilled and as much as you want), but also for the ritual: every customer has a disc with a green side to tell the waiter you want more and a red side to say you have finished. A good way to encourage your kids to get a little more adventurous with their tastes is through a *por-kilo* restaurant where food is selected from a buffet and paid for by weight. *Arroz* and *féijão* (rice and black beans) are often served as side dishes, but you can order chips, which come in generous portions, as do all the dishes. For dessert, fresh fruits will delight little mouths, as will cuscus de tapioca, a sort of coconut flan.

❶ Warning
⤳ A great deal of care is needed, especially in the cities and towns. Here, pickpocketing and armed robbery are not uncommon, nor on the major roads connecting São Paulo to the coastal towns. Never let your child wander off alone. Do not display any evident signs of wealth.

◐ Time difference
⤳ Time zones range from UTC−03:00 to UTC−05:00.

BOOKS FOR THE YOUNG TRAVELLER
› High adventure for pre-teens, *Journey to the River Sea*, by Eva Ibbotson, is set in the Brazilian Amazon.

CHILDREN'S SOUVENIRS
› Brazilian football team uniforms
› Customised Havaïanas flip-flops

CANADA

Canada will stun the family with its wild, endless spaces. Exploring is made easy due to the excellent facilities geared to children, particularly in many of the parks. Young travellers will discover its rich natural beauty during hikes and trips to ecomuseums, where they can learn about the First Nations cultures. In the cities, they will find an impressive choice of activities on offer.

Nature is on a grand scale for small travellers in Canada

CHILDREN WILL LOVE...
Being face to face with nature
» Wood Buffalo National Park (Alberta), with herds of roaming bison.
» Boat trips to see whales, rorquals, dolphins and seals (particularly in the St Lawrence estuary, Québec, or on the west coast of Vancouver Island).

» Gazing at Niagara Falls from a gondola in the SkyWheel, a boat, or galleries hollowed into the rocks behind the curtain formed by the falls.
» The amazing Northern Lights and polar bears of the Churchill region.
» Riding a dog sled or ski doo (from age eight) in one of the parks around Temagami.
» Camping in a real tepee! Or more simply under canvas, like the majority of Canadian families on a camping trip.

The favourite pastimes of young Canadians
» Attending a hockey game (the national sport) in the Bell Centre in Montréal, or a rodeo at the Calgary Stampede.
» Ice skating on the Rideau Canal in Ottawa, at the Atrium in Montréal and on a number of frozen lakes in winter.
» Exploring Ottawa: observing the changing of the guard, enjoying the capital's many festivals and museums set up with children in mind.

Travelling in time
» Uncovering the era of the dinosaurs in the town of Drumheller (Alberta): the creatures pop up everywhere across town. The remarkable Paleontology Museum is not to be missed.
» Learning about the First Nations by touring the reconstructed villages at the Canadian Museum of History (Gatineau, Québec), visiting the reserves to see the way First Nations people live today or by attending a powwow in summer.
» Stepping back in time with the Acadian people in the Arcadian Historical Village of Caraquet (New Brunswick), where buildings and scenes from the 18th to 20th centuries have been painstakingly re-created.

BEST TIME TO GO

In summer pleasant temperatures favour outdoor pursuits. The weather is also mild in September, October, April and May, and there are fewer tourists. Between November and April, 2.5m of snow falls on average in the cities of the south and temperatures can easily fall to -25°C. Nonetheless winter also lends itself to a great number of activities.

COST

Canada is more expensive than the rest of North America, though not quite as expensive as Western Europe. Accommodation is likely to be your biggest expense, but as fuel prices rise, transportation ranks up there too. Ontario, Alberta and British Columbia are more costly than other provinces, but not as bad as the three northern territories (Yukon Territory, Northwest Territories and Nunavut). Your dollar will stretch furthest in Québec, the Atlantic provinces, Manitoba and Saskatchewan. Discounts are widely available to children and students, and many attractions also offer a family admission price. Taxes of 6% to 14% are added to nearly all goods and services. Tipping is the norm here; in restaurants, 15% is standard. At hotels, tip bellhops about $1 to $2 per bag. Leaving a few dollars for the room cleaners is always a welcome gesture. Cab drivers also expect a tip, usually 10% to 15%.

HEALTH CHECK

» There are a lot of insects in June and July. Take some good-quality repellent.
» Medical facilities are excellent but can be costly, especially for hospital stays. Think about getting specific insurance.

BOOKS FOR THE YOUNG TRAVELLER
› *Under a Prairie Sky* by Anne Laurel Carter is a picture book about a young boy who wishes to be a mountie.
› *Garden of the Spirit Bear: Life in the Great Northern Rainforest* by Dorothy Hinshaw Patent is a beautifully illustrated look at the delicately balanced ecosystem of British Columbia's northern forests.

CHILDREN'S SOUVENIRS
› Small First Nations sculptures of animals or a furry toy elk
› A *pichenotte* game (a table top game similar to finger billiards) or a game of bean bag toss (target game with small sandbags)

GETTING AROUND

Hiring a car is the best option in summer but less certain in winter when snow and ice can make travel difficult. The extensive bus network is excellent and fairly cheap (half price for children under 12 years). The train is slightly more comfortable. For long distances, it has to be a flight: numerous carriers serve 150 destinations across the country.

Mealtimes

Many Canadian restaurants are exemplary in dealing with children (they have booster seats and waiters that listen). Menus often cater for them with chicken tenders or mini-pizzas, and you can usually order a half portion of any savoury dish. For dessert, maple syrup is delicious drizzled on pancakes and on 'Beavertails' (large, hot donuts), which also come covered in chocolate. Kids will also love the iconic Québecois dish *poutine*, a mess of french fries with gravy and cheese curds.

! Warning
→ Black bears and grizzlies are common in Canada especially in the Rockies. Follow the advice provided by the Parks Canada office.

Time difference
→ Time zones range from UTC−08:00 (including Vancouver) to UTC−03:30, with Ontario and most of Québec at UTC−05:00. Some parts of the country observe daylight saving time in the northern hemisphere summer.

CHILE

Young travellers will mainly appreciate the beauty and untamed character of Chile's wide, open spaces. They will find widely differing surroundings and climates in this long, thin land: coastal beaches, outdoor pursuits in the Chilean Lake District and, if the family sets its sights on still more daring adventures, Patagonia or the Atacama Desert.

Torres del Paine is accessible for adventurous older families

CHILDREN WILL LOVE...
Breathtaking nature

» The national parks, as numerous as they are varied. There's a choice of landscapes from lunar (volcanic regions), verdant (the Lake District) or frozen (close to the Antarctic).
» Andean wildlife, mainly camelids (guanacos, vicuñas, llamas and alpacas). You may also spot viscachas (related to the rabbit), pumas (rare), flamingoes, Andean condors, and, if you are very lucky, a huemul (south Andean deer).

Urban Chile

» Santiago, the capital, seen to best effect from San Cristóbal Hill. The summit is reached by funicular, and there is even an open-air pool for a swim.
» Valparaiso, the legendary port, where you can explore the hills via eccentric funiculars.

Water, ice and fire

» The beaches, though most are not really suited to swimming. Those who can stand the cold can plunge in to the sea from the northern beaches such as those at Viña del Mar, a very popular resort near Valparaiso.
» Easter Island (Rapa Nui), in the middle of the Pacific (3700km from the coast), and its fascinating *moai* (giant carved stone figures).
» The Andes mountains, with a number of family-friendly ski resorts with runs catering for children and beginners. Some resorts, such as Parva, are just an hour's drive out of Santiago.
» The Atacama Desert, in the north, said to be the most arid desert in the world. Its salt landscapes, dunes and geysers are fantastic.

Wild Patagonia

» Torres del Paine National Park, ideal for exploring Patagonia's many faces and its wildlife (such as condors, flamingoes and guanacos). If the superb hikes are deemed unsuitable for children, take a minibus tour.
» The quirky village of Caleta Tortel, where wooden walkways serve as roads. This is the main departure point for a number of hikes, boat trips or horse rides heading to the ice fields.
» An excursion to Isla Magdalena or the Otway Sound from Punta Arenas, to observe the penguin colonies.

BEST TIME TO GO

Due to its length (4300km from north to south), Chile has many different climates. Take advantage of the beautiful Chilean summer (December to February) to enjoy natural sites such as the Torres del Paine National Park; in winter they can be inaccessible. In spring and autumn, you can explore the centre of the country, including the Lake District. June to September is the season to head for Chile's ski resorts.

COST

Chile is not cheap by South American standards, but its standard of living is higher, and it is still more economical than Europe or North America. Prices can double during the late-December to mid-March high season, but travel just before or after the official season and you'll most likely score bargain accommodation. Excellent deals can be had for families in fully equipped cabins in the summer resorts. Internal flights devour travel funds at any time of the year. But surprisingly cheap and ridiculously filling set-menu lunches are served by most restaurants – even expensive eateries have very affordable lunchtime deals. It's customary to cough up an extra 10% of the bill as a tip in restaurants, except in family-run places.

Mealtimes

Chilean cooking is a little spicy (mainly due to the accompanying sauces). Fish and seafood take pride of place on the menu. Children who do not fancy this can tuck into *lomo* (or *bife*) *a la pobre* (steak and chips with eggs on top) or *pastel de choclo* (minced meat cooked with onions and raisins and topped with a creamed-corn gratin). The dessert menu is a bit thin: you will see *manjar* (caramel made from condensed milk) used in all kinds of cakes. Portions are hefty in restaurants and you might share with your child.

BOOKS FOR THE YOUNG TRAVELLER

› An imaginative interpretation for young readers of Easter Island's mysterious *moai* can be found in T A Barron's *The Day the Stones Walked*.

CHILDREN'S SOUVENIRS

› Soft toys and figurines of llamas
› Colourful knitted dolls and animals

HEALTH CHECK

» Santiago can suffer from high levels of pollution in winter. If a state of emergency is declared, keep children away from the city centre.
» The quality of care is good in medical centres in Santiago but guarantees of payment are required on arrival. It is best to have a credit card and medical insurance.

GETTING AROUND

Flying is the best way to deal with long distances. It is less tiring for children and sometimes less expensive than the bus. Buses are faster than trains and the network is far more extensive. In the south of the country you can easily transfer between islands and fjords by boat. However, at the end of the high season, the ferry service is less frequent. In cities you can use the collective taxis: like buses they have set routes, but are faster and more comfortable. A car will let you reach out-of-the-way places far more easily, but hiring one is fairly expensive and it can be very difficult, even impossible, to leave the car in a different location to where you hired it.

🛈 **Warning**
→ On some beaches the sea is quite choppy due to strong currents. Read the warning signs.
→ Stray dogs are common. Do not let your children play with them.

🛈 **Time difference**
→ Time zone UTC−04:00. Daylight saving time observed in southern hemisphere summer.

COSTA RICA

Playing Tarzan in the middle of the jungle, seeing a volcano up close, swimming with the fish or admiring the incredible flowers: children's dreams can come true in stunning Costa Rica. And this small, peaceful country has all of the practicalities that rank high with parents, plus a child-friendly culture. It is the family holiday destination to beat all others in Latin America.

Costa Rica is packed with family-friendly adventures

CHILDREN WILL LOVE...
Adventures worthy of Indiana Jones
» The bubbling, steaming volanic cauldron at Parque Nacional Volcán Poás, which has a stroller-friendly walkway along the observation area (one of the few national parks accessible in this way).
» An excursion through the jungle canopy on a series of suspension bridges, platforms and zip wires, or via a scenic train, in the Monteverde Cloud Forest Reserve.
» Family-friendly rafting and 'safari trips' through the tropical forest on Río Sarapiquí or Río Pejibaye.

Animal spotting
» Taking a boat tours through the canals of Parque Nacional Tortuguero or staying in a jungle lodge outside the village to uncover wildlife all around.
» Watching sea turtles lay their eggs under the cover of night, one of Costa Rica's truly magical experiences, possible on both the Pacific and the Caribbean coasts.

» Sloth Sanctuary of Costa Rica, the best place to meet some baby sloths, possibly the cutest creatures on the planet.
» Fundacíon Santuario Silvestre de Osa, a boat-accessible sanctuary which rehabilitates injured and orphaned animals and where friendly monkeys roam freely.
» Frog's Heaven, a tropical garden filled with all sorts of brightly colored (and transparent!) amphibians, including the iconic red-eyed tree frog.
» Capering on Playa Carrillo beach, south of family-friendly Sámara; this beach can be all yours during the week and is convivially crowded with Tico (Costa Rican) families on the weekends.
» Parque Nacional Manuel Antonio, where beach visits are usually enlivened by monkeys, coatis and iguanas.
» Playa Negra, a black-sand, blue-flag beach (meeting Costa Rica's highest ecological standards) with plenty of space to plant your own flag.

Meeting the Ticos and Ticas
» The sight of wandering street vendors and *mercados* (markets) with brightly coloured stalls in San José.
» Attending a *tope* – half rodeo, half village fete – in the Guanacaste, land of gauchos.
» Participating in the day-to-day life of an indigenous Guaymi family in the Golfo Dulce Forest Reserve.
» Taking a walk around the mountain village of Sarchi, the most famous centre for arts and crafts in the country, where you can stock up on colourful souvenirs.

BEST TIME TO GO

The Costa Rican summer (*verano*), which runs from December to April, is the best time to travel to the country. Winter (*invierno*) is the rainy season: there are fewer tourists but flooding can make travel difficult (though river crossings by 4WD can be a thrill for the kids!). It is more difficult to find accommodation in town between Christmas and New Year, as well as during Holy Week (Easter).

HEALTH CHECK

» Malaria is present all year in Limon province. The risk is insignificant elsewhere. Dengue fever is widespread, so protect yourselves from mosquitoes.
» Good medical care is available in most major cities but may be limited in rural areas. Most pharmacies are well supplied and pharmacists are licensed to prescribe medication.
» Tap water is safe in Costa Rica, but if you find yourself far off the beaten path it's best to avoid it.

Mealtimes

Costa Rican food is simple, not very spicy and, as such, enjoyed by children. Chicken, fish (fried or grilled), rice and black beans are more or less what you will see on your plate. For breakfast, if they're not keen on the traditional *gallo-pinto* (sautéed beans and rice dished up with eggs, cheese and cream), order them a tropical breakfast of bread and fresh fruits instead. *Batidos* (smoothies made with fresh fruit and water or milk) are refreshing for children, but the top drink will be *pipa fría*, a green coconut into which you slide a straw to drink the milk. If you're travelling with an infant or small child, stock up on formula, baby food and snacks before heading to remote areas, where shops are few and far between.

BOOKS FOR THE YOUNG TRAVELLER

> Nancy Drew fans will love the 'Eco Mystery' trilogy set in an adventure resort in Costa Rica. The first book in the series, by Carolyn Keene, is *The Green-Eyed Monster.*

CHILDREN'S SOUVENIRS

> Tropical-hardwood carved toys, such as masks, jungle animals or the uniquely Costa Rican, colourfully painted replicas of *carretas* (traditional oxcarts) produced in Sarchí.

COST

As it is so highly geared for tourism, Costa Rica can be pricey, and is the most expensive country in Central America. But it's also one of the safest and friendliest. Transport is good value (though children over three pay full fare on buses), and package deals can be an economical way to enjoy a number of attractions and activities.

GETTING AROUND

The bus may be slow but services are frequent and good value. More expensive are the tourist buses to most of the sights: they pick you up at your hotel (avoiding long waits with the children) and can be booked online, through your hotel or travel agents. Car hire is possible in San José and in cities and towns on the Pacific coast. Car seats are not always available, so bring your own or make sure you double check with the agency. Opt for a 4WD as the roads are mediocre, especially during the rainy season, and minor accidents are common. Thieves can easily recognise rental cars, so never leave anything in the car and if possible, park in a guarded parking lot over night. You can also hire a taxi for a few hours or for the day (often cheaper than an organised tour).

❗ **Warning**
↳ During bus trips, take care to keep important objects and papers in a bag with you in the bus: it is not unusual for items in the hold to disappear during a stop.

🕐 **Time difference**
↳ Time zone UTC−06:00.

129

CUBA

Beaches galore, thumping music and some of the friendliest folks on Earth turn what might seem like an unlikely family destination into a kids' wonderland. Despite the economic hardship, the atmosphere is always cheerful in the streets and on the beach. Visitors are sure of a warm reception and children are welcome everywhere.

Kids love Cuba's riot of colour

CHILDREN WILL LOVE...

Living history

» The streets of Habana Vieja (Old Havana). They can't have changed much since the days of the *Pirates of the Caribbean*, so your kids' imaginations will run wild in forts, squares, museums and narrow streets.

» The Hershey Electric Railway, near family-friendly Playa Jibacoa in Mayabeque, which passes picturesque farming communities and tiny time-warped hamlets.

» American cars from the 1940s and '50s, seen on every street. Some act as taxis for tourists: children will love to take a spin in one of these glamourous pre-revolutionary museum pieces!

The paradisal coastline

» The resort complex of Varadero, with the best beaches for children, plus amazing pools, an amusement park, organised activities and plenty of other kids for playmates.

» The *cayos* of the north coast: tiny enchanting islands perfect for more intrepid families.

» Snorkelling to watch the marine life teeming below the surface of the warm, turquoise waters of Playa Ancon, near Trinidad.

» A trip in a sea-going kayak (for older children) or boat, which can both be hired on the tourist beaches.

Animal encounters

» The 30,000-strong pink flamingo colony on the untamed Cayo Ramano (but be prepared for swarms of mosquitoes).

» Horseback riding, which is possible all over Cuba and usually run out of rustic ranches in rural areas such as Pinar del Río and Trinidad.

» Turtle watching at Parque Nacional Peninsula de Guanahacabibes.

» Having a whirl on the big wheel and bumper cars at Isla del Coco theme park, in the capital.

» Parque Maestranza, with bouncy castles, fairground rides and sweet snacks overlooking Havana harbour. Great for the under-fives.

» The surreal Valle de la Prehistoria, in Parque Baconao (Santiago de Cuba), where you can see 240 dinosaur models.

Music and dancing everywhere

» The Carnival in Trinidad in June, famous for its horse racing, and that of Santiago at the end of July, the most colourful in the Caribbean.

» Cuban concerts – they are happening almost everywhere all the time. Cubans turn up surrounded by family, why not you? Dance classes are also easy to find.

BEST TIME TO GO

Avoid June to August if possible: the temperatures and room rates rise uncomfortably. Choose February to March, rather than the period when hurricanes threaten (June to November), or the Christmas holidays: the heat is less intense so children will be able to enjoy the sunshine more – though it is still very strong for delicate skin.

COST

Cuba is not a cheap travel destination, being similar in cost to Western Europe. *Casas particulares* (rooms in private homes) are the most affordable accommodation and are a very child-friendly option. They are a great way to mix with local families, and many come with breakfast and other meals. Resorts are more expensive, but extremely family-friendly. Car hire is expensive – for short distances, it is often better value to take a taxi. Many museums and attractions are half price for children under 12. Disposable nappies (diapers) and baby formula can be hard to find; bring your own. Havana and tourist resorts are more expensive than elsewhere in Cuba.

Mealtimes

No need to waste time trying to convince your children to eat their greens; in Cuba they are rarely on the menu. Meat (pork or chicken, often fried or grilled) is served with slices of fried plantain, tomatoes, onions, cucumber, shredded white cabbage and a combination of rice and black beans known as *congrí* or *moros y cristianos* (Moors and Christians). Ice cream is popular on the island but preferably try those served in the best hotels or at Coppelia in Havana, a national institution! High chairs in restaurants are almost nonexistent, so you might like to bring a portable booster seat.

BOOKS FOR THE YOUNG TRAVELLER

> *Where the Flame Trees Bloom*, by Alma Flor Ada, is a collection of inspirational stories about a childhood in Cuba, great for pre-teens.

CHILDREN'S SOUVENIRS

> Musical instruments, such as claves or brightly painted maracas
> A lace fan
> A game of handmade dominoes

HEALTH CHECK

» The country has an efficient and extended network of medical centres. Nonetheless, carry a medical kit with everyday items as supermarkets and pharmacies often run out.
» Take a strong mosquito spray.
» Do not drink the tap water.

GETTING AROUND

The lack of signs and lighting and the poor state of the roads can hamper car travel. Note that car seats are not mandatory in Cuba, and taxi and rental-car firms don't carry them. Bring your own if you're planning to hire a car. Before hiring a car check the state of the vehicle (and the spare wheel!). The tourist areas are well served by the Viazul bus company (the only one available for tourists over long distances), which offers discounts for children under 12. The buses are punctual, comfortable and safe, unlike the trains. In town, children will love riding in a coco-taxi (yellow and shaped like an egg) or in a horse and carriage. Cuba's potholed pavements weren't designed with strollers in mind.

ⓘ Warning

→ The anti-smoking law banning cigarettes in enclosed public spaces is virtually ignored.
→ Don't let children approach stray dogs and cats.
→ Cots are rarely provided in accommodation.

🕐 Time difference

→ Time zone UTC−05:00. Daylight saving time observed in northern hemisphere summer.

131

ECUADOR

From the Pacific coast beaches to the Andean volcanoes capped with snow, from the equatorial forest to the stunning wildlife of the Galápagos Islands, Ecuador is packed with intriguing curiosities for children. What's more, there is the possibility of enriching encounters with the Amazonian and Quechua communities.

Wildlife spotting is a thrill in Ecuador

CHILDREN WILL LOVE...
Seeing animals in their natural habitat
» Searching for condors in the Parque Cóndor.
» Spotting giant tortoises, baby seals, penguins and sea lions in the Galápagos, a paradise for observing extraordinary creatures. Plus, using a snorkel to look at the rays and multicoloured fish.
» Watching monkeys (spider monkeys, titis, capuchins and marmosets) and jungle birds in the Parque Nacional Yasuni and the Reserva de Producción Faunística Cuyabeno.
» Whale watching off the coast of Puerto López.

The thrill of adventure
» A horse ride setting off from a *hacienda* (colonial ranch) in the Sierra du Nord.
» A cruise on the lower reaches of the Río Napo, broken up with a trip in a canoe or a walk to the top of the canopy.
» A train journey perched on the carriage roof (there are only two tourist lines and the roofs are designed for this purpose).
» Swimming and snorkelling in the Galápagos and at Isla de la Plata. For older children, there are surfing lessons at Canoa where the waves are great for beginners.

Compelling cities
» Quito, the capital perched at 2830m above sea level, with its beautiful monuments, atmospheric markets and view from the cable car.
» Cuenca, with its paved streets dotted with colourful stalls.
» The small spa city of Baños, backed up against a volcano and situated near some fabulous waterfalls perfect for a dip.

Living with the indigenous communities
» Spending the night in the middle of the jungle in a lodge run by an Amazonian community at Kapawi or in the Reserva de Producción Faunística Cuyabeno.
» The intense colours of the Indian markets along the Quilotoa loop, where you can stock up on small souvenirs.
» The villages of the northern plains such as Playa de Oro, adjoining the Reserva Ecológica Cotacachi Cayapas.

BEST TIME TO GO

In the Sierra the climate is spring-like all year with variations for altitude. The rainy season lasts from October to May on the coast and from January to May in the jungle. It is best to avoid July to October in the Galápagos when the sea is choppy; the water is around 22°C between January and April. During Easter the tourist areas are besieged.

COST

Ecuador is one of the cheapest countries to visit in South America. The best value is to be found in non-touristy areas. Accommodation, restaurants and tours aimed at tourists – especially package deals, where you are restricted in where you can stay and eat – can be quite expensive. With the exception of a trip to the Galápagos Islands, attractions are cheap, as is transport. Keep in mind that Ecuador has a cash-based economy; restaurants and tour companies expect cash, and if they do accept cards, will apply hefty surcharges.

Mealtimes

Ecuadorian cooking is more varied on the coast where seafood is prepared in several ways, but it is no doubt in breadcrumbs that children will like it best. In the Andes, potatoes, pieces of meat, corn and quinoa are omnipresent. Across the country, little restaurants serve *almuerzos* (lunch): for thrice nothing you will get a delicious soup (garnished with potatoes, morsels of meat and vegetables), a plate of white rice served with meat in a sauce and vegetables, and a *jugo* (fruit juice; delicious but check that water has not been added). Nourishing and well-suited to the younger diner.

BOOKS FOR THE YOUNG TRAVELLER

> *Island: A Story of the Galápagos*, by Jason Chin, is a stunning picture book tracing the evolution of the islands and their unique wildlife.

CHILDREN'S SOUVENIRS

> A small panama hat for a bit of style (despite the name the hat originates in Ecuador)

> A hammock made of vegetable fibre by the Amazonian communities

HEALTH CHECK

» Tap water is not safe to drink.
» Medical care varies according to the region. There are good but pricey health facilities in Quito and Guayaquil.

GETTING AROUND

Bus travel works well throughout the country but the journeys can seem long to children. Hiring a car is admittedly very practical: opt for a 4WD if possible, for the state of the roads varies from region to region and getting around can be hard during the rainy season. Take a flight to reach the Amazon jungle or the Galápagos. As for the train, there are only really two very popular tourist lines, which are worth it mainly for the scenery.

ⓘ Warning

→ Avoid excursions at altitudes that involve acclimatisation with children.

→ Make sure you take a range of clothing as the weather changes depending on the region and the altitude.

→ Safety is not guaranteed everywhere: avoid night buses on the Ruta del Sol (Sun Road) from Guayaquil, and night travel in general. Travel advisories warn against travel close to the Colombian border.

🕑 Time difference

→ Time zone UTC−05:00; UTC−06:00 in Galápagos Province.

MEXICO

From the pre-Hispanic pyramids lost in the jungle to the forests of cactus, the lively markets to the raucous festivals, Mexico is a mosaic of scenery, colours and sounds, with everything it takes to win over young travellers.

Mexico's intriguing history is waiting to be explored

CHILDREN WILL LOVE...
The spirit of adventure
» The Olmec, Toltec, Aztec and Maya sites. You can spend a whole day wandering around the biggest – Chichén Itzá; Palenque, half swallowed by the jungle; Teotihuacan, with grandiose pyramids – or spend an hour or two in the smallest, which are equally fascinating.
» Swimming through the turquoise waters in cenotes (natural wells) and exploring the mysterious caves in Quintana Roo on the Yucatán Peninsula.

Beach life
» Spending a night in a comfortable bungalow in Tulum (Yucatán), Zihuatenejo (Guerrero) or in the nearby villages around Veracruz (Tabasco), then jumping in the water on waking and admiring the pelicans in full morning flight.
» Snorkelling among fish and tortoises in Yucatán. Older children also have the opportunity to snorkel among whale sharks off Isla Holbox.

Animals in their natural habitat
» Seeing whales from December to March in the seas off Baja California.
» Spotting jungle mammals and birds in Chiapas or Campeche, or in the Yucatán lagoons. They can also be seen up close in a number of zoos.

Fun with the family
» Giant water slides and aquariums at Mazatlán, Puerto Vallarta and Acapulco, on the central Pacific coast.
» Dizzying rides and roller coasters in La Feria de Chapultepec park, in Mexico City.
» The park in Uruapan (Michoacán), on the very edge of the city. It has waterfalls in the middle of the jungle and free-roaming animals may join you on your walk.

A party atmosphere
» The floating gardens of Xochimilco (Mexico City) as seen from aboard a *trajinera* (a form of gondola) with mariachi music in the background.
» The vibrancy of the *zócalo* (the main square in a city or town) and its souvenir sellers, shoe shiners and mariachis. It is the compulsory place for an evening stroll.
» The brightly coloured markets and indigenous people in traditional costumes, particularly in Chiapas.

NEED TO KNOW

BEST TIME TO GO

Mexico makes a great destination any time of year. The coastal and low-lying regions, particularly in the south, are hot and humid from May to September. Inland the climate is milder, sometimes cool in the evening at altitude. During the rainy season (mid-April to the end of October), the Caribbean and Pacific coasts should be avoided due to cyclones.

COST

Mexico is cheap compared with the rest of North America, but it is one of the more expensive countries among its Latin neighbours. Tourist resorts and big cities are the most expensive areas, and the coastal regions and the north also tend to be pricier. Many hotels raise their rates during the high season. Keep your costs down by having a *comida corrida* (three- or four-course set lunch), served by many restaurants, and avoid the touristy eateries. Markets are a good source of cheap food. Almost all Mexico City museums are free on Sundays, and the city regularly stages free concerts on the *zócalo* on weekends. Finally, use the metro and the Metrobus to get around instead of taxis.

Mealtimes

Chicken cooked in every way; other meat and fish grilled; burritos, fajitas or nachos smothered in cheese… Mexican cooking is sure to leave children feeling satisfied, as long as they can stop themselves dipping their fingers in the accompanying sauces, where the chilli is usually hiding! Big family tables are common in restaurants at weekends and you will usually find a highchair for the youngest child.

BOOKS FOR THE YOUNG TRAVELLER
> *The Aztec Empire*, by Sunita Apte, is a thorough, colourful, not overly gory overview of this fascinating civilisation for ages seven and up.

CHILDREN'S SOUVENIRS
> Piñatas (papier-mâché figures filled with sweets)
> Chilli lollipops or those containing a *gusano* (the famous worm placed in the bottom of a bottle of tequila) are ideal to impress friends back home.

HEALTH CHECK

» Malaria is present year-round in certain rural areas, especially in Chiapas and in Oaxaca. An antimalarial treatment may be needed. Protect yourselves from insects. Dengue is also a risk, so take measures to prevent mosquito bites.
» Hospitals and private clinics (very expensive) offer good care in most regions in Mexico.

GETTING AROUND

Well-maintained asphalt roads extend across most of the country. Toll roads and motorways are the safest. The country has around 50 airports: internal flights are ideal when covering long distances with children. Very comfortable buses operate across the country, but journeys can be long. The train is not suitable for families.

! **Warning**
→ Safety is not guaranteed countrywide. Some regions are considered too dangerous to visit.
→ Avoid swimming on deserted or non-guarded beaches on the Pacific due to possible currents and groundswells.

⏱ **Time difference**
→ Time zones: UTC−06:00 most of Mexico; UTC−07:00 Baja California Sur, Chihuahua, Nayarit, Sinaloa and Sonora; UTC−08:00 Baja California. Daylight saving time observed in northern hemisphere summer.

PERU

The first encounter of young romantics with Machu Picchu and other Inca sites in this land where cities were reputedly made of gold will prompt unbridled imaginings. Junior adventurers will be captivated by the range of outdoor pursuits and the variety of wildlife. The more contemplative will be equally enchanted by grand cities with colonial architecture and small Andean villages.

Peru is a heady mix of mountains, ruins and llamas

CHILDREN WILL LOVE...
The mysteries and treasures of the Incas
» Machu Picchu, the most famous Inca city, still splendid and veiled in mystery.
» A flight over the Nazca Lines in a small plane to investigate one of the world's most enduring archaeological enigmas.
» The ruins of Chan Chan, the biggest Pre-Columbian city on the continent, and the nearby fabulous Sun and Moon temples.
» The remains of Kuelap, a vast fortified city that was lost in the jungle-covered mountains.
» Lima's Museo de la Nación and Museo de Oro del Perú, both offering a richer understanding of the Inca way of life through recovered objects and treasures.

Trips with the promise of adventure
» Crossing the breathtaking Cañón del Pato, between 1000m-high rock faces.
» A cruise on the Amazon from Iquitos, swinging in a hammock.
» Surfing on the giant sand dunes at Huacachina, an oasis lined with palm trees.

Sights in the cities and villages
» Coloured houses and baroque churches in Trujillo, a town tucked away in a corner of the desert.
» The stunning Monasterio Santa Catalina in Arequipa, a maze of lanes, courtyards and monastic cells.
» The church and convent of San Francisco in Lima, with catacombs housing 70,000 tombs.
» Lake Titicaca and the Islas Flotantes of the Uros people. The islands are made from woven reeds that support homes also made from reeds.
» Numerous festivals around Lake Titicaca, particularly festivals in Puno and Cuzco, which is the oldest inhabited city on the continent and is lined with Inca walls.

Animals on land and in water
» Spotting Humboldt penguins, Chilean penguins and sea lions during a boat trip to Islas Ballestas.
» Admiring the flight of the condors above the Cañón del Colca, leaving from Cabanaconde.
» Spotting Amazonian jungle fauna and flora at Tarapoto, without having to leave the comfort of the tarmac road.
» Visiting Lima Zoo and its 210 specimens of Peruvian wildlife, seeing up close the animals already encountered in the jungle.

BEST TIME TO GO

You can visit the country at any time of year – summer and winter cover different periods according to the region. From December to March, it is often rainy in the mountains, while it is hot on the coast. Except in the north, the coast disappears from May to mid-September hidden by the *garúa* (coastal fog). In the Amazon, temperatures climb to 35°C during the humid season (between December and April).

COST

Peru is relatively cheap compared with elsewhere in South America, similar to Ecuador but more expensive than Bolivia. Accommodation and food are well priced. Lima and destinations along the Gringo Trail will be more expensive. Tours to sights such as Machu Picchu and the Nazca Lines will be major expenses but are worth shelling out for.

Mealtimes

Potatoes originated in Peru, so it's no surprise they're everywhere. There are no chips on the menu, but potatoes most often turn up in soups, cold salads or in the shape of donuts. For a quick snack, avoid the street stalls and head to a *pollerías* (roast-chicken restaurant) or to a bakery, where children will love empanadas (pasties filled with meat or cheese) and various sandwiches. Best avoid ceviche (the national dish based on marinated raw fish and seafood), or at least only have it in a decent restaurant. Any hunger can be satiated by one of the many sugary desserts such as *suspiro limeño*, a sort of caramel pudding topped with meringue.

HEALTH CHECK

» An antimalarial treatment may be recommended (notably in the Amazon). Dengue is present in the country. Take measures to protect against mosquitoes.

» A large part of Peru is at high altitude (Machu Picchu is at around 2500m, Lake Titicaca is at 3820m and Cuzco at 3326m). It is inadvisable to take children under one above an altitude of 1200m and children under 10 above 3000m.

» Tap water is not safe to drink.

GETTING AROUND

The bus is the most common form of transport and the most practical in Peru. Day travel is safer. Internal flights may be a good alternative (check safety arrangements). In town travel by taxi (stick to licensed taxis), as they're much simpler than the bus. If you wish to hire a car, save it for trips around one of your stopovers. As for the train, take it to Machu Picchu.

❗ **Warning**
→ Travel is not recommended in the Amazonian area bordering Colombia.
→ Destinations over 3000m are only suitable for older children.

🕐 **Time difference**
→ Time zone UTC−05:00

BOOKS FOR THE YOUNG TRAVELLER

› *Up and Down the Andes*, by Laurie Krebs, is a rhyming picture book that takes young children through all the highlights of Peru, with explanatory notes for parents.

› For a look at the civilisation that spawned Machu Picchu, try Sandra Newman's informative and well-illustrated *The Inca Empire*.

CHILDREN'S SOUVENIRS

› Pan pipes and ocarinas (wind instruments) in various shapes

EASTERN UNITED STATES

New York City from up high, vast torrents of water shunting over Niagara Falls, sandcastles and lighthouses on a Cape Cod beach, eyeing up dinosaur skeletons…You visit the eastern United States in the same way you flick through a comic book: for fun! Here every town, every museum, every natural park is packed with activities for children of all ages.

New York teems with attractions for kids

CHILDREN WILL LOVE…
America XXL
» The skyscrapers of Chicago, viewed while enjoying a mini boat cruise.
» Manhattan, New York, seen from the top of a skyscraper; Times Square, for its giant screens, hustle and bustle, and mind-blowing shops – in particular Toys 'R' Us.
» The awesome Niagara Falls and Niagara Gorge Discovery Center, featuring interactive displays and activities for kids, including a rock-climbing wall.
» Cape Cod's oldest, tallest and brightest lighthouse, Highland Light. Kids must be 122cm (48in) tall to scale the 69 steps and steep ladder, but even just clamouring around inside a genuine lighthouse is exhilarating.

The best of the best attractions
» Orlando, the town of theme parks. Don't miss Walt Disney World®, Universal Studios and Islands of Adventure.
» Noah's Ark Waterpark, the biggest aquatic park in the USA, at Wisconsin Dells.
» The Chicago Aquarium, the biggest in the world.
» A musical on Broadway: *Shrek*, *The Lion King*, *The Little Mermaid*…
» The Kennedy Space Center in Florida, where space-capsule models and all kinds of NASA rockets are displayed.

Adventures in the great outdoors
» Bathing at the foot of waterfalls in Virginia's Shenandoah National Park, cycling through the lush countryside, fishing and bumping into a lynx.
» Weaving their way through swamps on a hydroplane in Florida's Everglades.
» Learning how to crack open a lobster and heading out on whale- and puffin-watching tours in Maine.
» The Florida Keys, a 200km string of islands with warm, shallow water and some of the country's best snorkelling – ideal for wannabe pirates.

Weird and wonderful experiences
» Feeding alligators in the Louisiana bayous (under supervision) at the Bayou Pierre Alligator Park.
» Visiting Miami in an amphibious bus to discover the city and the islands.
» Crossing the incredible road bridges that hover above the surface of the water en route to the Florida Keys.
» Paying homage to Elvis Presley in his Graceland residence with its rock'n'roll decor.

BEST TIME TO GO

If summer is the ideal time to cross the country, it is also the season when Americans go on holiday. There can be crowds, particularly in the national parks, and that is often reflected in the prices. Spring and autumn are just as pleasant whether you're at the Great Lakes or in Louisiana. In Florida the weather is great year-round. In New York and in all the northern states the winters can be harsh.

COST

The USA is huge, and prices vary greatly depending on what region you are in. Accommodation in New York is much more expensive than in other cities. But south of New York, the east coast is generally cheaper than the west. Public transport in the east is reasonably priced, and food is cheap, with lots of budget restaurant chains. Shopping is generally cheap and you can buy anything you need once you arrive. Don't leave home without health insurance. Operations and hospital stays can be phenomenally expensive, and with no public health system, the patient foots the bill. Tipping is not optional; only withhold tips in cases of outrageously bad service.

Mealtimes

Despite the clichés, there are myriad places where you can eat well in the United States. In New York City try slices of crusty pizza, hot dogs, super-sized sandwiches and pretzels (sold on virtually every street corner) – all ideal for a picnic in the park. Not to be missed, American diners are a good alternative for children to fast-food outlets; breakfasts here are hearty affairs and are usually delicious. There are so many foreign influences that children can take a tour around the world just by looking at their plate: Italian, Asian, Mexican, Cuban and Caribbean. And don't forget the famous Texan barbecue and the unique flavours of Louisiana – among many others.

BOOKS FOR THE YOUNG TRAVELLER
> Lonely Planet's *Not For Parents: New York City* is packed with tales of towering skyscrapers, deep subways and superheroes.

CHILDREN'S SOUVENIRS
> American sports clothes and accessories
> Beautiful American cars in miniature

HEALTH CHECK

» Mosquitoes can make life complicated. Use protection as mosquitoes can transmit the West Nile virus and its ensuing complication, encephalitis, as well as dengue.
» Air conditioning to the extreme. Always have something warm at hand to wear, even in intense heat.

GETTING AROUND

Outside the cities, where public transport is practical and efficient, hiring a car is a good way to see the country. That said, the distances are huge and taking an internal flight means a lot of time saved between stops. The Visit North America Pass, where the fare is worked out according to the number of miles covered, is an interesting proposition. Camper vans are a unique experience for children, but they can work out to be more expensive than a car and hotel deal when you factor in the camping pitch fee.

! Warning
→ If you rent a car, do not forget that the service stations are few and far between. Make sure you carry water to avoid the children becoming dehydrated.
→ Never leave your belongings on display in any big city in the United States, and be careful if travelling at night in some districts.

⏱ Time difference
→ Time zone UTC−05:00 or UTC−06:00. Daylight saving time is observed in northern hemisphere summer.

WESTERN UNITED STATES

The country of cowboys, hamburgers and vast, wild expanses is a dream destination and an endless land of discovery for young travellers. While cities such as Las Vegas, Los Angeles and San Francisco are emblematic and full of surprises, it is in the countryside that you will find the real spirit of the American West.

Kids fit right in to the ranch lifestyle

CHILDREN WILL LOVE...
The great Wild West
» The New Mexico Desert, seen from onboard former freight wagons in the Santa Fe region.
» Yellowstone National Park (Wyoming) for the incredible geyser display.
» Snapping the American Big Five (black bear, grizzly, moose, puma and lynx) during a Rockies photo safari.
» The giant sequoias at Redwood National Park in northern California.
» The cave dwellings dotting the cliffs of Mesa Verde National Park (Colorado), where Ancestral Puebloans lived.
» The Grand Canyon (Arizona) and Bryce Canyon (Utah) for a vertiginous walk.
» Rafting down the Colorado River in summer, when the current is not too strong.
» A sea excursion in Oregon to watch whales.

The world of cowboys and indians
» Visiting Wyoming for the rodeo in Jackson and the fascinating museums in Cody, the hometown of Buffalo Bill. For total immersion in the Wild West of yesteryear, spend a night in the reconstructed village of Rawhide (Arizona).

» Meeting Hopi and Navajo tribespeople in Monument Valley and sleeping in a *hogan* (traditional Native American home).
» Attending a powwow with traditional dances and songs at Window Rock (Arizona) or at Shiprock (New Mexico) in September.
» Playing at cowboys in the Big Bend National Park (Texas), a Stetson perched on their heads.
» Scenery like something straight from a Western, punctuated by waterfalls and canyons formed by the Rio Grande.
» Attending a rodeo and trying out a few country dance steps at Billy Bob's Texas in Fort Worth.

Sequins and stars
» A trip to Hollywood (Los Angeles), following in the footsteps of the stars and visiting Universal Studios.
» Las Vegas (Nevada) for its fantasy buildings, replicas of Paris and New York monuments and outstanding shows including Cirque du Soleil, the Bellagio Fountains displays and enchanting tours to the Puppet Magic Center.
» San Francisco with its legendary cable car, the Golden Gate Bridge – which can be driven, walked or cycled over or viewed from the ferry – and whale-watching in the surrounding area.
» Seeing the faces of American presidents immortalised in the rock of Mt Rushmore (South Dakota).

Attractions 100% for children
» Disneyland (California), the first of the genre, and the less hectic Knott's Berry Farm, an enormous fun park with a Wild West theme.
» San Diego Zoo (California), with 3200 animals in an exceptional environment.
» Santa Cruz Beach Boardwalk (California), an immense fun park on the beach.

BEST TIME TO GO

The differences in climate are massive between the desert south (dry all year, but torrid in summer) and the regions north of San Francisco where rain falls in abundance year-round. In summer, the sun warms up the northwest beaches and the mountains, but also inflames prices. If you wish to travel in winter, it will be warmer in the south and you can ski in the Rockies.

COST

Due to the vastness of this country, prices vary greatly depending on what region you are in. The cost of living is slightly higher in the western states than in the east. Save money by purchasing a national parks pass in advance. Shopping is generally cheap and you can buy anything you need once you arrive, including cheap, reliable umbrella strollers. Don't leave home without health insurance. Operations and hospital stays can be phenomenally expensive, and with no public health system, the patient foots the bill. Tipping is not optional; only withhold tips in cases of outrageously bad service.

Mealtimes

In the land of hamburgers, pizzas, chips and Coke, children will be delighted…at least the first few times! In larger cities the cuisine is more varied due to the cultural mix, but even small towns enjoy the ethnic offerings of local Chinese or Mexican restaurants. Fish and seafood appear on many menus, as do vegetables and fruit. Western US has some interesting food, including buffalo steaks on the Great Plains (or in Wyoming), or the Southwest's cross-border fare such as New Mexico's red and green chillies. Portions are always huge and it is possible to share a dish with a child.

BOOKS FOR THE YOUNG TRAVELLER
› *The Misadventures of Maude March*, by Audrey Couloumbis, is a rollicking Wild West–adventure novel for pre-teens.

CHILDREN'S SOUVENIRS
› Kachina dolls made by Hopi tribespeople

› A cowboy or Native American costume

› A cowboy hat

HEALTH CHECK

» Mosquitoes can make life complicated. Use protection as the insect can transmit the West Nile virus and its ensuing complication, encephalitis, as well as dengue.

» Air conditioning to the extreme. Always have something warm at hand to wear, even in intense heat.

GETTING AROUND

While hiring a car is perfect for crossing vast rural America, it may be better to consider domestic flights to reduce transit time – even if it costs more than the bus (for which children two to 11 can benefit from a 40% discount) or the train (which may be worth considering for the stunning scenery on certain railway lines). It is possible to buy a special air pass, but only in conjunction with an international flight. Buses, metro systems and taxis will get you around the towns, and San Francisco has an over-ground cable car.

! Warning
→ If you rent a car, do not forget that service stations are few and far between. Make sure you carry water to avoid the children becoming dehydrated.

→ Never leave your belongings on display in any big city in the United States, and be careful if travelling at night in some districts.

◐ Time difference
→ Time zone UTC−07:00 or UTC−08:00. Daylight saving time is observed in northern hemisphere summer.

VIRGIN ISLANDS

Waves to splash in, sand castles to build, sea turtles to visit, forts to explore – families will find activities throughout the US & British Virgin Islands. St Thomas, St John and St Croix hold the majority of kid-friendly resorts (plus there's no passport requirement for US visitors). The British Virgins have family offerings too, just not quite to the extent of the USVI. You may find yourself (as many do) bringing the kids back year after year.

Taking a delicious dip at the Baths

CHILDREN WILL LOVE...
Beachy keen swimming
» The USVI's most popular beach, Magens Bay (St Thomas), with lifeguards, food vendors, paddle boats and plenty of little playmates.
» Secret Harbour (St Thomas): the secret here is calm water and a swimming platform to jump from.
» Looking for hawksbill or green turtles in the protected, shallow water of Maho Bay (St John).
» Protestant Cay (St Croix), a wide beach in the shadow of a fort.
» Meeting local families who come to picnic on weekends at Cramer's Park beach (St Croix).

Creature features
» Visiting Coral World Ocean Park (St Thomas): touch starfish, pet sharks, feed stingrays or watch the turtles.
» Seeing leatherback sea turtle hatchlings at St Croix Environmental Association.
» Walking among butterflies and flowers at the Butterfly Farm (St Thomas).
» Spotting fish, lizards and crabs everywhere on the islands.

Adventures at sea
» A nighttime paddle through the bioluminescent water of Salt River Bay (St Croix).
» Kayaking through a mangrove sanctuary with VI Ecotours on St Thomas.
» Exploring grottoes and swimming in tidepools at the Baths (Virgin Gorda).
» Taking a sea trek on St Thomas: kids over age eight can go deep and walk around the reef.
» Learning to sail, windsurf, kayak and more at the Bitter End Yacht Club (Virgin Gorda).

History lessons
» Playing pirates using the cannons and dungeon at Fort Christiansvaern (St Croix).
» Exploring the red-brick battlements where slaves fought for, and got, their freedom at Fort Frederik (St Croix).
» Seeing Columbus' 1493 landing site at Salt River Bay (St Croix).
» Sailing aboard the historic *Roseway* schooner at the World Ocean School (St Croix).

BEST TIME TO GO

The weather will oblige whatever you do, but mid-December to April is when children's activities are in full swing at the resorts. The water is calmest for sailing, swimming and snorkelling in spring.

COSTS

The Virgin Islands are about middle of the range when it comes to Caribbean destinations. Cheap flight deals are often available, which can make all the difference. The islands offer a wide range of family accommodations for a wide range of budgets, including campgrounds, condominiums, private villas and luxury resorts. All-inclusive resorts can be great value if you are happy to stay in one spot. Rates tend to be lowest in spring. You can buy snorkel masks or anything else you forget at local shops, though it'll be costly.

Mealtimes

The vast majority of restaurants are family-friendly, especially the many beachside eateries. Many offer special children's menus, but if not they typically have burgers and pizza as part of their line-up. There are plenty of opportunities to introduce children to West Indian food, too, including stewed chicken with rice and peas, and fried fish. Watch out for hot sauces as they're really hot! The ambience tends to be informal and relaxed wherever you go.

BOOKS FOR THE YOUNG TRAVELLER

› *I am the Virgin Islands*, by Tiphanie Yanique, is a celebration of island culture in poetry and collage.

› *The Sea, the Storm, and the Mangrove Tangle*, by Lynne Cherry, is a beautiful picture book exploring the mangrove ecosystem.

› *Escape From Fear: A Mystery in Virgin Islands National Park*, by Gloria Skurzynski, is an adventure for pre-teens.

› For older teens, Tiphanie Yanique's novel *Land of Love and Drowning* chronicles the islands' history through the 20th century.

CHILDREN'S SOUVENIRS

› Sailing boats, sea animals or masks carved from mahogany

› St Croix hook bracelets, a traditional souvenir of the islands

HEALTH CHECK

» The water is considered safe to drink, but diarrhoea is the biggest risk, so it is advisable to stick to bottled water and do not eat fruits or vegetables unless they have been peeled or cooked.

» The islands are malaria-free but there are occasional outbreaks of dengue fever and chikungunya, so protect yourselves from mosquitoes.

» Avoid eating large reef fish such as barracuda as they can contain ciguatera toxin.

GETTING AROUND

Renting a car is definitely the easiest way for families to get around. Cars drive on the left in both the US and British Virgin Islands. The law requires all passengers in private cars to wear seat belts, and children under age five must be in a car seat, but this is rarely enforced. Most car-rental firms provide car seats, but supplies are limited, so reserve well in advance. Taxis are shared, and are often open-air vans. The many and frequent ferries are the best way to travel between islands.

🕐 Time difference

→ Time zone UTC−04:00

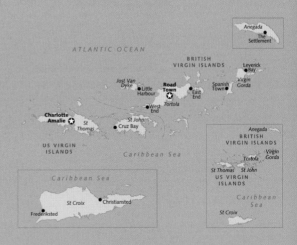

The Pacific

Are you drawn by the magic of the antipodes? From the vast expanses and unique animals of Australia to the turquoise waters and butterscotch beaches of the Pacific Islands, to the glorious and varied landscapes of New Zealand and its fervently embraced outdoors, the Pacific can satisfy any holiday wishlist.

These days the Pacific is more accessible than ever before. The airlines flying to this region, reputedly some of the best in the world, offer excellent facilities (video screens, films and games for children), which ease the rigours of long flights from the northern hemisphere. And depending on your point of departure, your family might consider breaking up the journey with a stopover in Singapore, Bangkok or Dubai.

Once you arrive, the feeling of being in a far-flung country forces you to forget everything else. With its exotic creatures, Australia seems like one giant theme park. Finding yourself face to face with a kangaroo, a possum, a wombat, a koala or a wallaby is an unforgettable experience for a child – and for many adults! In New Zealand the whole family will click into active mode and sample the vast array of outdoor pursuits on offer, in the grandiose setting of fjords, mountains and volcanic landscapes. The program may include canyoning, hiking, rafting and zorbing – in extremely safe, well-managed conditions. And do not forget to attend a rugby match, with all the passion and drama that entails.

In the Pacific Islands, fun in and around the water is on the agenda: learn to dive in a crystal-blue lagoon, watch manta rays and small sharks (harmless), gape in wonder as dolphins and whales swim past, and picnic on a desert island.

AUSTRALIA

Australia is a genuine El Dorado for families who want to play at explorers in total safety. Kangaroos, koalas and other strange animals will amaze the youngest members in the group, while pre-teens will prefer the pull of the surf, diving or the outback, which is a little bit like the Wild West.

The ultimate drawcard for kids: the beach

CHILDREN WILL LOVE...
Nature on a huge scale
» Kings Canyon (Watarrka National Park, Northern Territory), an impressive fault in the heart of the red desert.
» The Gold Coast (Queensland) and the aptly named Surfers Paradise, where they can learn to surf and admire the prowess of more accomplished children.
» The outback, the Australian bush, its arid landscape and its ghost towns worthy of a western.
» Beaches: there are 7000 in total, guarded by 112,600 lifeguards!
» The islands: Tasmania, best explored on the Wilderness Railway cog train, and the wild tropical landscapes of the Whitsunday Islands (Queensland) and Tiwi Islands (Northern Territory).
» The Great Barrier Reef (Queensland): admiring the coral in all its glory while snorkelling or peering through the bottom of a glass-bottomed boat – or even visiting the Sydney Aquarium.
» The tingle eucalypt trees as tall as cathedrals in the Valley of the Giants (Western Australia).

The land of kangaroos
» Discovering Australian animals with strange names such as wombats, quokkas (marsupials the size of a cat), cassowaries (like emus), emus and kangaroos. All can be seen in a number of zoos, particularly Taronga Zoo in Sydney, one of the most beautiful zoos in the world.
» Stroking gentle koalas at the Lone Pine Koala Sanctuary, near Brisbane.
» Seeing sharks, whales and…whale sharks from the south coast.
» Taking a boat trip on the Northern Territory's Adelaide River to view the jumping crocodiles, or visiting the calmer ones at the Crocodylus Park & Zoo in Darwin.

The magic of Indigenous culture
» The changing colours of Uluru (formerly known as Ayers Rock; Northern Territory), an enigmatic monolith and the most sacred of Aboriginal sites.
» Learning about this ancient, complex culture at Kakadu National Park or Cape York Peninsula in the extreme north.
» The marvellous Dreamtime paintings in the Cultural Centre at Uluru-Kata Tjuta National Park.

Perfect outings for little ones
» The leisure parks on the Gold Coast (Queensland): Infinity, Sea World aquatic park, and Warner Bros Movie World to meet Shrek and Scooby-Doo.
» Theme parks that take you back in time: The Pioneer Settlement in Swan Hill (Victoria), with a reconstructed paddle steamer, and Sovereign Hill, an open-air museum representing a gold rush town.

NEED TO KNOW

BEST TIME TO GO

You can travel around Australia year-round as the weather is always good somewhere. In the centre and the south the seasons are the reverse of the northern hemisphere (summer from December to February and a mild winter from June to August). There are two seasons in the north: dry (May to October) and the monsoon season (November to April).

COST

Travel in Australia always seems to cost more than people think. It's more expensive than North America, but not as bad as Western Europe. Getting there is the first big expense, and getting around is the second. Domestic flights are particularly pricey as there is very little competition. Then there's the strong Australian dollar. Accommodation and food are expensive, though both are of a high standard. Petrol costs shoot up as soon as you leave the populated coast. Package deals combining transport, hotels and tours can be an economical approach, and with the country's mild weather and wonderful wilderness, camping is a great way to save on costs.

Mealtimes

Delicious fish and crustaceans on the coast; tasty meats (sometimes ostrich and kangaroo!), fruit and vegetables in abundance inland: Australian cooking is varied. There are numerous foreign influences in the cities, where you can grab just about anything you want to eat, anywhere. Children will probably be happy with classic pub food such as sausage and mash, pizzas, pasta and mixed salads. On the beach you will often find fish-and-chip huts, usually of a very good quality (often using shark meat).

BOOKS FOR THE YOUNG TRAVELLER
> Two classics for younger children are Norman Lindsay's *The Magic Pudding* and May Gibbs' *Snugglepot and Cuddlepie*. The homes of both authors are now museums (both in New South Wales).

CHILDREN'S SOUVENIRS
> A soft toy koala or other Australian animal
> A boomerang
> A didgeridoo, a wind instrument that's as beautiful to look at as it is to listen to.

GETTING AROUND

If time is short, an internal flight is a must, as distances are vast. Buses are practical, admittedly (unlike trains), but the ideal option is to hire your own vehicle (an international driver's licence is required). Faced with the long distances involved, children will appreciate the comfort of a camper van, not least as campgrounds offer great facilities (swimming pools, barbecues) at a reasonable price. It is best to book before leaving home, especially during the holidays. Cars drive on the left here.

ⓘ Warning
> Never underestimate the distances and journey times when organising your trip, especially with children.
> If you travel by car in isolated desert areas of the outback, make sure you take plenty of water and a spare can of petrol.

🕑 Time difference
> Most of mainland Australia falls between UTC+08:00 and UTC+10:00 time zones, with daylight saving time observed in the southern hemisphere summer in some states.

FIJI

Fiji is a major family destination and the locals adore children – in fact, your little ones may tire of having their cheeks squeezed! Most of the islands offer quintessential tropical beaches with activities such as surfing, sea kayaking, coral viewing and horseback riding. World-class, free kids' clubs are a huge attraction here, and while the children are safely occupied, parents can indulge themselves as well.

Fiji is one big tropical playground

CHILDREN WILL LOVE...

Being on, in or under the water

» Snorkelling and swimming on the dreamy coral fringes of the Mamanuca and Yasawa isles.
» A jet-boat safari whirling up the Sigatoka River.
» Learning to scuba dive and visiting world-famous dive sites around the Mamanuca Islands.
» Paddle-boarding among the mangroves on the Salt Lake.

Environmentally aware activities

» Visiting Kula Eco Park wildlife sanctuary on Viti Levu to see hawksbill sea turtles, the Fijian flying fox, and an aviary full of quarrelsome kula parrots.
» Wandering around Colo-i-Suva Forest National Park, an oasis of lush rainforest, melodic bird life, walking trails and natural swimming holes.
» Getting muddy at the Sabeto Hot Springs and Mud Bath in a lush tropical setting.
» Exploring the impressive, rugged Sigatoka Sand Dunes, the site of many archaeological finds.
» Enjoying kids' clubs that focus on natural activities such as hunting for crabs, and traditional crafts such as palm-leaf weaving, as well as soccer, singing and storytelling.

The islander lifestyle

» Riding the old sugar train on the Coral Coast Scenic Railway on Viti Levu.
» The Arts Village on Viti Levu, where they can ride an old-style canoe around an artificial village with local actors dressed the part.
» Hindu Holi (Festival of Colours), held in February/March – a great chance to squirt each other with coloured water.
» The villages of the Nausori Highlands on Viti Levu, where they can watch Fijian fire- and knife-dancing and singing.
» The produce market of Suva, a kaleidoscope of tropical fruits and brightly coloured Indian sweets.
» The captivating Fiji museum in Suva, especially the chiefs' whale-tooth necklaces, the Fijian war clubs and the cannibal utensils!

BEST TIME TO GO

Fiji has pleasant weather year-round and is a great place to escape winter, whether you live in the northern or southern hemisphere. The Fijian 'winter' (dry season), from May to October, is perhaps the best time to visit. It has the lowest rainfall and humidity, milder temperatures and a reduced risk of cyclones and dengue-fever outbreaks. High season runs from June to September. Crowds also increase during the Australian and New Zealand December and January school holidays, though this is cyclone season.

COSTS

Fiji is a reasonably affordable destination, especially if you're travelling from nearby Australia or New Zealand. Prices are nowhere near as expensive as those in Tahiti and French Polynesia, but nor are they as cheap as Southeast Asia. The 12.5% value-added tax pushed prices up. There are plenty of accommodation options to suit all budgets. Most resorts are all-inclusive, which can be a bargain if you are prepared to stay in one spot. There are even a few resorts that provide free accommodation and/or meals for kids. Food is more expensive on the islands than on the mainland due to the cost of transporting it. Prices rise 10% to 20% in high season, peaking in June and July.

Mealtimes

Most family resorts provide children's meals, and the quality will be fine, but the menu probably won't be anything to write home about. Restaurants usually offer Western, Indian and Chinese foods with some Polynesian dishes thrown in. Traditional Fijian foods include fish served with coconut cream. As part of a village tour you may be offered a *lovo* (barbecue cooked in a pit with taro, sweet potato, pork or ham) – the kids will at least enjoy the novelty of it.

BOOKS FOR THE YOUNG TRAVELLER
› For young readers, Robin Peirce's *A Potter in Fiji* describes the life of a Fijian who makes pots without wheel or kiln.

CHILDREN'S SOUVENIRS
› Gloriously coloured *sulus* (sarongs)
› Carved wooden drums (be sure the wood is treated or you may not be allowed to take it into your home country)

HEALTH CHECK

» Large reef fish such as snapper, barracuda and grouper can contain ciguatera toxin. Ocean-going fish such as tuna, wahoo and Spanish mackerel are safe, and small reef fish that the locals eat should be okay.
» Water is generally safe in resorts but in villages drink only bottled water from containers with an intact safety seal.
» Fiji is malaria-free but there are occasional outbreaks of dengue fever in urban areas.
» Some resorts have an on-site nurse, which is a real plus as medical help can otherwise be a plane ride away.

GETTING AROUND

Check with your travel agent about transfer times to the resorts, as they can be up to two hours by bus from Nadi airport. Getting around is fairly easy, by car, bus, boat or plane. Ferry routes connect Viti Levu with the major islands, and smaller boats travel to smaller islands. Unless you take an organised cruise or charter your own boat, however, it can be difficult to hop from island to island. Car rental is expensive but worth the splurge for a day or two on the larger islands. Some rental companies provide baby seats. A baby carrier is useful around resorts, but it shouldn't be used in villages (nothing is carried on the shoulders, out of respect for the chief).

🕐 Time difference
→ Time zone UTC+12:00. Daylight saving time observed in southern hemisphere summer.

NEW ZEALAND

Do you need to spend time with the family, alone, somewhere peaceful, in the wilds surrounded by wide, open spaces? Then head to New Zealand! Home to the Maoris, the All-Blacks and the setting for *Lord of the Rings*, New Zealand is primarily a destination for lovers of the outdoors, a dynamic cocktail for young and old. On the agenda are sport, adventure and spectacular landscapes, with all the comforts of home to boot.

You won't sit still in activity-packed New Zealand

THE CHILDREN WILL LOVE...
Burning energy
» Setting off down the river aboard a raft, canoe, kayak, jetboat or bodyboard.
» Diving, with or without oxygen.
» Sailing and waterskiing.
» Skiing in the Southern Alps between June and October.
» Hiking, mountain biking, skiing or horse riding.

The *Lord of the Rings* landscape
» Visiting the sublime Tasman Glacier, the longest in the country, on a tour in a Zodiac boat. The Antarctic Centre in Christchurch is a must for getting the low-down on glaciers.
» The Waipoura Forest, the kingdom of kauri. Some of these giant trees are 2000 years old!
» The fjords and waterfalls seen from a mini-cruise along Doubtful Sound.
» The Moeraki Boulders (huge sphere-like rocks on Koekohe Beach) and the Oamaru Blue Penguin Colony.
» The geysers of Blowhole and Te Puia, and the geological phenomena at the Wai-O-Tapu Thermal Reserve.
» The majestic volcanoes of Ruapehu and Ngauruhoe in the Tongariro National Park.
» Walking the 660m-long pontoon at Tolaga Bay.

Kiwis, kiwis and...more kiwis
» Kiwis (nickname for New Zealanders), whose culture is a mix of Anglo-Saxon influences and Maori traditions such as dancing, singing, tattooing and, of course, the impressive ceremonial war dance: the haka.
» Kiwi fruit: don't miss the Kiwi360 Experience in Te Puke, where you can visit kiwi orchards in little trucks in the shape of...kiwis!
» Travelling to Kapiti Island Nature Reserve, home to over 1000 kiwis – the flightless bird that is the symbol of the country.

BEST TIME TO GO

The warmer months from November to April are best for outdoor activities; they're also when most festivals and many sporting events take place. Between June and August, the ski resorts are very busy, while the seaside towns are quieter. Be careful to book a holiday for the New Year period well in advance, as transport and hotels can be very busy. Generally, it is colder in the south than the north, and it rains more in the west than the east. The marine climate means the weather can change rapidly.

COST

In recent years the NZ dollar has gained ground against international currencies such as the greenback, and burgeoning tourism has seen prices rise with demand. However, if you're visiting from Europe or North America, it's still a fairly economical destination. Tours and adventure activities such as jetboating generally top the expense list. Gastronomes will find food to be surprisingly pricey. Food in remote areas also costs more, without necessarily being of better quality. Museums, cinemas, and tour and activity organisers usually offer discounts for kids, and there are plenty of open-air attractions available for free!

Mealtimes

Many restaurants provide a games area for children, and a children's menu is usually provided – often fish and chips or burgers. Meat, especially lamb, is excellent, as are many other local products: fruit, vegetables and a wide variety of cheeses. Fish and seafood are also famously good: the children will be amazed at the mussels – delicious but giant! For dessert, children can opt for tasty ice cream and the national favourite, pavlova (meringue with fruit).

BOOKS FOR THE YOUNG TRAVELLER
> The stories in *Taming the Sun: Four Maori Myths*, by Gavin Bishop, are beautifully retold and illustrated for young children.
> For older readers, *The Whale Rider*, by Witi Ihimaera, tells the story of a young girl living in contemporary New Zealand who can communicate with whales.

CHILDREN'S SOUVENIRS
> A poi, two balls attached to cords that you swing around, or Kiwodo, a modern version with a ribbon attached.

GETTING AROUND

The best way to travel around New Zealand is by car: it's cheap and the roads are good (you drive on the left and an international driver's licence is required). Many families opt to hire a camper van. There are frequent ferry shuttles between the two islands; and airfares to cross the country are reasonable. The train is fast, but the network is patchy on the South Island, unlike the bus network (but this can be slow and costly).

ⓘ Warning
→ 'Lock it or lose it': This sign commonly seen at car parks sums up the risk of leaving belongings in your car.
→ Even in summer, the sunny weather can quickly change to heavy rain and high winds. Equip yourself accordingly.
→ Rips and undertows can make some beaches hazardous. Heed local warnings when swimming, surfing or diving.

🕔 Time difference
→ Time zone UTC+12:00. Daylight saving time is observed in southern hemisphere summer.

TAHITI & FRENCH POLYNESIA

Tahiti, Bora Bora, the *vahinés* (dancers) and the sweet scent of *monoï* perfumed oil… French Polynesia is a dream for parents and a paradise for children. Climate, nature, fun in the water and general comfort – these islands live up to their reputation. The other Polynesian islands, less busy but just as beautiful, will charm children with their simple lifestyle, and parents with their more reasonable prices.

The lushness of Mo'orea is captivating

CHILDREN WILL LOVE...
The lands between sky and sea
» Tahiti, the most famous Polynesian island, and its capital, Pape'ete. Just an hour's boat ride away is the second best-known of the Isles du Vent (Windward Islands), Mo'orea, with its lagoons and archaeological remains.
» Huahine, Ra'iatea and Tahaa, Bora Bora (the most touristy) and Maupiti: these islands, named after princesses and boasting stunning lagoons, form the archipelago of Isles Sous-le-Vent.
» The Tuamotu, an archipelago of 77 atolls and lagoons, teeming with more fish than anywhere else in the world.
» The Gambier Islands, a tiny archipelago, 1700km from Pape'ete. They feel like the end of the world.

» The Marquesas Islands' rugged landscapes covered with thick forests, cliffs tumbling into the sea and numerous archaeological sites.
» The Austral Islands, 90 minutes from Pape'ete and a leader in ecotourism.

Underwater adventures
» Seeing Nemo's friends – they're everywhere and are clearly visible even from above the surface as the water is so crystal clear.
» Diving (from age eight) at one of the licensed centres.
» Walking underwater in a coral garden at a depth of 3m with Aqua Safari in Bora Bora, and Aqua Blue in Mo'orea. A fantastic experience for all the family (from age six) thanks to a diver's helmet.

Island adventures
» Riding in a 'truck' (big multi-coloured bus fitted with wooden planks), on a bike or in a 4WD to explore the interior.
» Sleeping in a bungalow built on stilts.
» Travelling by motorboat to the *motu* – tiny, unspoilt islets set on the coral reef where the best beaches can be found.
» Watching humpback whales and dolphins during a boat excursion and feeding the rays.

Tikis and ma'ohi festivities
» Hunting for tikis (traditional statues). The biggest are on Hiva Oa island (Marquesas) at the archaeological sites of Taaoa and Lipona.
» Attending a *heiva* (fete) in Pape'ete and on the other isles between the end of June and the end of July. On the programme: dance contests, Polynesian chanting, races in *va'a* (pirogues) and traditional sports, including lifting the stone.

BEST TIME TO GO

Even though the climate changes from one island to the next, the temperatures are mild all year. The most pleasant period is during the dry season, between June and October, when the temperatures are kinder. Avoid the rainy season between November and March, when it can often rain several days in a row.

COST

Tahiti and French Polynesia are expensive by anyone's standards and travel costs are some of the highest in the world. Flights alone tend to be a substantial cost, but once you arrive you may be shocked to find even the cheapest meal is a blow to your pocket. Over-water bungalows might be everyone's dream, but they start at around US$500 per night – about three times the cost of a hotel room. To score the best deals (and there are good package deals out there) book well in advance. Many places offer half-price discounts for children under the age of 12. Food is expensive: you can keep costs down by including breakfast in your accommodation, making lunch your main meal at a local restaurant and keeping things light at dinner. Value-added tax is another bugbear here: it adds 6% to your hotel bill, plus there's the 5% government tax and the *taxe de séjour* (accommodation tax or daily tax), which top off the bill.

HEALTH CHECK

» Take precautions against sunburn and mosquito bites.
» Make sure you thoroughly clean any cuts from the coral.

GETTING AROUND

The Air Tahiti inter-isles air passes are a good, efficient way to plan your trip. Ferries are another way of island hopping. To travel around an island, opt for trucks (buses) and bikes for short trips. Hiring a car is easily done, but know that conditions (the state of the roads and terrain) vary considerably from island to island.

Mealtimes

Even if poultry and red meat are on the menu, fish – cooked or raw – should be tried. Cuisine is most varied in Tahiti, Bora Bora and Mo'orea, with a number of restaurants offering French, Chinese and Polynesian specialties. The combination of rice and fish predominates in the atolls of Tuamotu. A celebratory dish, *ahima'a* (roasted suckling pig) will be a sure winner. For dessert, little ones can choose from French-style cakes, fruits and more typical *faraoa coco* (tasty coconut cake).

❗ Warning

→ When diving, ensure the equipment is designed to fit a child (mask, size of the tank etc).

🕓 Time difference

→ Tahiti UTC–10:00; Gambier Islands UTC–09:00; Marquesas Islands UTC–09:30.

BOOKS FOR THE YOUNG TRAVELLER

> Rai Chaze has published a series of books for young readers called *The Imaginary Tales of Tahiti*, each illustrated by a different local artist.

> *Treasure in Tahiti*, by Connie Lee Berry, is a fun adventure for pre-teens that manages to pack in educational content about the islands.

> *Another day in Bora Bora*, by Titi Becaud, is an amusing tale for little ones of a hoarding crab.

CHILDREN'S SOUVENIRS

> A ukulele or a *pu* – a shell that makes the sound *'puuu'* when you blow in it

Asia

There is no better destination than Asia for teaching your children that there are many different ways for people to live in the world! Eating with chopsticks, learning the story of Buddha on the steps of a pagoda, and trailing an elephant through the jungle are all rare experiences and will provide wow factor from one end of your trip to the other.

Of all the continents, Asia is probably the most exotic for young travellers. Coming face to face with teenagers in Tokyo or young monks in Laos will be far more intriguing for them than Tintin and his blue lotus, which could swiftly be relegated to the shelf for old-fashioned books. From Nepal to Japan, via China, Mongolia or Indonesia, life is a production in which you and your family can take part during your travels.

These totally different worlds may pique curiosity and perplex parent and child in equal measure. Never-ending journeys in China and crowds in Bangkok or in Indian railways stations mean no rest for the little ones. However, apart from Japan, the cost of living in Asia will alleviate many concerns. Once the flights are paid, you will be able to afford the very best, which should help your family handle the fatigue of long journeys and changing time zones. A car with a driver falls within anyone's budget in Sri Lanka, as does a bijoux hotel on a Malaysian beach or an internal flight to avoid endless hours on a train in India.

Wonders such as the Taj Mahal, Angkor or the Great Wall of China will transform children's dreams into reality and result in images, flavours and sounds that will linger long after you return from your family holiday in Asia.

CAMBODIA

Exploring the temples of Angkor, coming face-to-face with an elephant, taking a boat on the Mekong or a trip in a tuk-tuk, and then stretching out on a beach after one of these adventures – budding explorers (and their globetrotting parents) will love it!

Children will be amazed by Cambodia's magnificent temples

CHILDREN WILL LOVE...

Extraordinary temples and sites
» Angkor Wat, but also the more eccentric Ta Prohm or Beng Mealea, partly swallowed up by vegetation.
» The Royal Palace in Phnom Penh, particularly the Silver Pagoda, with its impressive silver-tiled floor and its Buddhas.

Jungle life
» Walking with elephants in their natural habitat and learning about each elephant's history and behaviour at the Elephant Valley Project.
» Observing (sometimes with difficulty!) Irrawaddy dolphins in the Mekong River, around Kratie.
» Phnom Tamao Wildlife Rescue Centre, south of the capital, for an overview of the country's wildlife, including tigers and sun bears.
» An organised trip in the Koh Kong conservation corridor from the Cardamom Mountains to the untouched tropical forest populated with animals.

All kinds of swimming
» Swimming, diving or riding on a banana boat on the beaches of Sihanoukville, and especially on the popular Ochheuteal and Serendipity beaches.
» Playing castaway on the stunning, virtually deserted beaches on the islands around Kep.
» The Phnom Penh Water Park, with its pools and water slides.
» A dip in the famous Bou Sraa waterfall (Mondulkiri) in the middle of the jungle.
» Diving into the crystal-clear waters of Boeng Yeak Lom crater lake, one of the most beautiful places in the country.

Learning about other ways of life
» A cruise on Tonlé Sap lake to explore the floating village of Chong Kneas and the spectacular drowned forest of Kompong Phluk with houses on stilts.
» The Cambodian cultural village museum in Siem Reap with its reconstructed villages and reproductions in miniature of the major monuments.
» Staying the night in a resident's home in a village in Mondulkiri to learn about the culture of the Phnong people.

BEST TIME TO GO

You can visit Cambodia year-round, but the best time is December and January when there is less humidity and the heat, which can reach 40°C or more, is not so intense. The rainy season (June to October) is not so bad, as any showers are usually short lived.

COST

Cambodia is a budget holiday destination, cheaper than Thailand, and you can sample excellent food and comfortable accommodation at very affordable prices. US dollars are the preferred currency, and the only one accepted for hotels, though you may pay less for food and small items if you pay in riels. Visitors to Angkor will have to factor in the cost of entrance fees, which are US$20 for one day, US$40 for three days and US$60 for one week. An additional expense is transport to get to, from and around the ruins, and food and shops nearby inflate their prices.

HEALTH CHECK

» Malaria is present year-round except in Phnom Penh and around Tonlé Sap, Siem Reap. A preventive treatment is recommended as well as protection (sprays, mosquito nets), which will also serve to prevent dengue fever.
» Health facilities are fine in the cities and towns. Beyond, it is better to see a doctor than go to hospital.
» Tap water is not safe.

GETTING AROUND

The bus network is extensive and the vehicles are generally comfortable. Avoid the minibuses in rural areas where the drivers can be reckless. Travelling on the waterways is fun, but be aware of safety issues. Most of the boats running between Phnom Penh and Siem Reap do not offer sufficient safety guarantees. Children will love riding in a *cyclo* (bike rickshaw), tuk-tuk or *remork-moto* (trailer pulled by a bike). If you hire a car, get a driver too. The railways are limited to freight transport.

Mealtimes

Rice is a must, of course. Children will love it steamed, fried or in a form of porridge *(bobor)*, served with chicken or grilled fish. Watch out for the spices, which could put them off some dishes. Certain sweet foods are eaten between meals such as *akao* (balls of sticky rice and palm sugar). Exotic fruits such as mangos and rambutan, also known as hairy lychees, will be very much to young diners' liking.

! Warning

→ A number of landmines litter the countryside. Keep a close eye on children and do not let them wander off the path.
→ Traffic in the capital can be dangerous; always hold your child's hand when crossing the road.
→ Beware of thieves on Sihanoukville beaches.

🕐 Time difference

→ Time zone UTC+07:00

BOOKS FOR THE YOUNG TRAVELLER

› Younger readers will enjoy *Angkat: The Cambodian Cinderella*, retold by Jewell Reinhart Coburn – a great picture book based on a Khmer legend.
› For an insight into the life of a street flower-seller find a copy of Frederick Lipp's *The Caged Birds of Phnom Penh*.

CHILDREN'S SOUVENIRS

› A bamboo jaw harp or a buffalo-skin drum
› A traditional ball made from rattan
› Puppets made from cow or buffalo hide

CHINA

A visit to the third-biggest country in the world requires a finely tuned itinerary. Whichever path you choose to tread, your young emperors will marvel at China's wonders: historical and present-day, manmade and natural. Surrender to the massed terracotta armies, mind-boggling fortifications, vibrant cities, wondrous landscapes and rare wildlife – you won't have a choice.

What child hasn't dreamed of the Great Wall?

CHILDREN WILL LOVE...
Millennium China
» The Terracotta Warrior Army of Emperor Qin and his 6000 life-sized soldiers at Xī'ān.
» The Summer Palace in Běijīng, the Imperial Court's summer home located in a park irrigated by a peaceful lake.
» Walks along the Great Wall, the world's longest man-made structure.

Běijīng parks
» Flying a kite in Temple of Heaven Park.
» Watching a session of water calligraphy before it evaporates, then climbing into a duck-shaped pedal boat in Běihǎi Park.
» Watching Běijīngers sing, dance or play mah-jong on the hills of Jǐngshān Park.

China – big, bigger, biggest
» Hong Kong's Central-Mid-Levels escalator, which stretches 800m, and the huge Ocean Park theme park.
» Panoramic views of Shànghǎi from atop its skyscrapers.
» The Three Gorges Dam, seen during a cruise starting from Chóngqìng.
» The 71m-high giant Buddhas at Lè Shān in Sìchuān, and the 34m-high version on Lantau Island, Hong Kong, reached via a glass-bottomed cable car.

China by bike or train
» Exploring the Li River scenery around Yángshuò (Guǎngxī) by bike.
» Catching a bike rickshaw in the country or through Běijīng's *hutong* (alleyways).
» Kicking back in a first-class train sleeper for an exciting overnight journey.

A walk on China's wild side
» Spending a day with the pandas at the Giant Panda Breeding Research Base in Chéngdū, or the Yǎ'ān Bǐfēngxiá Panda Base.
» Exploring the incredible landscapes of Shílín, the stone forest in Yúnnán.

Martial arts and the circus
» The Shànghǎi circus, where contortionists, jugglers, acrobats and spinning-plate acts do a turn. Even parents will be wide-mouthed.
» A *biàn liǎn* show (where an actor changes masks at great speed) in Běijīng.

BEST TIME TO GO

Visit from March to May and from September to the beginning of November to avoid the summer heat and harsh winter. The major tourist sites get very crowded during the Chinese holidays: Labour Day (three first days of May), National Day (first week in October) and Chinese New Year.

COST

China is a considerably cheaper place to travel than Western Europe, but it is more expensive than Southeast Asia. It's a large country, and prices will vary depending on where you are – luxury hotels in Shànghǎi and Běijīng can be as expensive as those in the West. Food and accommodation are generally good value, but admission prices can be significant.

HEALTH CHECK

» Malaria is a risk in southern areas such as Yúnnán and Hǎinán; a preventive malarial treatment is recommended. In the other southern regions and in the centre, protective measures against mosquitoes will suffice (dengue is also present).
» Hand, foot and mouth syndrome is present in some regions (wash your hands regularly).
» Avian flu is present in some southern areas, especially during winter.
» Watch out for spikes in pollution levels, particularly in Běijīng during winter.

Mealtimes

Whether at a small street stall or in a crowded restaurant, eating is always a sociable experience. But it is not easy to decipher a menu in Chinese! Happily there are often pictures. You can also point at your neighbour's plate and sometimes go into the kitchen to choose. Your children's stomachs may need a period of adjustment. In big towns, there are often children's menus; they usually comprise chicken or fried fish.

BOOKS FOR THE YOUNG TRAVELLER
› Lonely Planet's *Not for Parents: China* has tales of ancient empires, martial arts, the discovery of gunpowder and the first cup of tea, among many other fascinating titbits.

CHILDREN'S SOUVENIRS
› Puppets, traditional figurines, stuffed pandas
› Cheongsam or kung-fu costume

GETTING AROUND

The best way to visit tourist sites outside the main cities (Great Wall, Terracotta Warrior Army) is to hire a car and driver for the day. It is almost impossible to rent a car without a driver. Trains are efficient and comfortable, especially if you travel in soft seats or sleepers (first class), and are perfect for medium-length journeys (take something to eat). Reserve your seats as soon as you arrive at your point of departure, either through an agency or your hotel. Keep a close eye on your children at stations, which are always packed. Flying is better for longer journeys. In the city, you can often hire bikes near tourist attractions (bring your own helmets). The big cities have metro systems, which are easy to use and generally free for small children.

❶ Warning
→ The cities and towns are heavily populated and polluted. Things are quieter in the countryside, but there can be difficulties with transport and hygiene.
→ When visiting the Great Wall, you may find it easiest to choose the areas nearest to Běijīng or those accessible by cable car, such as Bādálǐng and Mùtiányù (these are more crowded, however). Avoid the most remote parts with difficult access. Take water, snacks, hats and sunglasses.
→ Crossing the road in China is dangerous: always hold your child's hand. Use underpasses and pedestrian bridges wherever possible.

🕐 Time difference
→ Time zone UTC+08:00

NORTHERN INDIA

The country of glittering saris and Ganesh, the elephant god, can be alarming. But despite the crowded cities and poverty, travelling in India with the family is much easier than it seems. For one thing, low prices mean you can travel in comfort. From the Taj Mahal to the Rajasthan forts, the culturally and historically rich north will leave the young traveller with an indelible memory of a magical country.

India's colours and vibrancy are irresistible to children

CHILDREN WILL LOVE...
The colourful cities and amazing palaces
» The white marble mausoleum of the Taj Mahal, which looks like something from an eastern fairy tale.
» The sound-and-light show at the Red Fort in Delhi.
» The peaceful green spaces of Lodi Gardens in Delhi, and the birds, butterflies and picnickers that inhabit them.
» The cities of Rajasthan. Relatively close to Delhi are the white city of Udaipur, with its tranquil lake; the blue city of Jodhpur; the pink city of Jaipur and the golden Amber Fort; Pushkar and its camel fair (October to November); and the indescribable maharajas' palaces that dominate each of these cities.
» The citadel of Jaisalmer, standing proudly in the middle of the Thar desert with 99 crenellated towers.

Climb to the roof of the world
» A visit to Darjeeling (at an altitude of 2000m) to see the Himalayas in the distance, before exploring the tea plantations, the zoo and a narrow-gauge railway known as the 'Toy Train'.
» The colourful Buddhist monasteries, adventurous 4WD rides and relaxing mountain-meadow walks in Sikkim.
» The markets and bazaars, with their riot of colours and scents, and cows wandering down the middle of the roads!

Camels and tigers
» Tracking a tiger in the tiger reserves of Madhya Pradesh or the Corbett Tiger Reserve (Uttarakhand).
» Seeing the rare Asiatic lion at the Gir National Park and Wildlife Sanctuary (Gujarat).
» Taking a safari on camel-back in the desert dunes of Thar, near Jaisalmer (Rajasthan).

Gods and goddesses
» Hindu temples, ranging from small village temples with colourful frescoes to the temples at Konark and Puri (Odisha), and Akshardham Temple in Delhi.
» The Golden Temple of Amritsar, the main place of pilgrimage for Sikhs. The intricate, glittering temple is strikingly situated on a manmade lake.

BEST TIME TO GO

Winter (November to February) is generally the best season to visit, even though it can be cold at night in Delhi and elsewhere in the north. From April to June, the heat is unbearable on the northern plains and in the centre of the country. During this season, it is better to head for the Himalayan region, though it's very busy. Best to avoid the monsoon rains; they begin in June and can persist until September.

COST

On the financial front, India pleases all pockets. Comfortable accommodation won't bust the bank, a delicious array of eateries at all price points allows you to fill your belly without emptying your moneybelt, and it's possible to zip around economically thanks to the country's comprehensive public-transport network. Delhi is expensive when compared with the rest of India. However many of the city's attractions are cheap or free, and hiring a car and driver is very affordable. While tourist restaurants are more expensive than street stalls, they are definitely the safer option with kids. Whatever you do, you're bound to find it a bargain.

Mealtimes

Dishes are often *hot!* In restaurants offering regional cuisine, children will enjoy rice, naan, *paratha* (pan-fried flatbread), chapatti and yoghurt, washed down with a glass of lassi (yoghurt drink). *Pakora* (fritters), *dosas* (savoury pancakes) and *idli* (rice cakes) will also appeal to young palates, while guesthouses commonly offer pancakes and omelettes. For dessert, young foodies will be won over by *kheer* (rice pudding), *firni* (sweet cream) and *kulfi* (milk ice cream). Do not let children be tempted by fruit juices, ice creams or lassi sold in the street. Fried rice and Western fast food (available in larger cities) are fall-back options.

BOOKS FOR THE YOUNG TRAVELLER

> Teens will enjoy the gently comic novel about Westerners trying to find their place in Delhi in Ruth Prawer Jhabvala's *A Backward Place*.

CHILDREN'S SOUVENIRS

> Indian puppets

> Princess outfit: sari, bracelets, bindis…

> Small wooden painted deities

HEALTH CHECK

» In many regions, particularly the northeastern states, malaria is present all year below 2000m.

» Hygiene is generally poor and disease caused by water and food is common. Avoid ice cubes and fruit juices mixed with water. Avoid raw fruit and vegetables. Never use unpurified water, even when brushing your teeth.

GETTING AROUND

The ideal choice is a car and driver – guaranteed flexibility, comfort and ease. Avoid buses, which are usually packed, particularly at night as there are many accidents. Flying, which is cheaper than in Europe, can help reduce journey times. The night train may be a good option for long distances, especially with children; book tickets through the special foreigner booking desks at major stations to avoid scams. And of course, you cannot travel in India without using a rickshaw – an adventure in itself!

! Warning

→ Before leaving home, prepare your children for the poverty they are likely to encounter.

→ The big cities are sometimes quite oppressive; there is heavy traffic and it is dangerous to cross the road.

→ Monkeys can be aggressive.

→ Be aware of altitude limits for children.

🕐 Time difference

→ Time zone UTC+05:30

SOUTHERN INDIA

For a first trip to India with the family, there is nothing like the laid-back and beautiful south. On the western coast there are well-appointed beaches hemmed with palm trees where young and old can relax before catching the little train to explore tea plantations and incredible temples worthy of *The Jungle Book*. Or sample the endless possibilities of the sprawling megalopolis of Mumbai.

Find a slower-paced India in the south

CHILDREN WILL LOVE...

The beaches

» Goa, with its blue and white buildings and sublime beaches lined with guesthouses where you can cycle or play Robinson Crusoe.
» The fabulous beaches of Kovalam and Varkala, south of Kerala.

Unusual trips

» A houseboat cruise on the backwaters that weave their way through the lush vegetation of Kerala. An unforgettable adventure!
» The miniature steam train to Ooty (Tamil Nadu), to breathe the fresh mountain air, admire the verdant scenery and explore the tea plantations.
» Climbing aboard a 4WD for a journey through the Wayanad district and the natural reserve of Periyar (Kerala).

Mumbai (Bombay), Kochi (Cochin) and Puducherry (Pondicherry)

» Chowpatty Beach (Mumbai), to wallow not in the water but rather in the town's festival atmosphere.
» A boat excursion to the caves of the Elephanta Island in the middle of Mumbai port. A maze of sanctuaries carved into the rock – there is nowhere else like it in the world.
» The Matheran hill station, not far from the heat of Mumbai. Take the little train at Neral Junction for an epic climb. On arrival you'll find horses, red earth and pure air!
» Kochi, one of the few calm Indian cities. On the agenda: colonial architecture and *kathakali* shows – actors in this stylised dance drama interpret Hindu sagas.
» Puducherry, with its colonial residences and French cuisine.

Colourful temples and maharajas' palaces

» The temples and cave paintings of Ajanta and Ellora (Maharashtra).
» The giant multicoloured temple of Madurai (Tamil Nadu), where the popular devotion is impressive.
» The Mamallapuram Temples (Tamil Nadu), on the edge of the sea, set in a calm, friendly atmosphere amid pleasant gardens.
» The Mysore Palace (Karnataka), a kaleidoscope of coloured glass and mirrors.
» The ruins of Vijayanagar city near Hampi (Karnataka).
» Cave temples, giant statues and dramatic sandstone scenery at Badami and Sravanabelagola.

BEST TIME TO GO

The dry and rainy seasons set the pattern for the year. The climate is generally pleasant from December to March (high season), and particularly in January and February, the best months for travelling in southern India. The monsoon, which starts in June, brings torrential rains. The south coast endures heavy rains from October to the start of December.

COST

South India is a very cheap travel destination. You will pay more for accommodation in the larger cities, especially Mumbai, as well as at popular tourist destinations during peak season. As Goa is a tourist hotspot, it tends to be expensive when compared with the rest of India. But once accommodation is paid for, you can get by on a matter of dollars a day. Eating out is sizzling-hot value, attractions are cheap, and hiring a car with a driver is surprisingly good value.

Mealtimes

Beware: the food is spicy! Children should love the rice, *pakora* (vegetables fried in batter), *dosa* (savoury pancakes) and *idli* (rice cakes). They can fill up on fresh fruit as long as is has been carefully peeled and rinsed with purified water. By the sea, fish, prawns and crabs are sold from huts on the beach from the end of October to the end of March, but check their freshness. Indian-Chinese food is comparatively child-friendly, with fried-rice an easy fall-back option. Western fast-food is widely available in larger cities.

BOOKS FOR THE YOUNG TRAVELLER
> Pack a copy of (or a retelling of some of the stories from) Rudyard Kipling's classic *The Jungle Book*.
> *Espi Mai Is Stuck Again... and other Goan Tales*, by Anita Pinto, is a collection of colourful stories for young readers from this equally colourful region.

CHILDREN'S SOUVENIRS
> Indian puppets
> A sari and bracelets
> Small wooden or papier-mâché figurines

HEALTH CHECK
» Malaria is present all year below 2000m. An anti-malarial treatment is recommended.
» Hygiene is generally poor and disease caused by water and food is common. Avoid ice cubes and fruit juices mixed with water. Avoid raw fruit and vegetables. Never use unpurified water, even for brushing your teeth.

GETTING AROUND

Even if you save time by flying between cities, the train is sometimes a better option: there are more routes and night travel tends to be treated as an adventure by children. It's worth it to pay more for a better carriage with air conditioning. Unless there is no other option, avoid the bus: it is uncomfortable and unreliable. It's quite cheap to hire a car and driver, ideal for travelling freely. In the towns and villages, use taxis and rickshaws.

⚠ Warning
> Before leaving home, prepare your children for the poverty they are likely to encounter.
> Beware of currents on the coast; on the eastern shores swimming is virtually impossible.
> The big cities are sometimes quite oppressive; there is heavy traffic and it is dangerous to cross the road.
> Monkeys can be aggressive.

🕐 Time difference
> Time zone UTC+05:30

PAKISTAN

BANGLADESH

Bhubaneswar

Mumbai (Bombay)

Hyderabad

ARABIAN SEA

Panaji

Vijayawada

BAY OF BENGAL

Bengaluru (Bangalore)

Chennai (Madras)

Lakshadweep Islands

Kochi (Cochin)

INDIAN OCEAN

SRI LANKA

INDONESIA

Of all the islands in the Indonesian archipelago, Bali is the best for children, with its beaches, comfort and array of activities. But other islands will also enchant youngsters: there's Sulawesi, with its traditions; Nusa Tenggara, with its Komodo dragons; and Java, with all its teeming vibrancy.

Sublime dances in Bali will dazzle children

CHILDREN WILL LOVE...
Curiosities from the living world
» Finding rare animals amongst the abundant wildlife and many parks, including the Sumatran tiger, Sumatran orang-utans and, of course, Komodo dragons.
» The rafflesia, the biggest flower in the world (1m wide). But be sure your children are warned: they also have the worst smell!
» Discovering rich underwater life while snorkelling at Bunaken (north Sulawesi), around the Sunda Islands and in the Gili Islands.

Daredevil activities
» Visiting the extraordinary Borobudur Buddhist Temple (Java), with amazing sculpted friezes that read like a comic book. Be careful, the many steps are challenging and difficult for smaller children!
» The many volcanoes on the archipelago. There are around 400, of which more than a quarter are active.
» Climbing Mt Batur (Bali), Kawa Ijen and Bromo (Java); feasible for teens and some older children.
» An acrobatic treetop walk in the magnificent botanical gardens at Bedugul (Bali).
» A trip to the Sindang Gila waterfall and a stroll among the rice paddies in Lombok.
» Rafting on calm stretches of water such as Ayung or Telaga Waja (Bali), or on Antokan (Sumatra).

Colours and traditions
» Watching *bedoyo* (dance theatre) in Ubud (Bali): princesses, gods, demons and warriors come to life with fascinating gestures and rich costumes.
» The Wayang Museum in Java, dedicated to Javanese *wayang* puppetry. Extend the visit with a show.
» Festivals and everyday ceremonies such as weddings, and Hindu offerings to the gods on Bali.
» Getting around by *becak* (bicycle rickshaws) and *bajaj* (three-wheel scooter), or by *dokar* (horse and cart) – often brightly painted and decorated with tinkling bells.

BEST TIME TO GO

It is hot (between 22°C and 32°C) and humid all year, with some variations depending on the region and altitude. The dry season (roughly May to September) is generally best for children, though in places such as Bali and Kalimantan changing seasons make little difference.

COST

Costs vary depending on where you go, but Indonesia remains one of the cheapest travel destinations in Asia. Hotels, food and transport are all inexpensive. Accommodation is usually the greatest expense. Travellers' centres with lots of competition, such as Bali and Yogyakarta, can offer superb value for accommodation and food. Sulawesi and Nusa Tenggara are also good budget options. Elsewhere, budget accommodation can be limited and prices are higher because competition is less fierce. Transport expenses also increase once you get into the outer provinces.

Mealtimes

Fairly spicy food could be a problem for children. The youngest will be able to eat a number of rice-based meals, the staple ingredient. This can be fried in *nasi goring*, the national dish, which little ones will be certain to appreciate. They will also like *mie goring* (sautéed noodles), *perkedel* (donuts), satay (meat on a brochette or skewer with peanut sauce) and *pisang goring* (banana donuts). The fish is unbeatable but there are also duck and pork dishes in Bali. In the tourist areas, little tummies will be relieved to find Western food. Fruit, delicious and sometimes oddly shaped, will arouse their curiosity and whet their appetite.

BOOKS FOR THE YOUNG TRAVELLER
> Give the kids a fright with Peter Sis' *Komodo!* – the story of a young boy's fascination with dragons, which takes him to the Indonesian island.

CHILDREN'S SOUVENIRS
> *Surakarta*, a strategy game very popular in Java
> A puppet made according to Balinese tradition

HEALTH CHECK

» Malaria is present all year except in urban areas and the main tourist spots in Java and Bali. An anti-malarial treatment is recommended. Dengue is also a risk, so take measures to prevent mosquito bites.

GETTING AROUND

Hiring a car to explore the islands will save precious time and ensure greater comfort. You must have an international driver's licence. Buses, minibuses *(bemo)* and boats are slow and uncomfortable (due to the heat or over-efficient air conditioning). Certain boats are not safe. If your holiday is short, flying is the best way to travel between the different islands. Check that the carrier meets all the safety criteria before buying a ticket (several operators are banned in Europe).

! Warning
> Security concerns and lack of tourism infrastructure do not make Papua, Central Sulawesi and Maluku ideal for children.
> Check before you swim: there are dangerous areas on every island due to undercurrents, jellyfish and the like in the water.
> Wear conservative clothing outside Bali.
> If you're visiting during Ramadan be prepared for the limited opening hours of many businesses.

🕑 Time difference
> Time zones range from UTC+07:00 to UTC+09:00.

JAPAN

In a country of mangas and games consoles, children will quickly find their feet. But, perhaps surprisingly, they will be equally thrilled by the discovery of the more traditional side of Japan: temples, imperial sites, and a landscape where mountains meet the sea. Japan is an Asian holiday destination that is easy to explore with young travellers and, with planning, less expensive than you might imagine.

With something for everyone, Japan tickles all fancies

CHILDREN WILL LOVE...
Robots and mangas
» Toyko's Ghibli museum, a magical place conceived by Hayao Miyazaki, the writer and director of the animated features *Princess Mononoké* and *Spirited Away*.
» The National Museum of Emerging Science and Innovation in Tokyo, with robotic humanoids and housing modules for a space station.
» Tokyo's Harajuku bridge at the weekend, where they can watch the *cosplay zoku* – groups of young people in outrageous costumes and make-up like something straight out of a manga.
» The Sony Building in Tokyo, where you can see the manufacturer's latest gadgets.
» The Kyoto International Manga Museum with its children's library and designers at work.

Temples and samurai
» Total immersion in the Japan of yesteryear in Kyoto. As well as the countless temples, pretty wooden houses and the shogun castle, do not miss the Tōei Uzumasa Movie Village, a sort of theme park where samurai films were made. You can walk around the film sets, help with fights and dress up.
» The great Buddha of Nara, one of the biggest bronze statues in the world, and Nara-Koen Park with its 1200 deer, who are eager to accept treats.
» Sendai City Museum (Tōhoku region), where they can see the helmet that inspired that of Darth Vader.

Volcanoes and beaches
» The Pacific coast of Shikoku, for its beaches and whale-watching trips.
» The wilds of Hokkaidō, with its mountains and volcanic scenery.
» The beaches and semi-tropical vegetation on Amami-Ōshima, Yoron-tō, Aka-jima and Iriomote-jima islands.

Quirky Japan
» Kyoto boutiques where professionals transform parents into geisha or samurai.
» Karaoke in their own room in a karaoke parlour.
» A *bunraku* show, where large puppets are carried around the stage by black-clad puppeteers.
» Coming face-to-face with a huge whale shark at Osaka Aquarium, one of the best in the world.

BEST TIME TO GO

Spring (March to May) and autumn (September to November) are the most pleasant times to visit. The heat and humidity of summer can be disagreeable; there is also the risk of typhoons at the end of August. In winter the snow is an extra worry when travelling in Hokkaidō and on the coast. Nonetheless, there are plenty of deals on holidays, especially in Kyoto, and though it's freezing in Honshū, autumn and winter are perfect for topping up the tan in Okinawa.

COST

It's no secret that Japan is on the pricier end of the scale when it comes to Asian travel destinations. You can't expect Southeast Asian prices, but in terms of what you get for your money, Japan is good value indeed. Accommodation is the top reason you'll burn through your money. If you're travelling in the peak periods of spring and autumn, you'll be competing against domestic tourists as well as foreign visitors, so booking accommodation and transport well in advance is vital. There are cheap food chains everywhere where you can grab udon noodles, curry or ramen; otherwise self-catering is a good way to go.

⚠ Warning

→ During meals, remind your children not to stick their chopsticks upright into their rice, as this action is associated with funerals.

→ In the cities, make sure you have a good map in Japanese and English, and a plan of the underground system in Tokyo and Kyoto.

🕐 Time difference

→ Time zone UTC+09:00

BOOKS FOR THE YOUNG TRAVELLER

› Pre-teens will enjoy *Shipwrecked: The True Adventures of a Japanese Boy*, by Rhoda Blumberg.

CHILDREN'S SOUVENIRS

› Knick-knacks, small toys, decorative objects – even at rock-bottom prices, the attention to detail is such that it is hard to resist Japanese gadgets

› *Ningyo* (traditional dolls) are little works of art in porcelain, wood and fabric; alternatively there are ninja or samurai dolls

› Wigs and other items to dress up as a geisha or samurai

GETTING AROUND

Train or plane, there are several formulas for substantial cost cutting (usually involving reserving tickets well ahead). Flying is the best way to reach the smaller islands, although a longer ferry ride can be an enjoyable mini-cruise. Whether it is the Shinkansen (bullet train) or the express train, the Japanese rail network is extensive. The Japan Rail Pass, valid for seven to 21 days of unlimited travel, is good value. Slower and almost as expensive, buses are sometimes the only way to reach off-the-beaten track places. In the cities the subways (or trams) are the easiest and quickest way to get around. In the countryside, and especially in Hokkaidō, a car is often the easiest way to get around quickly.

Mealtimes

Japanese food is tasty and varied; except for *shokudo* (family restaurants) and *izakaya* (Japanese-style pub), establishments specialise in one type of cuisine. Children will find just what they want in *yakitori-ya* (restaurants serving skewers of grilled chicken and vegetables) and *ramen-ya* (for Japanese noodles) and perhaps, with greater difficulty, in *sushi-ya* (sushi). They can also try *okonomiyaki* (savoury pancakes) and *omuraisu* (rice-filled omelettes). *Kaiseki ryotei*, the temples of gastronomic cuisine (often very expensive), are not ideal for teaching your children to use chopsticks. Everywhere else, the clumsiness of foreigners is borne indulgently.

LAOS

Less equipped for tourists than its neighbours, and with no beaches, Laos is probably the most difficult country in the region to explore with a family. But this relaxed, welcoming, well-kept secret will delight young adventurers and their parents. All will be spellbound by the magical temples and a cruise on the Mekong River – memories that will last a lifetime.

Laos is a relaxed, if not always comfortable, destination with children

CHILDREN WILL LOVE...
Sites that spark the imagination

» The former royal city of Luang Prabang and its imposing temples. Your children will be struck by the vibrant colours (flowers, temples, the monks' robes) and can wander around in complete safety in a city where cars are rare.

» The mysterious Plain of Jars, near Phonsavan, strewn with enormous stone jars dating back well over a thousand years and whose origin is unknown.
» The caves of Vieng Xai (northeast), in one of the most beautiful regions of Laos.
» Xieng Khuan (Buddha Park), in the capital, Vientiane, with its concrete sculptures showing both Hindu and Buddhist influences – look out for the giant pumpkin on three levels representing Earth, Heaven and Hell.

Playing explorers

» Exploring the limestone hills of Vang Vieng. The popular Tham Sang cave (Elephant Cave) is linked to other grottoes by a marked path.
» Swimming in the natural basins at the foot of the waterfalls of Tat Sae or Tat Kuang Si, around Luang Prabang.
» A boat trip on the Mekong to savour the fabulous scenery and discover some of the 4000 islands.
» An encounter with elephants or a hike with a guide in the Phu Khao Khuay National Protected Area, north of Vientiane.
» A ride on a camel in the Sé Pian National Protected Area, in Ban Na (near Vientiane), or the Tat Lo waterfalls (on the Bolaven Plateau).

Discovering Lao traditions

» The lively festivals including Makha Busa in February and Bun Bang Fai (Rocket Festival) in May.
» Pi Mai (the Lao New Year), a three-day fete held in mid-April with elephant processions and traditional costumes.
» A game of *petang*, the local version of bowls or, for the more athletic, *sepak takraw* (kick volleyball) with young Laotians.

BEST TIME TO GO

The best time to visit Laos extends from November to February, when the humidity lessens and temperatures are milder. It is also the main period of *'bun'*, national and regional festivals. If you are heading for the mountains, go in the hot season (from March to May) to enjoy more moderate temperatures. However, this is the time to avoid if you want to head south, where the temperatures can climb to 40°C.

COST

Laos is a bargain for travellers. It's cheaper than Thailand, and similar to Vietnam. The exception is transport, which is disproportionately expensive, with drivers charging the most in Luang Prabang. Meaning that getting to sights can eat into your budget. Guesthouses (well presented and clean) are an economical form of accommodation. Food is very cheap. Prices rise in touristy areas, but portions are often big enough to share.

HEALTH CHECK

» The clinics and hospitals leave a lot to be desired in terms of hygiene, equipment and qualifications. In case of serious illness, go to Bangkok.
» Malaria is present year-round throughout the country, except in Vientiane. An anti-malarial treatment is recommended. Dengue is rife, so take measures to prevent mosquito bites.

GETTING AROUND

Hiring a car and driver is a great option, even though the roads are in a poor condition. In town, try cycling (take a helmet), or a tuk-tuk ride or bike rickshaw, which will provide children with some unforgettable memories. Buses are often slow and uncomfortable. If you doubt your children have the patience, take a plane; they're faster but not necessarily more reliable, as cancellations are commonplace. Do not leave Laos without taking a trip on the Mekong River or one of its tributaries, by slow boat or river taxi; avoid *héua wái* (speed boats), which are uncomfortable and dangerous.

Mealtimes

No surprise that rice is the staple ingredient in Lao cooking. *Khào niaw*, sticky rice, is everywhere: you eat it with your fingers and children love it. The food is always fragrant with coriander, basil and lemongrass etc, but rarely spicy. However, the accompanying *jaew* (sauces) can be very spicy, so are best avoided. For breakfast there are baguettes (a hangover from the days as a French Protectorate), often spread with *sai nâm nóm* (sweet concentrated milk). This milk is also used in desserts such as banana pancakes.

! Warning

→ In rural districts, do not venture off road without a local guide: there are still unexploded ordnance dating from the Vietnam War. Keep an eye on the children and make sure they do not wander off.
→ Beware of snatch thieves, on the rise in the tourist towns.

Time difference

→ Time zone UTC+07:00

BOOKS FOR THE YOUNG TRAVELLER

› *Tangled Threads: A Hmong Girl's Story*, by Pegi Deitz Shea, is a novel for young teens about a Laotian refugee trying to adjust to life in modern America.
› The picture book *Nine-in-One, Grr! Grr!*, by Spagnoli, retells a Laotian folk tale with illustrations in traditional Hmong embroidery.

CHILDREN'S SOUVENIRS

› Pretty fabric dolls
› Woven rattan balls for playing *sepak takraw*

MALAYSIA

Malaysia holds some major trump cards for families: its lush, easy-to-explore countryside and palm-fringed beaches. The cultural mix of Malaysian, Indian and Chinese allows children a real insight into Asia's diversity. Another advantage is the hotels are good and reasonably priced.

Palm-fringed beaches are part of the fun in Malaysia

CHILDREN WILL LOVE...
Playing Tarzan in the jungle

» Exploring the Taman Negara (Pahang) National Park, the country's 'green lung', by pirogue (boat), or from the top of the Canopy Walkway swaying 40m above the ground between the treetops.
» Prowling the huge caverns of Niah (Sarawak), reached by a long, wooden walkway through the jungle.
» Hiking in the depths of the jungle on the Forestry Research Institute Malaysia walkway, not far from Kuala Lumpur.

Animals in their natural habitat

» Observing rescued orang-utans at the fantastic Sepilok Orang-Utan Rehabilitation Centre.
» Visiting elephants at Kuala Gandah (Pahang) or, even better, swimming with these gentle pachyderms.
» Keeping their eyes peeled for the seldom-sighted Sumatran rhinos in the Endau-Rompin National Park (Johor).
» Discovering Asian monkeys, cute gray langurs and their macaque cousins in Bako National Park (Sarawak) or Kuala Selangor Nature Park.
» Exploring caves in the Gunung Mulu National Park (Sarawak), home to stalagmites, stalactites and bat colonies. The bats emerge every evening between 5pm and 7pm, an amazing (and deafening!) event that's not to be missed.

Fun in the water

» Swimming from the fabulous white beaches of the Pulau Perhentian, where you can see turtles laying their eggs in certain seasons.
» Diving or snorkelling in the small archipelago of Pulau Redang, well known for its coral reefs and rich marine life, and on gorgeous Pulau Tioman.
» Building sandcastles on the beautiful beaches of Langkawi, which also boasts forests full of birds and waterfalls and a full complement of kid-friendly resorts.

Butterflies and towers in Kuala Lumpur

» Watching wings beat at the bird and butterfly gardens in Lake Gardens, a huge park of more than 90 hectares.
» Climbing the Petronas Twin Towers (452m), which dominate the capital. The 41st-floor Skybridge links the two soaring structures.

BEST TIME TO GO

You can visit most of Malaysia at any time of year and experience favourable conditions. One exception is the eastern coast of the peninsula, which experiences abundant rain from November to mid-February, and most accommodations close. Another exception is Malaysian Borneo, which receives high rainfall year round, though it's heaviest from October to March.

COST

Most visitors to Malaysia will find it very affordable, although it is the most expensive country in Southeast Asia after Singapore. You can get by very cheaply staying in guesthouses and eating at hawker centres, or you can splash out on a luxury hotel and restaurants without breaking the bank. Attractions are reasonably priced.

HEALTH CHECK

» Urban areas and coastal regions are free from malaria, but there are several affected zones in Borneo. A preventive treatment is recommended depending on the destination.
» Dengue is present all over the country, so take measures to avoid mosquito bites.
» Do not drink the tap water.

GETTING AROUND

To reach Borneo from peninsula Malaysia you'll need to fly – and flying is often the easiest way to get around. Ferries only connect neighbouring islands (do not embark if you consider ferries to be overloaded or too old). Buses are economical and comfortable, but accidents are not uncommon. You can also opt for long-distance taxis, which are practical and widespread. If you hire a car, drive on the left. The roads are in an excellent state of repair and driving is enjoyable.

ⓘ **Warning**
↳ For trips into the jungle, get children to wear long sleeves and trousers (made from cotton) and shoes that cover the ankles to protect them from insect bites, stings and leeches.

ⓘ **Time difference**
↳ Time zone UTC+08:00

Mealtimes

Children will love dining in a hawker centre, a sort of lively covered marketplace packed with food stalls offering Malay, Indian, Chinese and Indonesian specialities. Be careful, the food can be spicy, but the skewers of beef or chicken marinated and grilled are safe and kids generally relish them. For dessert young connoisseurs can sample many different tropical fruits such as rambutan, dragonfruit and – for the adventurous – durian.

BOOKS FOR THE YOUNG TRAVELLER
› *Kampung Boy*, by Malaysia's beloved cartoonist, Lat, provides a whimsical introduction to Malay ways.

CHILDREN'S SOUVENIRS
› A kite *(wau bulan)* is highly prized in Malaysia, where there are a number of organised festivals
› Puppets made from dried buffalo hide
› A traditional spinning top *(gasing)*

MALDIVES

In a country where the Indian Ocean is 99% of the country, holidays can be summed up in two words: sand and sea. It would be hard for children to find fault with such a program and in such a safe, heavenly setting. Choose a big hotel geared towards families, with a bigger range of activities on offer.

Shallow, warm and crystal-clear water is perfect for snorkelling

CHILDREN WILL LOVE...
Swimming and water sports
» Swimming in the turquoise waters where the lagoons are shallow and the water temperature can reach 32°C – ideal for little children!
» Undertaking windsurfing lessons, water skiing and fishing expeditions where they can meet friends the same age.

Underwater diving
» Learning to dive at a registered centre, usually possible from age eight.
» Experiencing the joys of snorkelling. As long as they can swim, all but the smallest tots can don a snorkel and explore the undersea world.
» A dive on board the *Whale Submarine*, based outside the capital and accessible by boat.

Animals in their natural habitat
» Fruit bats, giants that sweep the skies at dusk.
» Comical geckos – these lizards run up trees and house walls.
» Hermit crabs, which find shelter in all kinds of shells, even the most unlikely.
» Studying amazing coral reef fish (butterfly fish, angel fish, parrot fish, stingrays etc) during a dive or while snorkelling.
» Taking a boat trip to watch the dolphins and whales. More than 20 species are common in these warm seas. In the southern atolls, you can encounter groups of up to 500 whales!

Robinson Crusoe–style excursions
» Exploring the atolls with a trip on a catamaran.
» Having a barbecue at night on a deserted beach.
» Undertaking a foray to an inhabited island (with prior permission) to connect with the local population.
» Strolling around the markets in the tiny capital of Male, which is the size of 10 football pitches and surrounded by water!

BEST TIME TO GO

The dry season, which runs from December to April, is the best time to get the most out of the Maldives' natural beauty. As the destination is fairly expensive, it is best to travel with the family in April or November when the rates are lower and the climate is not too humid.

COST

This is no cheap destination. Even if you get a good flight-and-accommodation deal, unless it's full board you'll spend almost as much again on food and drink during your stay. For those with a modest budget, the best deal is usually a full-board or all-inclusive package that includes flights and transfers. It is also possible to stay at family-run guesthouses, eating your meals with the family, which can work out much cheaper. Activities such as diving can be a real budget killer.

HEALTH CHECK

» Serious health issues can only be treated in Male, as services are limited outside the capital; certain emergency operations will require an airlift to Colombo, Singapore or back home.
» Ensure children wear plastic sandals in the water to guard against sharp coral and sea anemone stings.

GETTING AROUND

Speedboats are the most widespread form of transport between the islands – or there is the *dhoni* for short distances, a vessel under sail or with an engine. There are nine regional airports in the Maldives, all of which are linked to Male by regular flights. Helicopters and seaplanes will often complete the final leg of the journey to resorts once passengers reach the main international airport at Hulhumale. There are taxis in Male. Some small islands can be explored on foot and some by bike.

! **Warning**

→ Never let your children go outside without high-factor sunscreen, sunglasses or hats. The UV rays are particularly fierce here. Avoid the heat of the day.

→ Keep an eye on them swimming as the currents can be strong.

→ If you plan to let them learn to dive, make sure you get a medical certificate before leaving home.

⏱ **Time difference**

→ Time zone UTC+05:00

Mealtimes

Resorts prepare food with travellers in mind, so there ought to be ample kid-friendly options. Resorts also offer plenty of sweet treats, including *bondi bai* (sweet rice cakes) and imported tropical fruit. If using prepackaged baby food, bring it with you as it is not available here. Maldivian cuisine is principally made up of rice and fish (mainly bonito, a type of red tuna) and can be spicy.

BOOKS FOR THE YOUNG TRAVELLER
› Older children might like to check out Rosaline Ngcheong-Lun's *The Maldives*, in the Cultures of the World series.

CHILDREN'S SOUVENIRS
› Carrom, a traditional game similar to billiards
› Carved wooden fish and animals

MONGOLIA

A dream destination for the adventurous, Mongolia is a challenging country in which to travel, but all the effort made by your family comes with a rich reward. Surveying the vast steppe, sleeping in yurts, staying with nomads…these unforgettable experiences will bring your brood closer together while giving everyone a taste of what really counts.

Mongolia offers a cultural experience like no other

CHILDREN WILL LOVE...
The great outdoors and time standing still
» Sleeping in yurts: cosy tents with big beds and a table for eating.
» Galloping across the steppe like ancient adventurers Genghis Khan and Marco Polo.
» Wandering nomadically from one camp of yurts to another in the Gorkhi-Terelj National Park, easily reached from Ulaanbaatar.
» Taking a horse trek to Burkhan Khalduun, the sacred mountain of Genghis Khan, or to the Eight Lakes (Naiman Nuur).

Incomparable wonders of nature
» Exploring the 'singing dunes' of Khongoryn Els (Duut Mankhan) in the Gobi Desert by camel – don't forget to jump down and do a few roly-polies in the sand.
» The seasonal Orkhon Khürkhree waterfall or a dip in the Mogoit hot springs.
» Undertaking adventurous activities such as fishing, kayaking and mountain biking at gigantic Lake Khövsgöl, on the border with Siberia.
» Glimpsing wildlife: horses, camels and yaks, of course, but also argali (mountain sheep), ibex, bears, sables, elk, gazelle and onager (wild donkeys).

Animals from another age
» The *takhi*, or Przewalski horse, in the Khustain Nuruu National Park – the last ancestor of the modern horse.
» Dinosaurs! Discover ancient skeletons and eggs at the Museum of Natural History in Ulaanbaatar, and bones and fossilized eggs at the Flaming Cliffs (Bayanzag) in the Gobi Desert – everything budding palaeontologists are crazy about.

Experiences simply out of the ordinary
» Experiencing daily life with the Mongols: milking mares, caring for the herd, preparing traditional meals, making felt…
» The Naadam festival in July, three days of traditional contests, horse races and archery competitions.
» Watching a demonstration of hunting with an eagle at Ölgii in the Altai Mountains of western Mongolia.

BEST TIME TO GO

'Extreme' aptly sums up the Mongolian climate! Winter is long and glacial, and summer is short (June to August, the high tourist season) and warm – even scorching in the Gobi Desert. June and July are dry but there is frequent rain in August. In May and September, the weather varies, tourists are rarer and certain yurt campsites close. The temperatures are particularly icy in December and January. Winter activities include dog sledding, ice skating and skiing.

COST

Mongolia is a reasonably cheap Asian country, less expensive than China. There are a wide range of places to stay in the capital, with some of the best deals at the bottom and top ends. During the week surrounding the Naadam festival, accommodation may be in short supply and prices are often higher. Camping in rural areas is obviously the cheapest accommodation option. Fresh foods such as fruit can be expensive as they have to be imported. The cost of an organised tour or prearranged package may seem high, but can actually work out cheaper than organising your own accommodation, meals and transport.

Mealtimes

Mongolian cooking is simple and filling. Dishes are meat based (and animal fat is often used in soup), usually served with bread, rice or potatoes. Green vegetables are rare. In restaurants, children will like *buuz* (meat dumplings) and *boortsog* (sweet fried bread similar to a donut). With all the fresh air, they will not be fussy and will be glad of the hearty meals. And to wash it all down: tea with salty milk?

BOOKS FOR THE YOUNG TRAVELLER
› For pre-teens, *Sorghaghtani of Mongolia*, by Shirin Yim Bridges, tells the story of the 13th-century princess, mother of Kulai Khan, who helped create one of the great empires of the world.
› *Horse Song: The Naadam of Mongolia*, by Ted Lewin, is a celebration of the Naadam festival in modern-day Mongolia.

CHILDREN'S SOUVENIRS
› Buddhas, small paintings or calligraphy to decorate a bedroom
› Silver jewellery

HEALTH CHECK
» Outside Ulaanbaatar, health facilities are basic.

GETTING AROUND

Due to a lack of transport infrastructure, travelling around Mongolia can be difficult. Flying is a good way to cover the vast distances. Relatively comfortable buses link Ulaanbaatar with the regional capitals. For more freedom, you might hire a car (with driver if you don't want to get lost), but this will not save you from all the jolting! Then there is always the sense of adventure that comes with a Trans-Mongolian Railway journey. And for outings, headstrong yaks or quarrelsome camels are available for the whole family. Unless you prefer horses, that is.

❗ **Warning**
→ In view of the often spartan facilities and sometimes tiresome transport conditions, Mongolia is best visited with children over the age of five or six.
→ Road signs can be difficult to come by and trails criss-cross endlessly. To be safe, invest in a GPS!

🕐 **Time difference**
→ Time zone UTC+08:00 most of Mongolia; UTC+07:00 the provinces of Khovd, Uvs and Bayan-Ölgii.

NEPAL

Nepal is a country of mountains. While there is no question of dragging your children up to 8850m, a carefully chosen trek will be an exciting adventure for them. With most hikes starting in Kathmandu and Pokhara, you can alternate to explore both cities. And there are also tropical forests and savannahs in Nepal, perfect for a safari packed with surprises.

Festivals and temples abound in Nepal as well as lakes and mountains

CHILDREN WILL LOVE...
Hikes within their capabilities
» Climbing up to Sarangkot (1592m) to admire the Annapurna Himalaya.
» Easy walks in the Annapurna Mountains from Pokhara.
» Day-long walks from Bandipur (from 1000m to 1830m maximum) and Tansen (from 1372m to 1600m maximum).
» Treks from Helambu and from Langtang. These are easy to organise from Kathmandu, short and at moderate altitude; depending on the trail chosen, you will be walking between 2000m and 3500m.

Nature beyond the mountains
» Observing rhinos and tigers in the Chitwan National Park or the (less busy) Bardia National Park.
» Gentle kayaking on Pokhara's Fewa lake, and moderate kayak or rafting descents on Nepal's rivers.
» Exploring the Nepalese plain, allowing little legs to recover after a trek.

Encounters and celebrations
» Nights spent in lodges during a short trek, or getting closer to nature on a camping trek, with staff on hand to set up camp, haul luggage and cook meals.
» Tibetan New Year, 15 days of festivities starting from the new moon in February, and the Nepalese New Year (Bisket Jatra), held in April or May.

Temples and mythic sites
» The hustle and bustle of Kathmandu, with its bazaars and snake charmers on street corners, and Durbar Sq, home to Kathmandu's most famous temples and palaces.
» Buddhist sanctuaries in Swayambhunath and Bodhnath, near Kathmandu. They cannot fail to fascinate children, with oil lamps, fluttering prayer flags and prayer wheels to spin under the watchful eyes of Buddha.
» The Hindu temple of Manakamana, reached via an impressive cable car. (Avoid Saturday, the day of animal sacrifice.)
» Lumbini, the birthplace of Buddha, where you can bike from temple to pagoda, each one as impressive as the last.

BEST TIME TO GO

October and November (just after the monsoon) and in spring (March to May) are the most pleasant times to visit, particularly for hiking in the mountains. The monsoon period (mid-June to September) should be avoided, as should winter (December to February), which is cold almost everywhere. At altitude, warm clothes are needed year-round.

COST

Nepal is a very cheap destination for travellers, a little more expensive than India but certainly less than China. Hotels and guesthouses are very affordable, so it's worth going a bit upmarket. Food, transport and attractions are also good value – your biggest expense will be organised treks and the equipment needed for them (though good-quality equipment is cheaper here than in the West). Pokhara is the tourist favourite so prices are a little higher here than in Kathmandu, especially during the high season.

Mealtimes

While the tourist areas prepare food from around the world, you may have to make do with *daal bhaat* (rice with stewed lentils), noodles, omelettes and instant soup in out-of-the-way places. Make sure you take snacks if you hike with children. *Masu* (meat) is quite rare, as many Nepalese are vegetarian. You will find more in the Kathmandu Valley, where the spice and heat may deter sensitive young palates. Children will prefer *momos* (Tibetan dumplings served fried or steamed) and Chinese-inspired dishes such as *chow mein* and noodle soup. For dessert, sweets made from milk and palm sugar, as well as the famous *juju dhau* (king of yoghurts) of Bhaktapur, will be sure to please.

BOOKS FOR THE YOUNG TRAVELLER
> A scrapbook-style book for pre-teens, *The Boy Who Conquered Everest: The Jordan Romero Story*, by Katherine Blanc, may inspire your youngsters to new heights.

CHILDREN'S SOUVENIRS
> Papier-mâché masks and colourful puppets
> A *bagh chal*, the national game of strategy comprising a tray of 20 goats and four tigers. Cerebral and very attractive!

HEALTH CHECK
» Malaria is present all year in the rural areas of Terai; an antimalarial treatment is recommended. Dengue is also a risk, so take measures to prevent mosquito bites in low-lying areas.
» Beware of leeches in wooded areas during the monsoon; take a bag of salt with you, which will make the leeches let go.

GETTING AROUND

Travelling around Nepal is not always easy. In town, taxis are practical and cheap. Elsewhere, hire a car (a 4WD if possible) and driver (obligatory for tourists), ideally through a travel agent. Fuel shortages can be a problem, but many villagers sell fuel informally. More expensive tourist buses are faster and more comfortable and take rest stops en route. Internal flights run to many destinations but safety is a serious concern and most airlines use small, cramped aircraft that are not comfortable for children. Check an airline's safety record before booking a ticket.

🛈 **Warning**
→ It is inadvisable to take children under one above an altitude of 1200m and children under 10 above 3000m. On average a child aged seven to eight can walk for about three hours a day, alternating time spent walking with being carried (in wicker baskets!).
→ Beware of bogus guides who approach clients in the tourist areas but have very little knowledge of the mountains and the dangers. Book through a well-established agency.

🕐 **Time difference**
→ Time zone UTC+05:45

PHILIPPINES

While they have fewer tourist facilities than other destinations in Southeast Asia, the 7000 paradisal islands of the Philippines are no less perfect for a Robinson Crusoe–style family escapade. With a little planning and a sense of adventure, children can learn new water sports and discover some fabulous scenery.

The Philippines is a great place to play castaway

CHILDREN WILL LOVE...
Beach activities

» Boracay, the star island in the very popular Visayas archipelago with kilometres of dazzling white sandy beaches. Children can throw themselves into a number of water sports (diving, windsurfing, water skiing) or simply collect *puka* (cone snail shells) to make bracelets and necklaces.

» Puerto Galera, 'the pearl of Mindoro': this collection of bays and splendid beaches is one of the most beautiful sites in the world for diving (from age eight) and snorkelling.

» Seeing the marine species that inhabit the Philippines at Manila Ocean Park, walking in a cultivated tropical forest or splashing about in the big swimming pool.

Novel experiences

» Peering into the simmering craters of Taal Volcano rising out of the middle of a lake from the safe vantage point of Tagaytay Ridge. The town of Tagaytay is popular with families as it is cool, clean, gorgeous and a bit of a foodie haven.

» The Palawan Wildlife Rescue and Conservation Center: a breeding centre for endangered crocs, with regular tours for families.

» Swimming in the hot thermal springs or the cool plunge pool below Katibawasan Falls on the island of Camiguin (Mindanao).

The promise of adventure

» Climbing Mt Pinatubo (1450m) near Manila; a memorable 4WD journey involving action-packed river crossings followed by a two-hour hike to the volcano's crater.

» A boat trip on the underground Sabang River in St Paul Subterranean National Park in Palawan; if you raise your eyes you will spot the bats.

» An excursion into the caves of Timbac (near Kabayan, Luzon), which contain mummies that are hundreds of years old. Attempt this only in the dry season, when you can reach the site by 4W, avoiding a long, difficult walk for little legs.

» A tricycle race to the stunning 2000-year-old Banaue rice terraces, which rise like stepping stones to the sky.

BEST TIME TO GO

Be sure to avoid the typhoon season (June to December). Unless you book well ahead it is difficult to find accommodation during Holy Week (Easter), when prices shoot through the roof. From January to May, the weather is guaranteed to be fine and you can make the most of being outdoors.

COST

The Philippines is a bit more expensive than Thailand or Indonesia, but still quite affordable by Western standards. Of course, location is the operative word. Prices in Manila or Cebu City aren't indicative of expenses for the rest of your trip. In particular, Manila's accommodation is pricey compared with the provinces. Likewise, the famous resort of Boracay is a lot pricier than most other islands. The season also plays a huge role: you can expect up to 40% discount in the off-season. Fortunately, no matter where you go, basic necessities are amazingly cheap all year round. Likewise, transport, with the exception of private boat and car hire, is also a great bargain.

Mealtimes

The staple ingredient in Filipino cooking is rice: it is even eaten at breakfast and made into cakes (the hearty *bibingka*). Children will enjoy barbecued skewers of meat and coconut-milk stews. For dessert, they will happily overdose on sugar with the famous *halo-halo*, a mixture of ice shavings, ice-cream, fruit, cereal and sweet beans, amongst other things! Let them experience delicious exotic fruits such as durian, santol and rambutan, and enjoy the world's best mangoes – but make sure they are peeled in front of you. You can buy infant formula and long-life milk in the big towns, but stock up if you are going further afield.

BOOKS FOR THE YOUNG TRAVELLER
> For a mischievous illustrated folktale, pack a copy of Robert San Souci's *Pedro and the Monkey*.

CHILDREN'S SOUVENIRS
> Wooden reproductions of houses on stilts or *bangka*, traditional boats with outriggers
> Musical instruments such as flutes or gongs

HEALTH CHECK

» Malaria is present all year below 600m; an antimalarial treatment is recommended. Use protection against mosquitoes, as dengue is also present everywhere.
» Health facilities are often inadequate outside the big towns.

GETTING AROUND

A number of airlines operate domestic flights, but note that there are safety concerns for all Filipino airlines except Philippine Airlines and Cebu Pacific Air. You can travel between islands on ferries, *bangka* (motorised pirogues) or hydroplanes. Avoid overcrowded boats and do not venture out to sea when the weather is bad. On the islands, buses are frequent and inexpensive. Other forms of local transport are jeepneys and tricycles (the Philippine rickshaw: a little roofed sidecar bolted to a motorbike or bicycle). Driving is dangerous in Manila, and outside the towns the roads are in a poor state. It is almost impossible to arrange a taxi with a child restraint.

! Warning
↪ There is unrest in some regions. Avoid parts of Mindanao Island, Basilan Island and the Sulu and Tawi Tawi archipelagos.
↪ Avoid displaying signs of wealth (such as jewellery and cameras), and do not accept services from strangers you meet in the street or hotel lobby.

(Time difference
↪ Time zone UTC+08:00

SRI LANKA

Smaller and much easier to visit with children than neighbouring India, this legendary island extends a warm welcome to visitors. Beaches, animal reserves, colourful temples and giant Buddhas will transfix your brood.

Sri Lanka is warm beaches and warm welcomes

CHILDREN WILL LOVE...
Beaches lined with palm trees
» The beaches on the southern coast, such as Bentota and Mirissa, and eastern coast, including Passekudah and Kalkudah.
» Arugam Bay, considered to be the best surfing spot in the country. It is ideal for admiring the prowess of surfers, for learning to surf in calm areas, and for testing their newly acquired skills.

Animals from *The Jungle Book*
» Pinnewala Elephant Orphanage, where elephants roam freely. The feeding and bathing sessions for the babies are a huge hit with kids.
» Safaris to spot elephants, leopards, monkeys and peacocks at very close quarters in the Minneriya, Uda Walawe, Yala or Kaudulla National Parks.
» Seeing blue whales and dolphins from a boat along the southern coast, or in the east, out of Nilaveli.
» Being a nest protector at the turtle hatcheries of Kosgoda, on the west coast.

Unusual outings
» Riding in a tuk-tuk – the unmissable motorised three-wheeler.
» Peering at fish, rays and tortoises through the hull of a glass-bottomed boat.
» Exploring the ancient cities of Polonnaruwa or Anuradhapura by bicycle.
» Spidering up a ladder suspended on a rock wall (yes, kids can do it) to reach the captivating ruins of Sigiriya, a citadel perched on an outcrop of red rock.

Colourful temples
» Stone Buddhas lost in the jungle, camped on a beach or safe in their temple.
» Hundreds of golden or multicoloured Buddhas, seated or prone in the Dambulla caves.
» Indian divinities, which decorate the coloured frescoes of even the smallest village temple.

Fairy-tale festivals
» The Esala Perahera of Kandy, a 10-day festival held between July and August, with great parades of decorated elephants, dancers and drums.
» The Poson Poya Buddhist festival, held in May. Fabulous paper lanterns light up houses and streets. Puppet shows and theatre pieces are staged in the open.

BEST TIME TO GO

Thanks to the climatic variations on the island, there is always one corner of the coast where you can enjoy the beach at any time of the year. The driest season lasts from December to March on the southern and western coasts and in the mountainous centre. April to September is your best chance to enjoy good weather across the entire island.

COST

Sri Lanka is a good-value destination: it's not quite as cheap as India, but compared to a similar destination such as the Maldives, it's a steal. Accommodation and public transport are very cheap. Hiring a car and driver makes getting around more of an expense, but with a family it is worth it. Entrance fees to attractions, including national parks, are surprisingly steep, especially as tourists must pay a much higher price than Sri Lankans. And there are a variety of taxes added to just about everything. You are expected to bargain over hotel prices and shopping; you are also expected to tip for any service.

Mealtimes

Certainly spices are at the heart of Sri Lankan cooking, but grilled fish and rice dishes will get your children's taste buds working. Hopper (fried pancakes), string hopper (steamed noodles) and vegetable roti (a type of pancake) are not very spicy. Sri Lankans have a sweet tooth, as can be seen from the menus. What is more, the island is one big orchard where fruit is abundant, with avocado, mango, pineapple, melon and papaya, among others.

BOOKS FOR THE YOUNG TRAVELLER
› For teenagers Michael Ondaatje's *Running in the Family* is an insightful look at Sri Lankan culture.

CHILDREN'S SOUVENIRS
› *Peralikatuma*, a game of strategy a bit like draughts
› Wooden toys, skittles, spinning tops

HEALTH CHECK
» An antimalarial treatment is recommended for holidays of more than a week, and dengue is present throughout the country. Use mosquito protection.

GETTING AROUND

Even though the country roads are often narrow and potholed, driving is easy in Sri Lanka. It is normal to hire a car and driver for a day or more. If you choose to drive yourself, you will need an International Driving Permit. The rail network links most tourist towns. Once you leave the towns behind, bike rides can be very enjoyable, if you avoid mountain roads. The famous tuk-tuk is a practical, go-anywhere mode of transport.

⚠ Warning
↝ Look out for warnings restricting access, which means there are mines. Avoid forest areas, rice fields and ruined houses in the eastern and northern provinces where there could be unexploded ordnance.
↝ Watch out for empty beaches where currents may be strong.
↝ The archaeological sites at Sigiriya and Dambulla are remarkable, but you need to climb several hundred steps to reach them.

🕐 Time difference
↝ Time zone UTC+05:30

THAILAND

Thailand is a magical kingdom for families. After hectic Bangkok – where the crowds can be frightening for youngsters – children will relish the mysterious jungle in the north. Southern Thailand offers islands and paradisal beaches, with all the necessary facilities at a reasonable price for parents.

Children will finally be able to pinpoint paradise on the map!

CHILDREN WILL LOVE...

The island paradises
» Ko Samui and Ko Samet, Ko Pha-Ngan or Ko Phi Phi islands.
» The isles in the Ang Thong Maritime Park, ideal for playing castaways.
» Spotting whale sharks from the islands off the Similan Islands Marine National Park between January and April.

The real jungle
» Exploring the national parks of the Kanchanaburi Province, which are populated with elephants, tigers and gibbons.
» Khao Yai National Park, near Bangkok, home to elephants, monkeys, leopards and birds. They will also see superb waterfalls here.
» The Erawan Waterfalls and the caves and subterranean galleries of the Khao Sok National Park, where the forest – one of the most ancient in the world – conjures up *Jurassic Park*!
» ElephantsWorld (near Kanchanaburi) and Elephant Nature Park near Chiang Mai, where kids can learn the elephants' stories, and participate in feeding and bathing.

Folklore and traditions
» Shows with striking 1m-high puppets that relate popular legends with music, and the shadow theatre of flat puppets. Even if they cannot understand the language, children will be transfixed by the enchanting performances.
» Ten days of shows (parades, battle reenactments, acrobatics) staged during November in Surin – all in a festive atmosphere.

The most beautiful Buddhist temples
» The famous Emerald Buddha in Wat Phra Kaew, Bangkok, and the impressive 46m-long reclining Buddha situated not far away in the Wat Pho compound.
» A perambulation through Sukhothai Historical Park, an ancient ruined city with serene Buddhas in the centre of the jungle.
» Glimpsing the past at the ruined temples and palaces of Ayuthaya, a Unesco World Heritage Site and an easy day trip from Bangkok.

BEST TIME TO GO

The ideal season to travel to the region is between November and April. The heat is not overwhelming, the rains are less frequent and the principal festivals take place during this time. March to May or July and August are good times to head to the mountainous northern regions. The temperatures are milder at altitude.

COST

While it's not the cheapest country in Southeast Asia, one the reasons Thailand is so popular with tourists is its affordability compared with the rest of the world. The busiest tourist spots, such as the islands, are the most expensive. Accommodation and food are very cheap, even at the higher end. Local agencies offer the lowest rates for car hire, but their vehicles are often less well maintained; check before committing.

HEALTH CHECK

»   Malaria is present year-round, especially in the forests and mountains, and close to the international frontiers. There is no risk in the towns, in Ko Samui and in the main tourist resorts of Phuket. Dengue is present in the country; take anti-mosquito precautions.

»   Hand, foot and mouth disease affects the country.

»   Do not drink the tap water.

GETTING AROUND

Air travel is the easiest and fastest way to travel south. Train is the best way to travel from Bangkok to Chiang Mai, but otherwise is only an option if you are not in a hurry. Thailand has an extensive bus network, which lets you cover the country easily. Use reliable BKS buses. You can hire a car and drive yourself (good roads, driving on the left), but in town there is nothing more fun than a tuk-tuk or bike rickshaw. In Bangkok, you can get around on the *klong* (canals) on board long-tail boats.

! Warning

→   Traffic in Bangkok is particularly dangerous.

→   Do not feed or try to touch monkeys; they can carry rabies.

→   For safety reasons, there are formal warnings against travelling in the extreme southern provinces (Narathiwat, Pattani, Yala, Songkhla). Care is needed in the border areas with Myanmar. Also avoid the temple regions of Preah Vihear and Ta Muean Thom, on the Cambodian border.

🕐 Time difference

→   Time zone UTC+07:00

Mealtimes

Thai cuisine is delicious but often spicy. Fortunately restaurants will reduce the level of spice on demand. Children should like the mild chicken dishes – be they grilled (*gài yâhng*), fried (*gài tôrt*) or sautéed in peanuts (*gài pàt mét má-môo-ang*) – served with sautéed rice (*kôw pàt*). They will gorge themselves on tropical fruits, particularly mangoes. Mango with sticky rice (*kôw nĕe-o má-môo-ang*) will probably be a hit too.

BOOKS FOR THE YOUNG TRAVELLER

> Check your library for a copy of *Thai Tales: Folktales of Thailand*, retold by Supaporn Vathanaprida.

CHILDREN'S SOUVENIRS

> Dolls dressed in rich batik recalling the cultural diversity of the kingdom

> Scaled down 'royal puppets'

VIETNAM

Red dragons, green rice fields, conical hats, junks floating on an azure sea, colourful fruits…Vietnam is a bit like the Asia you dream about as a child. For parents it is an easy and welcoming destination, ideal for a first family holiday in Asia.

Vietnam offers a colourful cultural experience

CHILDREN WILL LOVE...
Picture-book scenery
» Walking or cycling through rice fields and terraces in the north, from where pointed straw hats emerge.
» Boarding a junk or taking a mini-cruise on Halong Bay through scenery that is almost unreal.
» Observing traditional ways of life up close while on a boat trip through the Mekong Delta, a real jungle on water.

Quirky and unusual experiences
» Watching a puppet show on the water in the Hanoi theatre dedicated to this art.
» Catching bicycle rickshaws to cross the towns.
» Staying in a B&B on stilts in and around Mai Chau in the north.
» Spending a night in a bungalow on a beach on Cat Ba Island.

The joys of swimming
» The tropical island of Phu Quoc, with its heavenly beaches.
» Fun and games and swimming on the beaches in Nha Trang.
» Suoi Tien theme park, a water park dedicated to Buddhism, 15km from Ho Chi Minh City. Kitsch and spectacular!
» The island complex of Vinpearl Land at Nha Trang, with a cable car over the sea and a huge wave pool.

Temples, ruins and pagodas
» One Pillar Pagoda and the Temple of Literature in Hanoi.
» The Imperial City, tombs and pagodas of Hue as seen from a boat on the Perfume River.
» The delightful city of Hoi An, with its wooden homes and lanterns lit up at night.
» Exploring the Cham monuments at My Son, on the trail of a lost civilisation.

Colourful markets packed with discoveries
» Gaping at the frogs, salamanders and other curiosities in the Hanoi markets.
» The floating markets of the Mekong Delta.
» Meeting the ethnic tribes of the mountainous north wearing their traditional dress at Sapa market.

BEST TIME TO GO

The climate varies according to region. Winter (January to March) only exists north of Danang; the change of season is marked by cooler temperatures (down to 3°C in Hanoi) and drizzle that can be unpleasant. It is always warm in the south. From July to November, violent and unpredictable typhoons occur in the centre and north of the country. The best periods for visiting Vietnam are December to February in the south; February to May in the centre; November to the start of May in the north.

COST

Your money goes a long way in Vietnam, which is one of the cheapest countries in Southeast Asia, if not the world. Hanoi, Ho Chi Minh City, and Sapa tend to be a bit more expensive than other places. Accommodation and food are low expenses, as are museums, attractions and even day tours. Haggling is part of life in Vietnam.

HEALTH CHECK

» Malaria is fairly rare in the country, apart from a few at-risk areas. Urban areas are free from malaria as are the Red River Delta and the central coastal plains.

» Do not drink the tap water.

» Outside the big cities (Hanoi and Ho Chi Minh City) health services are sorely lacking.

GETTING AROUND

The international driver's licence is not recognised in Vietnam. Hiring a car and a driver is by far the best way to cross the country with the family. It works for any itinerary and any diversions in between, even those covering just several kilometres. For long-distance travel, bus journeys will seem long to children, as the different stages can last six to seven hours minimum. Take the plane or train instead (book at least the day before; several days ahead for sleepers). Before taking a boat on Halong Bay, check out the safety arrangements.

❗ **Warning**
→ Keep your distance from monkeys as they're often aggressive.
→ Avoid meals prepared in the street or on the pavement; stick to food places in buildings.

🕑 **Time difference**
→ Time zone UTC+07:00

Mealtimes

Based on rice and noodles, Vietnamese cooking is not too spicy, so children can tuck in without too much problem. Really fussy eaters will find Western dishes in the major tourist destinations. On the sweet side, young travellers will get all the vitamins they need from the delicious fruits, in particular *pitaya* (dragon fruit).

BOOKS FOR THE YOUNG TRAVELLER
› *A Taste of Earth and Other Legends of Vietnam*, by Thich Nhat Hanh, should get kids in the right mood.
› Darell HY Lum's *The Golden Slipper* has bright illustrations to impress the littlest travellers.

CHILDREN'S SOUVENIRS
› *Tha dieu* (kites)
› Coloured *to he* figurines modelled from rice powder

Africa & the Indian Ocean

Africa is a riot of colour and sounds, and a welter of animals. The migration of the gnus in the Serengeti (Tanzania), the lions in the Kruger National Park (South Africa) and the lemurs of Madagascar will all leave indelible memories for children and their parents too, as will the Cairo bazaar and the colourful markets of Dakar on this confronting, kaleidoscopic continent.

Parents must be intrepid as well as organised to visit Africa. Perhaps more so than anywhere else, time spent researching destinations, activities and operators will be richly rewarded when your feet hit African soil. Throughout much of the continent, health problems persist, malaria in particular. A few precautions will prevent children from becoming ill. By paying a bit more and choosing top-end hotels and lodges or hotel-clubs for seaside resorts, it is possible to travel in a manner suited to very young children.

North Africa, especially Morocco and Tunisia, is a good place to start. Transport links are good, and it offers a broad range of activities for every age, as well as beaches, mountains, desert, healthy and varied food, and good accommodation. The shifting sands and remarkable vistas of the desert will appeal to the whole family, just make sure you use a specialist tour operator to prepare a suitable tour. Experience in person something you normally see on TV at famous animal parks of eastern and southern Africa, where lazing lions and ear-flapping elephants will leave you and your children goggle-eyed. Then there's the mesmerising islands of the Indian Ocean. Here your children can play Indiana Jones in the jungles of Madagascar, or chill-out in comfort on Mauritius or in the Seychelles, where they can tickle the giant tortoises.

EGYPT

This is a country that will kindle any early archaeological ambitions! Egypt, the land of the pharaohs, with its pyramids and temples, is unlike anything else anywhere in the world. Young and old will be drawn together by a shared passion for this lost civilisation. A cruise along the Nile or a diving course in the Red Sea provide refreshing interludes between history lessons.

A camel ride is a must-do experience in Egypt

CHILDREN WILL LOVE...
Cairo, from the bazaars to the pyramids
» The pyramids and the Great Sphinx of Giza, which has lost none of its mystery. To get away from the crowds, visit the step pyramid of Djoser in the Necropolis of Saqqara.
» The treasures of Tutankhamun and the mummies in the Egyptian Museum.

» Going back to the time of the pharaohs in the Pharaonic Village.
» Strolling around the timeless bazaars of old Cairo, where donkeys still thread their way through crowds.
» The camel market at Birqash.

Gods and pharoahs
» The giant array of columns at Karnak; the unusual Mummification Museum; Luxor Temple, which is fun to discover at night when the stonework is illuminated; the Valley of the Kings and the Valley of the Queens.
» The Temple of Horus at Edfu.
» The museums in Aswan, with a sound-and-light show on Philae Island.
» Crossing Lake Nasser to reach the Temple of Ramses II at Abu Simbel.

Desert adventure
» Taking 4WD excursions into the White Desert to admire the unearthly chalky formations, and into the Black Desert, where dark conical formations break the surface.
» Enjoying a camel ride across the dunes in the Great Sand Sea.

Keeping cool down by the waterside
» A mini-cruise in a *feluka* (sailboat) at Aswan.
» Taking a horse-drawn carriage along the cornice and from the fort at Alexandria.
» Exploring the bed of the Red Sea aboard a Sindbad submarine at Hurghada.
» Discovering magical oases, cooling havens hidden in the desert, such as Dakhla Oasis and its lush palm groves or Bahariya and its museum of ornate golden mummies.

BEST TIME TO GO

May, October and November are the best times to explore the whole country. Winter (December to February) is ideal for discovering the Upper Nile region (disregarding hotel rates). Temperatures from March to April are pleasant, but sandstorms can mean outings are cancelled. Avoid the hottest months (June to August) when visits are carried out at dawn and sunset to miss the heat of the day.

COST

Egypt is a very cheap travel destination, and is one of the cheapest countries in Africa. Touristy areas such as Luxor are naturally more expensive. Luxury accommodation is quite affordable, vegetarian meals are good value, and transport (including car and driver hire) is particularly cheap. Children and students get into most attractions for half price. The big-ticket sights can be quite pricey, but smaller museums are cheap. Water activities around the Red Sea are available at appealing prices. When shopping, everything is negotiable and you are expected to haggle. You will undoubtedly pay too much, but your purchases will still be inexpensive. Tour prices are also negotiable, and it can be a good idea to join a tour to the big sights just to avoid being hassled by prospective guides. Touts are very insistent: just say 'no' firmly and move on. *Baksheesh* (tips) are expected for just about everything.

Mealtimes

Restaurant food is varied. Children will be happy to find potatoes, often chips, on the menu, along with rice, pasta, lamb and grilled chicken. They can also pick at the mezze (including the famous *fuul* – broad-bean purée in olive oil). Pita bread in many guises (kebab, kofta, felafel, vegetables) is delicious. Avoid raw vegetables at all costs.

BOOKS FOR THE YOUNG TRAVELLER

> Locally produced kids' history books, such as Salima Ikram's *The Pharaohs*, are excellent for kids and reasonably priced for parents.

CHILDREN'S SOUVENIRS

> A board game from ancient times: *senet* (a game of '20 squares'), *mehen* or *seega*

> A painted sheet of papyrus

HEALTH CHECK

» Take mosquito repellent and wear long trousers and sleeves to cover up, particularly in the Nile Valley. No need for an anti-malarial treatment.

» The air in Cairo is very polluted: avoid it with very young children or those prone to asthma.

» Do not drink the tap water.

GETTING AROUND

Outside Cairo, hiring a car or, even better, a 4WD allows you to explore areas beyond the reach of public transport. Though public transport is well developed, the journeys can be tiresome for small children. 'Deluxe' buses are better even though the air conditioning and video only operate at full pelt. The rail network is ancient, but it is an option on some lines, such as Cairo to Alexandria. Internal flights can save time but the fares are high. Some 250 cruise ships tour the Nile from Aswan to Luxor in three to four days. To get to the Red Sea, take a plane or boat shuttle.

❗ **Warning**

→ Political instability and recent acts of terrorism mean warnings relating to travel in Egypt are in place. Large gatherings should be avoided in major cities. The situation is changeable, so keep abreast of the news and government travel advice before booking and departing.

🕐 **Time difference**

→ Time zone UTC+02:00. Daylight saving time is observed in northern hemisphere summer (but suspended during Ramadan).

KENYA

Kenya is a legendary safari destination. The many different species of wildlife to be seen wandering through absolutely breathtaking scenery will leave children open-mouthed in wonder. Maasai guides will add to the magic of the experience. But once you are done with the parks and reserves, gather up your brood and head out to the beaches facing the Indian Ocean.

Learning is hands-on with Maasai guides in Kenya

CHILDREN WILL LOVE...
Exploring parks and reserves

» The great reserves in the south: Masai Mara, Tsavo and Amboseli (with Kilimanjaro providing the backdrop!). These parks provide the very best conditions for seeing the animals, which is why they are the most visited!
» The lakeside reserves Nakuru, Baringo and Bogoria, nestled in the Rift Valley: thousands of birds are often spotted here, especially in January and February.
» Visiting the Kakamega Forest in the west, the only reserve in the country located in the middle of a tropical forest.
» The heights in the Mt Kenya park (where there are even glaciers) or in the Aberdare mountains dotted with torrential waterfalls.
» Investigating Samburu and Buffalo Springs reserves, still pretty wild and awkward to reach, but perhaps the most beautiful.

Adventures for young explorers

» Camel rides on the beach. Or, for older children, a camel safari south of Lake Turkana.
» Crossing the Masai Mara in a hot-air balloon: there's nothing quite like it for seeing the huge gatherings of wildebeest and zebra, and herds of elephants and antelopes.
» Exploring the mangrove swamps in a boat from the pretty village of Kilifi.
» Spending a night under canvas in one of the park campsites and hearing the roaring of wild animals in the middle of the night.

Water and marine life

» The beaches that stretch from the south of Mombasa to the border with Tanzania, in particular Diani Beach.
» Studying marine life while snorkelling in the sea reserves of Watamu, Kisite and Malindi.
» Rafting (from age five to 10, depending on rapids) or kayaking along one of Kenya's rivers.

NEED TO KNOW

BEST TIME TO GO

January and February, when it is warm and dry, offer the best weather. From June to September, the weather is equally nice but cooler, except on the coast. July to September is when the wildebeest migration takes place in the Masai Mara – perhaps the most spectacular wildlife sight in the world. Rain falls heavily from March to May (many hotels close) and less heavily from October to December.

COST

Overall, Kenya is not an expensive destination. However, compared to other countries on the continent, it is not always the cheapest place for safaris, and the biggest outlay for most visitors will be visiting the national parks, whether on a safari or independently. Nairobi is notably more expensive than other African cities. But you are better off paying a bit more for luxury accommodation, tours, etc, as quality drops quickly along with price. Hiring a car with a driver is worth the extra expense, as you will be covered for insurance and won't be liable for any excess. Drivers will look after the car at night, and are also incredibly helpful when it comes to fulfilling your travel plans. Note that there is a 16% value-added tax on goods and services.

Mealtimes

In Kenya all kinds of establishments serve up worldwide cuisine familiar to children, including Italian, Lebanese and Asian. Otherwise, restaurants offer beef or lamb (often from the barbecue, which is called *nyama choma*), accompanied by beans, potatoes, plantain bananas and other carbohydrates. Fruit is on every menu: mango, papaya, pineapple, passion fruit, bananas, guava. Watch out for the buffet in the lodges, which are often of lamentable quality compared to the top establishments.

BOOKS FOR THE YOUNG TRAVELLER

› *Mama Panya's Pancakes: A Village Tale from Kenya*, by Joice Cooper Arkhurst, for ages four to eight.

› *Masai & I*, by Virginia Kroll, is a picture book that makes the Maasai culture very relatable.

CHILDREN'S SOUVENIRS

› *Kikoi* (pieces of brightly coloured fabric)

› Objects made from soap stone (chess pieces)

HEALTH CHECK

» Malaria is prevalent; a preventative treatment is advised.

GETTING AROUND

Although expensive, hiring a 4WD with a driver is a great way to visit the reserves, especially in the north, where public transport is virtually nonexistent. There are a number of airports dispersed throughout the country, so flying is a good option and a guaranteed way to reach Amboseli, Masai Mara and Samburu reserves. There's a train line from Nairobi that allows you to reach Mombasa, but avoid 3rd class: it's testing for the children. There is also an extensive network of buses, *matatu* (minibuses) and shared taxis, but these are best avoided with small children.

❗ Warning

↱ Almost all parks refuse entry to children under seven. In any case, the safari lifestyle (early rising, lots of waiting) is not particularly suitable.

↱ Certain campsites do not accept children under 12.

↱ Never leave your children unsupervised in the lodges or campsites.

↱ Nairobi is often an unavoidable stopover but certain districts should be avoided.

↱ Travel warnings are in place for several areas. Check your government's latest travel advice before booking and travelling.

🕐 Time difference

↱ Time zone UTC+03:00

MADAGASCAR

Madagascar is an island that reveals itself less easily than its smaller neighbours, Mauritius and Réunion. You need a sense of adventure, so often found in children, to appreciate its raw beauty. Transport is tiresome and accommodation far from ideal, but with some careful preparation, these inconveniences can be overcome!

The Avenue of Baobabs is a memorable Madagascan sight

CHILDREN WILL LOVE...

The wonders of nature

» The Tsaranoro Valley, an exceptional site at the foot of the awe-inspiring granite mountains dominating the Tsaranoro.

» The fabulous sandstone rock formations in the Isalo National Park, notably the impressive Canyon des Makis.
» The Avenue of Baobabs (near Morondava), where 20 or so of these giant trees are silhouetted above paddy fields and indolent zebus (a type of cow).

Dreamy beaches

» Nosy Be, an island off the northwest coast, and the islets that surround it, such as Nosy Komba and Nosy Sakatia. The beaches get very busy and there are excellent hotels offering activities for the whole family, such as diving and canoeing along the coastline.
» Île Sainte Marie, a former pirate den on the east coast. Known as Nosy Boraha it's ideal for playing castaway. The water is shallow, so it's perfect for children.

Lemurs and other rare creatures

» Ring-tailed lemurs, the island's symbol, which play in the easy-to-access Anja Park.
» The acrobatic sifakas lemurs; see them in the Berenty reserve.
» Geckos and chameleons, which you will see while walking.
» Humpback whales off the Île Sainte Marie. Hundreds hug the coastline from July to September.

Bright local crafts

» The artisans of Antsirabe, who will enchant your children with their range of unusual creations (rickshaws, zebu carts, miniatures and sweets).
» The paper workshop producing *antaimoro* (something like papyrus) at Ambalavao.

BEST TIME TO GO

Avoid the rainy season (November to March), when the heat is intense and getting around can be difficult. Cyclones can strike the island from the end of December until the end of February. In the north, the climate is wetter than it is in the south and west. July to October is the best time to visit. During this time, temperatures can fall to below zero at night on the high plateau.

COST

Aside from the cost of getting there, Madagascar is a generally inexpensive destination. Accommodation is good value, and food is particularly cheap. It's an excellent place to go camping, which is not only cheap but allows you to get really close to the wildlife. National park entry fees are reasonable, but note that you are required to enter with a guide, which can add substantially to the price. Shop around for tours as prices can vary enormously, and be prepared to negotiate. Fuel is expensive, adding to the cost of hiring a car and driver.

Mealtimes

The food served in the tourist restaurants (largely recommended for hygiene reasons) is mainly French influenced. Children will enjoy fresh fish as well as grilled meats (zebu is a local speciality). Rice is almost obligatory in a true Malagasy meal, but visitors can also have chips or vegetables. On the dessert trolley, let children taste *koba ravina* (cake with peanuts cooked in banana leaves), deep-fried banana and, of course, tropical fruits. Milk products are rare.

BOOKS FOR THE YOUNG TRAVELLER

> *Torina's World: A Child's Life in Madagascar*, by Joni Kabana, is a revealing portrait for young children.

> *The Pirate's Son*, by Geraldine McCaughrean, is a swashbuckling adventure for pre-teens.

> Teens will enjoy the humorous exploits of naturalist Gerald Durrell in his *The Aye-Aye and I: A Rescue Mission in Madagascar*.

CHILDREN'S SOUVENIRS

> Toys made from recycled material such as cars made from tin cans

> Solitaire or a chessboard made with semi-precious stones

HEALTH CHECK

» Malaria exists across the country, particularly in the coastal regions; anti-malarial treatment is recommended. Dengue fever is also present. Take measures to prevent mosquito bites.

» Hospitals lack drugs and equipment. In the case of serious infection it is essential to be repatriated.

» Avoid wild dogs, as rabies is rife.

» Do not drink the tap water.

GETTING AROUND

Hiring a car with a driver is by far the best way to get around, but you need to know that only 5500km of the 30,000km road network is paved. Cycling is also possible, if you are prepared for those rough roads. For longer distances it is better to fly (while remembering that cancellations are commonplace). The *taxi-brousse* (small bus) is the most popular form of transport on the island, but they are generally packed, slow and uncomfortable.

! Warning

→ Do not let children swim in stagnant water.

→ The country is poor and theft is common.

→ Overloaded, unroadworthy vehicles and cavalier drivers make road travel potentially dangerous. Minimise risks by avoiding night travel.

🕐 Time difference

→ Time zone UTC+03:00

MAURITIUS & RODRIGUES

Life is sweet in this paradise set between Africa and Asia. Children can enjoy the wonders of nature – swimming in the lagoons or under waterfalls, studying the coral gardens and exotic fish of the deep – and take advantage of the many cultural and sporting activities set up with children in mind.

This tropical paradise could have been designed for kids

CHILDREN WILL LOVE...
The sights of Port Louis

» The Natural History Museum with its dodo skeleton – the now extinct creature remains the symbol of the isle.
» Fort Adelaide, an impressive fortified 19th-century citadel dominating the port.
» Champ de Mars, the oldest racecourse in the Indian Ocean region and a great place for families to watch the races with a passionate but friendly crowd.

Water fun

» A trip on a glass-bottom boat so as not to miss any of the abundant underwater life in the Blue Bay Marine Park.
» An undersea walk (from age seven) equipped simply with a weight belt and diver's helmet to admire the marine life.

Family activities

» The Mauritius Aquarium, at Pointe-aux-Piments. Children can feed the fish and watch a show with turtles, giant moray eels and sharks.
» Hiking in the Casela Nature Park (from eight to 10 years). Or taking a photo safari in a small open bus or a mini-safari by quad bike (from age eight) to see the antelopes, zebras and ostriches.
» L'Aventure du Sucre, a museum with everything you need to know about processing sugar cane (with an interactive tour for children).

Fascinating nature

» The Tamarind Falls, one of the most beautiful places in Mauritius. They are awkward to reach (better to have a car), but it is possible to swim in some of the pools.
» L'île aux Aigrettes and its giant tortoises, a natural reserve that also acts as a sanctuary for a number of at-risk bird species.
» An excursion to the isles of the Rodrigues lagoon, including Ile Aux Cocos and Ile Aux Sables, for a picnic on the beach.

BEST TIME TO GO

You can visit Mauritius year-round, as the climate is pleasant during any season. The heat can be a little overwhelming between mid-December and mid-March and there is a chill in the air (everything is relative) at the end of the day during the southern winter from June to September. Prices rise sharply during the Christmas festive period, in November and December (a holiday for Mauritians), and July to August, when Europeans have their summer holidays.

COST

Mauritius is slightly more expensive than neighbouring Madagascar or mainland African countries, but is nonetheless a well-priced destination. Luxury is affordable here, and there are some great packages available. In the low season, rates can be half what they are during the high season. Tours and activities can be pricey but not exhorbitantly so. Car hire is cheaper with small local firms.

Mealtimes

Mauritius has everything you need to provide your children with a healthy diet including grilled fish and meat, and quantities of fresh fruits and vegetables. The only issue is the often spicy Creole- and Indian-influenced food. Better to avoid dishes with sauces (such as *cari* and *rougail*) or ask the chef to add less spice for the children. If the children are not keen on vegetables, they may like sweet potato or pipengaille. Everyone will almost certainly appreciate the extra sweet fruits (mango, guava, coconut or pineapples).

BOOKS FOR THE YOUNG TRAVELLER
> *Mauritius: Grandma Ruby Went to Maritius and Met a Giant Tortoise*, by Ruby Cavanaugh Koerper, is a picture book in which youngsters meet a variety of animals in addition to the tortoise.

CHILDREN'S SOUVENIRS
> Model boats, a local specialty
> Wooden dodos

HEALTH CHECK
» Health care is usually free for visitors in public hospitals, but the services are often better in private clinics. In case of serious health problems, it is better to be transferred to Réunion.

GETTING AROUND

Mauritius is a small island and is navigable by bus; they are usually old but the service is generally frequent, at least in the main places. The road network is in a reasonable condition, except for a few secondary roads. Consider hiring a taxi and driver. If you hire your own car, remember to drive on the left!

! Warning
→ Taxi drivers can earn commissions from certain businesses to which they take passengers. Keep this in mind, if your driver tells you your chosen destination is closed, full or otherwise not worth visiting.

🕐 Time difference
→ Time zone UTC+04:00

MOROCCO

The vivid colours of the souks, walking in the Atlas Mountains, a camel ride in the Sahara dunes, swimming in the Atlantic: Morocco is the ideal destination for letting your children get their first taste of adventure in total safety.

The red walls of Marrakesh are straight from the Arabian Nights

CHILDREN WILL LOVE...
A stroll around the *ksour* in the medinas
» Djemaa el-Fna Sq in Marrakesh, with its snake charmers, monkey handlers and fakirs. While you're there, take a horse-and-carriage drive around the city walls.
» The imperial architecture of Fès and walks around the medina, unchanged for 1000 years.

» The *ksar* (fortified town) of Aït Benhaddou and the Glaoui kasbah, just a few kilometres away in Telouet, lying in ruins, but still a worthy rival to the Bahia Palace in Marrakesh, which it once hoped to eclipse.
» The beautiful ruins and Roman mosaics of Volubilis – even though the crumbling alleys show few signs of life these days!

Refreshing dips
» Swimming at the Atlantic beaches around Rabat and Salé, at lifeguard-patrolled Agadir, or at Essaouira, at the foot of the city's impressive ramparts.
» The splendid Parqué Maritimo del Meditteraneo, a leisure park at Ceuta (a Spanish enclave) on the edge of the Mediterranean.

Desert magic
» A visit to the cinema studios in Ouarzazate, on the threshold of the desert, to revisit scenes from *Asterix and Cleopatra* or *Gladiator*.
» Camel rides in the dunes at M'Hamid or Merzouga.

The alluring Atlas Mountains
» The Drâa and Aït Bougomez valleys, and the gorges of Todra, dotted with Berber villages that provide relief from the heat.
» A short donkey ride or a few days hiking through the villages and valleys of the Middle Atlas.
» The lunar landscapes of Anti-Atlas, folded like a millefeuille.
» The town of Tafraoute set in a stunning cirque of red granite mountains in the heart of Anti-Atlas, and the small villages of the Ameln Valley with houses anchored to the rock.
» The 110m-high Ouzoud waterfall in the heart of the Atlas Mountains.
» Walks in the gorgeous Cèdres Forest, in the central Middle Atlas.

BEST TIME TO GO

Spring (mid-March to May) and autumn (September to November) are the best seasons to visit. Winter proves the truth of the old adage 'Morocco is a cold country with a hot sun', for if the temperatures are mild during the daytime, the nights are chilly, even freezing in the mountains and desert. If you are travelling in summer, stick to the coast and the higher reaches of the Atlas, as the heat is suffocating in the interior.

COST

In global terms Morocco is a reasonably priced destination. It is more expensive than Egypt and Tunisia, but cheaper than nearby Spain. Competition keeps accommodation prices low, but luxury riads can approach Western prices, as can meals bought in hotels (local restaurants are much cheaper). Larger cities such as Marrakesh are more expensive, as are remote areas including the High Atlas where goods have to be transported in. Sights are generally free or cheap. Always bargain prices down when shopping in the souks.

Mealtimes

With juice, omelettes, small pancakes and pastries, breakfast comprises hearty fare and is eagerly devoured by children. On the other hand, the salad starters might take them aback with all the spicy flavours. If they are put off by the savoury-sweet combination of many tagines (stews) or *pastillas* (meat pies), they will tuck into the couscous with relish. For fast food there are snacks of grilled brochettes, *keftas* (meatballs), pizzas and *brouats* (flaky pastry pasties). For dessert, as well as the classic *kaab el ghazal* (almond cookies shaped like gazelle horns), sweet couscous and orange salad usually go down well.

BOOKS FOR THE YOUNG TRAVELLER

› For young readers, *The Storytellers*, by Ted Lewin, is the evocative tale of a boy and his grandfather who work as storytellers in the medina of Fès.

› For older children, *Tales from Morocco* is Denys Johnson-Davies' translation of six Moroccan folk tales.

CHILDREN'S SOUVENIRS

› Beautiful wooden games: chess, drafts, dominos

HEALTH CHECK

» Medical facilities can be non-existent or poorly equipped beyond the big towns.

GETTING AROUND

If you hire a car, you will soon discover the charms of driving in Morocco and the liberal use of the horn. Avoid driving at night as there are no street lights and passing through villages can be dangerous. The Moroccan rail network (ONCF) is one of the most modern in Africa, but serves only a few big towns and does not extend south of Marrakesh. Buses are numerous and good. Taxis are an easy way to get around town; hire one for the day or week if you prefer not to drive. If you have limited time, consider an internal flight.

ⓘ Warning

→ Henna tattoos can be tempting for children, but sometimes there are added substances that can set off allergic reactions. In any case, only accept the traditional red henna, never black.

→ If children are travelling with a single parent, the Moroccan authorities may demand a letter of authorisation signed by the absent parent. Find out before you leave home.

🕐 Time difference

→ Time zone UTC+0. Daylight saving time observed in northern hemisphere summer.

NAMIBIA

Thanks to the diversity and intensity of its landscape and culture, Namibia is an ideal introduction to southern Africa. Young explorers will be exhilarated by the wild animals and outdoor pursuits. In fact, everything you need to enjoy a great family adventure in complete safety and comfort can be found here.

Nature can take your breath away in Namibia

CHILDREN WILL LOVE...
Picture-book scenery

» The great expanse of Namibian dunes, the oldest in the world, with every possible variation in tone from cream to orange, and red to violet.
» The Deadvlei, a cracked white-clay pan dotted with the spooky black skeletons of dead acacias.
» The vertiginous Fish River Canyon (at least 160km long, 27km wide and 550m deep!), set against a lunar landscape.

A date with wildlife

» A safari in the Etosha National Park, where elephants, rhino, oryx, giraffes, zebras, wildebeest and antelopes, among others, seem to have arranged to meet at the watering holes. However, there are many other parks, with Namib-Naukluft and Mahango top of the list.
» A visit to the centre for the protection of cheetahs (CCF) on the Waterberg Plateau, to find out everything about this threatened feline.
» Watching the fur-seal colony at Cape Cross, made up of some 100,000 lumpy, noisy and rather smelly individuals.

Signs of the past

» The Brandberg White Lady painting, an astounding rock painting.
» The magnificent reproductions at the National Museum of Namibia at Windhoek.
» Dinosaur footprints at Kalkfeld.
» The engravings and rock paintings at Twyfelfontein (Doubtful Spring) and, not far away, the enormous fossilised tree trunks in a petrified forest.

Extraordinary experiences

» Lying on a board and tobogganing down the dunes near Swakopmund – a thrilling ride!
» Climbing on board a small plane at Swakopmund, to take in the Brandberg Mountain, Sossusvlei or the Skeleton Coast from the air.
» Meeting the Kalahari Desert Bushmen and finding out about their way of life and environment.
» Admiring the world's largest known meteorite at Hoba West farm, near Grootfontein.

BEST TIME TO GO

The period from May to October is ideal for seeing wildlife, and is marked by cool, dry weather. Average temperatures are around 25°C with cold nights in the desert. From October to December it's generally warm and dry. The warm rainy season lasts from January to April, but this is when the light is at its most beautiful.

GETTING AROUND

It is almost essential to hire a car (or a 4WD) to travel around Namibia with children. You'll need an international driver's licence or an official English translation of your national licence. The country has a good network of roads and trails but having a GPS is vital. Access to the parks and reserves is often limited to enclosed vehicles (and is free for under-16s). Namibians drive on the left. Air Namibia provides regular flights between Windhoek and other domestic hubs. Trains connect major towns but are *sloooow*. Bus services are limited.

Mealtimes

Traditional meat dishes (such as beef, antelope, warthog and mutton) are often prepared as a stew and accompanied by cornmeal. Apart from locally grown squash, vegetables and fruit are rare. You do find German specialities – such as sauerkraut, sausages and *apfelstrudel* or *sachertorte*, for the sweet-toothed – which are a legacy from colonial times. Most tourist restaurants offer a version of typical foreign dishes as well as fish and seafood (in the coastal regions). Picky eaters may have to settle for pizza, available on nearly every menu.

HEALTH CHECK

» Malaria is present from November to June in certain regions and year-round in others; antimalarial treatment is recommended.
» The country has a satisfactory health-care system and poses less risk than other African countries (thanks to the dry climate).
» Ensure your children wear enclosed shoes to protect them from thorns, insects and scorpions.

COST

Namibia is not really a budget destination. It is more expensive than other African countries, including Kenya and South Africa, as well as some Western European countries such as Greece and Spain. But infrastructure, safety and the tourism industry are better developed here than in much of the rest of Africa. You can find accommodation to suit all budgets – guesthouses are reasonable but luxury lodges can be very expensive.

! Warning

↪ Certain tour operators and top-end lodges refuse to take very young children. In any case, a safari lifestyle is not suitable for the very young.
↪ Never leave your children unsupervised in the camps and lodges.

🕐 Time difference

↪ Time zone UTC+01:00. Daylight saving time observed in southern hemisphere summer.

BOOKS FOR THE YOUNG TRAVELLER

› *Secret of the Crocodile and Other Animal Stories from Namibia* is a book for young readers created by the Namibian Oral Tradition Project.

CHILDREN'S SOUVENIRS

› Handmade toys in metal or wood
› Material to decorate their rooms; stones or minerals

SENEGAL

Whether you opt for a relaxing beach holiday or a more challenging trip, Senegal is a window into West Africa. Children will be delighted by the beaches, where *djembes* beat out a rhythm; the atmosphere of the villages; and the chance to see wild animals during an outing in a pirogue.

Children will find playmates speak a universal language in Senegal

CHILDREN WILL LOVE...

Flora and fauna

» Observing from a pirogue (dugout canoe) the thousands of aquatic birds that live in the marshes and estuary islands in Langue de Barbarie national park, near Saint-Louis.

» Glimpsing rhinos, giraffes, gazelles and monkeys in the Bandia Reserve.

» Setting off from Palmarin, Dionewar or Djifer to meander through the mangrove labyrinth of the Siné-Saloum Delta in a pirogue, and to picnic on some heavenly islands.

Cultural activities

» Attending a painting workshop on the magical island of Gorée, after a moving visit to the Maison des Esclaves (House of Slaves).

» Mastering the *djembe* after taking the instant drum lessons on offer nearly everywhere on the coast.

» Taking a course in batik: there are places for children in Ziguinchor village, Casamance.

Unforgettable escapades

» Swimming in Lac Rose, not far from Dakar, where you float effortlessly thanks to the high salt content.

» Relaxing and splashing about in the water on the beaches around Saly on the Petite Côte.

» Taking a dip under the waterfall at the sacred site of Dindefelo, then sleeping in the village in a stone or bamboo hut.

» Playing Tarzan in the baobabs at Accrobaobab Adventure (65km from Dakar), a unique tree-top experience where there are walkways suitable for children 10 and over. There is also a mini version for smaller children.

NEED TO KNOW

BEST TIME TO GO

The dry season, from November to February, is the most pleasant time to visit: temperatures are mild, the lack of rain makes travel easier (particularly to out-of-the-way places) and there is less chance of mosquitoes. During the rainy season many parks close. October and November are generally dry and there are fewer tourists: it is perfect if you wish to avoid the crowds, but the heat can be sweltering.

COST

Senegal is averagely priced for Africa, and comparable to Eastern Europe. While cheap hotels are the norm, you will probably prefer to spend a bit more to ensure standards are acceptable. Unless you speak a little French, you may find communication difficult, in which case it pays to shell out for organised tours.

Mealtimes

Children will find traditional chicken *yassa* (or the beef alternative) delicious; it's grilled and marinated in an onion and lemon sauce and served with rice. They will also enjoy another national dish *tiéboudienne*, rice mixed with fish and vegetables. Grilled fish, particularly *thiouf*, are a real treat. Always ask if dishes are spicy before ordering: chilli is widely used and sensitive young palates might not appreciate it.

HEALTH CHECK

» Malaria is present in Senegal; a preventative treatment is recommended. Take all necessary precautions to prevent your children being bitten by mosquitoes, which will also help to prevent dengue and chikungunya.

GETTING AROUND

You can use buses to get around Senegal, but they are slow and the service is irregular. *Taxi-brousse* (a small bus) are more economical than a hire car, but the latter will guarantee flexibility and relative comfort. If you are not used to driving in Africa, it is better to hire a driver. Children will enjoy riverboat rides. Pirogues, it has to be said, may be more dangerous. Whatever the means of transport, do not expect to travel comfortably, quickly or safely. There are no seat belts in most *taxis-brousse* and no children's seats.

⚠ **Warning**
⤷ It is inadvisable to travel in some parts of Casamance, and also the border regions with Mauritania and Mali.
⤷ It's impossible to get around with a stroller, even in Dakar.

🕐 **Time difference**
⤷ Time zone UTC+0

BOOKS FOR THE YOUNG TRAVELLER
› Nine- to 12-year-olds might like *Senegambia: The Land of the Lion*, by Philip Koslow, a history of West African communities from the 12th to 20th centuries.

CHILDREN'S SOUVENIRS
› Percussion instruments (*djembes, balafons*…)
› Planes, cars and other toys made from recycled materials (metal, cans, cloth…)

SEYCHELLES

Children will love exploring the many creeks on these island paradises and discovering the flora and fauna. And when they tire of that, they can sample many water sports in the warm seas that lap the shores of the archipelago. Importantly, many Seychellois speak English – a huge help when you need a guide or a diving teacher.

Life is wild and free in the beautiful Seychelles

CHILDREN WILL LOVE...

Water sports
» Exploring the shallow, clear waters with a snorkel. For kids aged eight to 10, this is an ideal spot to have a go at diving.
» A trip in a glass-bottom boat: always fun and a little magical.

Rare animals
» The birds nesting in their thousands on small islets such as Aride, Cousin or Bird. Treat yourself to a guided tour with a naturalist for a lively explanation.
» The giant tortoises in the tortoise parks or in their natural habitats on Curieuse, Bird or Cousin Islands.
» Whale sharks, which pass around Mahé between August and October.
» The turtles, which lay their eggs between October and February, particularly on Bird Island.

Quirky nature
» The curious-looking coco de mer (double coconuts or sea coconuts), a symbol of the country that are found in the Vallée de Mai on Praslin.
» The towering granite blocks that surround the beach of Anse Source d'Argent on La Digue, which looks like a film set. The scenery is amazing, and the water is shallow and safe.

Exploring on foot, by horse or by...cow
» A hike in the lush and verdant Morne Seychellois National Park. Take a guide and pick the short, shaded Copolia circuit.
» A ride in an ox cart on the delightful La Digue island.
» A horse or pony ride on Mahé.

BEST TIME TO GO

The water is inviting and the temperatures mild at any time of year, but the sun does not always make an appearance. From December to February, rainy spells are more frequent, but that does not stop the tourists flooding in during the Christmas period, nor the hotels from upping their prices. From June to September the rain peters out, but the wind can make some beaches unfit for swimming. The best times to visit are between seasons, from October to November and April to May.

COST

An isolated location and a pristine environment don't come cheap: the Seychelles is quite an expensive place to visit. While there are cheaper guesthouses available, accommodation is usually booked as part of a package, which can be a good deal if it's all-inclusive. If meals are not included, stay away from hotel restaurants and touristy places to keep costs down. Supermarket food can be expensive too, as it is largely imported – it can be a good idea to bring your own pre-packaged snacks with you. Car hire and activities are also pricey, so shop around.

Mealtimes

Bougeois, cordonniers, capitaines…odd names for fish! These species are among the most prized in the Seychelles, where they come grilled, fried or stewed. If your children were not fans of fish before, they may well change their minds. The sauces are delicious, garnished with spices and herbs, but are not too hot and are often toned down with coconut milk. For dessert, there is a real bonanza of fruits such as bananas, mangoes, corossols (or soursop) and pineapple. They are tasty all on their own, but children will also love them cooked in tarts or cakes.

BOOKS FOR THE YOUNG TRAVELLER

› Teenagers may enjoy the mix of fact and fiction in *Voices: Short Stories from the Seychelles Islands*, by long-term resident Glynn Burridge.

CHILDREN'S SOUVENIRS

› Shells to make necklaces or start a collection

› Puppets made from bamboo and coconut in La Digue

HEALTH CHECK

» Pharmacies are few in number and poorly stocked. Take a kit containing any medicines used regularly and the usual items for treating cuts and bruises.

GETTING AROUND

It is easy to reach Praslin from Mahé, thanks to inter-island flights. A regular boat service connects the three main islands of Mahé, Praslin and La Digue. Buses circulate on Mahé and Praslin, but you may have to wait a long time by the side of the road on certain routes (and the stops offer no shelter). Get information on the services from your hotel or the bus station in Victoria. Hiring cars is possible in Praslin and Mahé, but check that the insurance covers damage suffered, as well as damage caused. Driving is on the left. Cars are banned on La Digue, so your choices there are to walk, ride on an ox cart, or cycle.

❗ Warning

→ On some beaches the currents can be dangerous: check before letting children swim.

🕑 Time difference

→ Time zone UTC+04:00

SOUTH AFRICA

With a profusion of natural parks, beaches, hiking paths, and an unrivalled level of comfort for the African continent, South Africa is the perfect destination for a family holiday. It is here, in the national parks and reserves, rather than anywhere else, that children will have the best chance of seeing the 'Big Five'.

High adventure in South Africa

CHILDREN WILL LOVE...
The wildlife

» Trying to find the Big Five: rhinoceros, Cape buffalo, elephant, leopard and lion. The Waterberg Biosphere Reserve, among others, is a particular favourite for families, as it offers the chance to see the Big Five in a virtually malaria-free region.
» Seeing southern right whales from the beaches or cliff paths in Hermanus between June and December.
» Encountering proud ostriches and loveable meerkats at Oudtshoorn.

» Learning about elephants in the Addo Elephant National Park and Tembe Elephant Park.
» Spotting white sharks and their fellow sea creatures during specialist boat excursions.

Activities for everyone

» The bevy of swimming and water sports offered along the 3000km of coastline lapped by two different oceans. Certain beaches around Port Elizabeth and Durban, among others, are perfect for splashing around in the surf.
» Cape Town. Here, children can experience the Two Oceans Aquarium, with its sharks, seals and penguins; ride on a camel at Imhoff Farm; take the cable car to the top of Table Mountain, from where you can see the whole town; and visit historic sights such as Robben Island, where Nelson Mandela was imprisoned, and Slave Lodge, where slaves were held.
» The incredible Gold Reef City theme park, near Johannesburg, based on the 1880s gold rush.

Glimpses of traditional Africa

» The brightly painted, round thatched houses of the Xhosa people.
» Matsamo village, a living museum, dedicated to Swazi culture.
» The Venda people's region, with its forests and sacred lakes.

Landscapes to behold in wonder

» The Drakensberg Escarpment, an awe-inspiring tangle of serrated cliffs, plunging canyons, sweeping hillsides and temperate, thickly forested valleys.
» The red sand of the Kalahari desert.
» Outstanding fynbos (shrubland vegetation) seen in the Cape Floral Region and the regions on the west coast from the end of August to the end of October.

BEST TIME TO GO

The climate is variable, depending on the region, but the periods halfway through the season (March to April, September to November) are generally ideal thanks to warm temperatures that are not excessive (23°C on average during the day). It can be rather cold and wet from June to August. Try to avoid South African school holidays (especially mid-December to the end of January), as prices soar.

COST

Travelling in South Africa is not as cheap as in many less-developed African countries. However, it usually works out to be less expensive than travelling in Europe or North America, and the quality of facilities and infrastructure is generally high. Among the best deals are national parks and reserves, which offer excellent, accessible wildlife-watching at significantly lower prices than you would pay in parts of East Africa.

Mealtimes

South African cuisine is cosmopolitan and children will soon spot many familiar dishes among those offered. In every small town there are steakhouses and pizzerias. Avoid chicken-based fast food, as it is often very poor. Near the Cape, children will love fillets of fish in breadcrumbs. You'll need to adapt to South African hours, with dinner generally served around 6pm.

HEALTH CHECK

» Malaria is present year-round in the northeast, particularly in the border regions with Mozambique and Zimbabwe, including Kruger National Park. An antimalarial treatment is recommended.

» Private hospital care is very good but expensive. Take out international assistance insurance.

GETTING AROUND

The best way to get around South Africa with children is to rent a car (the road network is excellent). For long distances you can choose between the plane and train, which serve the major towns. Municipal buses, taxi mini-buses and ordinary taxis are great for travelling across town. From Cape Town to Durban, children will love climbing on board a *rikki* (small open lorry) or tuk-tuk (motorised tricycle).

> ❗ **Warning**
> → Many lodges refuse to take children under 12, which limits your choices to camping or bungalows.
> → For safety reasons, do not travel at night on foot or by car. Avoid deserted places and lock car doors.
> → When you swim, keep a close eye on your things. Theft is not unusual.

> 🕑 **Time difference**
> → Time zone UTC+02:00

BOOKS FOR THE YOUNG TRAVELLER

> *Indaba My Children*, by Vusamazulu Credo Mutwa, is an interesting book of folk tales, history, legends, customs and beliefs.

> For older children, *Waiting for the Rain: A Novel of South Africa*, by Sheila Gordon, is a story about a black boy and a white boy whose friendship is torn apart by apartheid.

CHILDREN'S SOUVENIRS

> A game of *jukskei*, a traditional sport where you throw a wooden skittle at a wooden baton stuck in the sand

> *Mefuhva*, a strategic board game

TANZANIA & ZANZIBAR

Tanzania offers children plenty of opportunities to be downright amazed! There is the incredible wildlife in the national parks, lakes as vast as the sea, stunning beaches on the Indian Ocean, and the shimmering island of Zanzibar. The unfailingly warm welcome from locals only adds to the country's appeal as a great family-holiday destination.

Traditional dhows make an exciting excursion

CHILDREN WILL LOVE...
The kingdom of wild animals

» Seeing the Big Five (lion, buffalo, rhinoceros, elephant and leopard), plus wildebeest and zebras by the thousand, during a safari in the Ngorongoro Crater or on the plains of the Serengeti, where you can trade the 4WD for a hot-air balloon.
» Discovering the baboon colony, pink flamingos and giraffes in the Lake Manyara National Park, and elephants in Tarangire National Park.
» Exploring the less busy parks and reserves in the south. Head out on the River Rufiji amid hippos and crocodiles in the Selous Reserve, or visit the really wild Ruaha National Park.

» Watching the animals, boating along the Wami River and enjoying the beaches along the coast in the small Saadani Park.
» Visiting Arusha National Park. The easiest to visit without a great deal of organisation (a simple 4WD will suffice), it's perfect for children as it's not too big and has lots of animals including giraffes, buffalos, monkeys and flamingos – all with the mythical Kilimanjaro in the background!

The colours of the Indian Ocean

» Playing Robinson Crusoe on the beaches of Zanzibar – Bwejuu, Matemwe and Pongwe are among the most beautiful – and its tiny islands, including Mnemba and Chumbe.
» Exploring Stone Town, the old town of Zanzibar, and the Maruhubi Palace ruins, and soaking up the atmosphere in the markets.
» Taking an excursion on board a *dhow* to reach the island paradises close to the coast or to admire the sunset from out at sea.
» Snorkelling to better observe the fish and coral in the marine parks on the island of Mafia, at Mnazi Bay or from any beach on Zanzibar.

Magical landscapes and towns

» The fabulous region of Lushoto, dotted with volcanic calderas, and the Usambra Mountains with picturesque villages.
» Boating on the great lakes of Tanganyika, Malawi (Nyassa) and Victoria, making stops in small ports.
» The village markets, exploding with colour, and *mnada* (fairs) organised by the Maasai once a month.

BEST TIME TO GO

Tanzania can be visited from July to March. The parks in the north can be cool in July, but the November showers are not usually a problem. During the rainy season (April to June), most of the park roads are impassable, and on the coast many hotels close.

COST

Tanzania is not the cheapest country in Africa, and thanks to tourism, prices in Zanzibar keep rising. That said, they are still good-value destinations in Western terms, and reasonably priced accommodation is not hard to find. Restaurants geared towards tourists can be expensive; the places where locals eat (which often serve Indian food) are cheaper. Although seafood is plentiful, it can be expensive, so check out a few restaurants before you dine, and look out for the daily specials. In Stone Town, cheap, freshly caught fish is fried in front of you at the nightly waterfront market. Museums and sights are cheap or free, but boat excursions are pricier. Don't fall for the unbelievably cheap safaris and tours offered on the street by scammers; book through an established and reputable agency.

Mealtimes

Delicious beef or chicken is often on the menu (watch out for the spices), served with rice or chips. There is also a lot of *nyama choma* (roasted meat). Lodges generally offer top-notch cuisine to suit Western tastes, using very fresh ingredients. The fish and seafood are delicious on the coast and on Zanzibar and Pemba islands. Near the lakes, tilapia, a freshwater fish with tender meat, is much appreciated by children. Tanzania is one giant orchard where children can get their fill of juicy, sweet fruit.

BOOKS FOR THE YOUNG TRAVELLER

> *The Clever Tortoise: A Traditional African Tale*, by Francesca Martin, is an illustrated book that young children should enjoy.

CHILDREN'S SOUVENIRS

> Maasai bracelets and necklaces

> Maasai blankets

> Tingatinga paintings (named for the artist)

HEALTH CHECK

»   Malaria is rife across the country, and dengue is also present. A preventative treatment is necessary.

»   For Tarangire and the parks in the centre, take thick clothes, preferably pale colours, to protect you from tsé-tsé fly bites, which are very painful.

GETTING AROUND

Hiring a car (usually a 4WD) normally includes a driver in Tanzania, except in Zanzibar. Buses are often the only way to get around; choose the express, which stops less frequently and is less crammed. Use the *dalla-dalla* (minibus) for short journeys, but not with very young children. Avoid the train. Be careful of old and overloaded ferries. You should only use shuttle services with modern catamarans to reach Zanzibar from the mainland. Regular ferry lines on lakes Tanganyika, Malawi (Nyassa) and Victoria cannot be recommended.

ⓘ Warning

⤳   Under-sevens are excluded from most parks. In any case, the safari lifestyle is not ideal for young children.

⤳   Certain camps refuse children under 12.

⤳   Never leave your child unsupervised in the camps or lodges.

🕐 Time difference

⤳   Time zone UTC+03:00

TUNISIA

The hotel clubs on the Tunisian coast welcome young children with open arms to the country's many superb beaches – all just a short hop from Europe. Older children can get a glimpse of a more adventurous Tunisia by heading for the desert dunes and the famous *Star Wars* set.

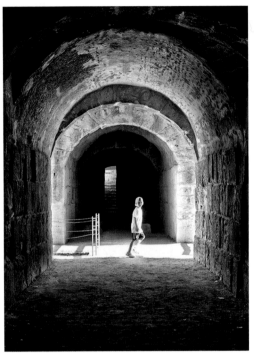

In the footsteps of gladiators

CHILDREN WILL LOVE...
Refreshing paddles
» The combination of warm seas (23°C) and some of the most beautiful beaches on the Mediterranean.
» The waterfalls at Tamerza, a fortified mountain village.
» The warm springs in the shade of a palm grove at Ksar Ghilane oasis.

Underground houses and *The Phantom Menace*
» Berber houses built underground at Matmata. The children will love sleeping in a troglodyte hotel, and the Sidi Driss Hotel was Luke Skywalker's childhood home in the *Star Wars* movies.
» The *Star Wars* locations near Tozeur, including the village of Mos Espa (Ksar Hadada), which was built for *The Phantom Menace*; admiring the dunes at Tatooine desert (Onk Djemel); Tatooine canyon (Sidi Bouhlel); and Tatooine desert and Lars homestead (Chott el-Djérid), where Luke is arrested in front of a crater.

The East as depicted in legend and picture books
» An hour-long ride on a camel at Douz to see the magnificent dunes.
» The El Jem amphitheatre, the biggest Roman amphitheatre in North Africa, where gladiators once fought.
» The hectic, colourful souks in Tunis, Sousse or Hammamet, where they might unearth the genie's lamp or Aladdin's slippers.
» The Chak Wak Park, on the threshold of Tozeur, which tells the story of our planet: from the dinosaurs to the Punic Wars, with more than a nod to biblical times. The best bit: a reproduction of Noah's Ark with the animals!
» Carthage Land, a Punic theme park, featuring rides and entertainment based on the epic story of Hannibal.

BEST TIME TO GO

Spring and autumn are the best seasons for discovering Tunisia with children, particularly May to June and September to October. In summer, stick to the Mediterranean coast, where it is cooler (but the beach resorts are jam-packed). Swimming is possible until the end of October, when the water temperature is still above 20°C. In winter the temperatures are cooler and most hotels close.

COST

Tunisia's prices lie between Morocco and Egypt. There are resort towns existing almost solely for tourism, which can get very expensive, but generally speaking it is good value. Taking tours, staying in luxury accommodation and travelling in the high season will greatly increase your expenditure.

Mealtimes

In the coastal resorts, chicken, pasta, pizza, pancakes and sandwiches go side-by-side with snacks such as chapati (folded flat bread filled with tuna, eggs and chopped potato). But for most children, Tunisia will be couscous heaven (with meat, fish or vegetables). While doughnuts sprinkled with *yoyo* (sugar) or *babalouni* (honey) may soon be the only thing that will do for a sweet snack in the afternoon. Be careful in the *gargotes* (cafes), where the food can be heavily spiced.

HEALTH CHECK

» Health services are good in the big towns. Elsewhere, medicines and equipment can be patchy.

GETTING AROUND

When you hire a car, make sure it has air conditioning. International agencies usually have child seats available. Otherwise, the transport network – buses, communal taxis (*louages*), trains – is pretty good. For long journeys, take night buses to avoid the heat.

! **Warning**

→ Bear in mind the political uncertainty. Demonstrations are often held in the towns. Check government travel advice before booking and departure, and avoid mass gatherings.

→ Sometimes there are jellyfish. Swimmers should check with local residents before diving in.

→ Be careful not to lose your children in the souks.

🕐 **Time difference**

→ UTC+01:00.

BOOKS FOR THE YOUNG TRAVELLER

› Editions Alif makes an excellent series of pop-up books about Tunisian life; the only English title is *The Tunis Medina: A Walk Through an Arab City*.

› Look out for a series of books about Tunisian crafts aimed at seven- to 10-year-olds by author/illustrator May Angeli.

CHILDREN'S SOUVENIRS

› A Berber doll

› A cuddly toy camel

Middle East

In the Middle East, children are kings and yours will be no exception. Travelling with the family opens all doors. In tourist areas you will attract sympathy and kindness, on buses people will give up their seats, you will get the best rooms in hotels, and no-one will take offence if your children play up in restaurants.

It will be a fantastic experience to explore the souks together: throw yourselves into it and give your offspring a rudimentary lesson in bargaining by buying a few trinkets.

The rich vein of archaeological sites throughout the region will rouse the children's intellectual curiosity and imagination. Set in a landscape worthy of The Arabian Nights, the ruined city of Petra in Jordan, the sultans' palaces in İstanbul or the old town in Jerusalem will take them on a journey through time. The Middle East also offers the chance to visit many sacred sites such as the Wailing Wall in Jerusalem.

After the cultural visits, there is time to relax and enjoy a swim. The Middle East has a large number of well-set-up coastal resorts like Aqaba in Jordan, Eilat in Israel, and Bodrum in Turkey. And why not sail on a gület along the Turkish coast or aboard a dhow around Muscat in Oman? Also take the family on a few trips into the desert: play at Lawrence of Arabia with the Bedouins of Wadi Rum in Jordan, hurtle down the sand dunes in the United Arab Emirates or explore Negev in Israel. All undertaken in comfort and less than four hours from Europe.

DUBAI & THE UNITED ARAB EMIRATES

A futuristic city perched on the edge of the Persian Gulf, Dubai is an easy holiday destination with children, as long as you take care in the sun. But there's a lot more to it than just sandcastles and sea. When you tire of the city, you can leave it behind and head off for a desert adventure in complete safety.

Every kid wants to slide down a sand dune

CHILDREN WILL LOVE...
Futuristic buildings
» The skyscrapers, including the Burj al-Arab, shaped like a sail hoisted above the water.
» The Burj Khalifa, the highest building in the world at 828m! Take the lift, which shoots up 124 floors in just a few seconds – quite an experience for anyone, but especially a child.
» Palm Jumeirah, an artificial peninsula in the shape of a palm tree with amazing villas and hotels.

Beaches and water sports
» Beaches, such as Jumeirah Beach Park, positioned on the edge of parks allowing you to play in the shade.
» Beaches at the luxury hotels (open to non-residents), offering water sports and great facilities for children.

Traditions full of Eastern promise
» An excursion on board a dhow (small, traditional sailboat). Set off from Abu Dhabi along the coast to see fishing ports and dolphins.
» Spectating at a horse race and going to watch the camels train at the camel racetrack.
» Watching a falcon on the wing at the Heritage Village (Abu Dhabi), a well thought-out museum on Emirate traditions.
» A glimpse of the Emirates before the oil boom at the small emirate of Umm al-Quwain, with its old town, superb beaches and bird colonies.
» The old district of Bur Dubai and of Shindagha, and the souks selling gold and spices in Deira.

Original experiences
» The water slides at the Wild Wadi Water Park – guaranteed thrills!
» Spending a morning surfing on the sand dunes, before throwing yourself down the slopes at Ski Dubai, the indoor snow dome at the Mall of the Emirates.
» Flying over the desert at dawn in a hot-air balloon (from age five).
» Taking a dip in the Hatta Pools in the Hajar Mountains. These natural bathing pools in the gorges are in the northeast of the Emirates.
» A 4WD excursion or camel ride into the desert from Abu Dhabi, followed by dinner in a tent with the Bedouins.

BEST TIME TO GO

October to November and March to April are the most pleasant times, as it is hot but not unbearable (30°C in the day, 20°C at night). From December to February, it is milder (24°C on average) with slightly cooler evenings. Apart from these times, the heat is infernal (48°C in July/August, and very humid) and the Emirates are best avoided, especially with children.

COST

Dubai is notoriously expensive, and it's true that those seven-star hotels are utterly exhorbitant. But more affordable (and still luxurious) accommodation is popping up all the time. On the other hand, there is practically no cheap accommodation in Abu Dhabi. Throughout the Emirates, if you avoid the top restaurants you'll find that delicious local food is quite cheap. Budget for activities such as indoor skiing, as they are quite expensive.

Mealtimes

There is a strong Lebanese influence in Dubai cuisine. Children will enjoy the mezze, and mixed grills, which let you try several different dishes. *Shwarma* (sandwiches made with pita bread) are everywhere and are tasty, filling and cheap. Specialities from Iran may be worth sampling; some kids love the spices and the sweet and savoury combinations. But with so many restaurants specialising in foreign food (European, Indian, American, Russian, Chinese) there is something for everyone. Most restaurants offer children's menus in any case.

HEALTH CHECK

» One tourist in two gets stomach trouble: avoid tap water (officially safe to drink), even for brushing teeth or in a four-star hotel.

GETTING AROUND

In Dubai, taxis, buses, *abra* (floating taxis) and the driverless metro make getting around easy. Collective taxis are practical for longer journeys. Driving in the Emirates can be epic – the Emirati tend to follow their own personal highway code. Nonetheless, with a little care, hiring a car can be the best way to tackle a one- or two-day trip from Dubai.

ⓘ **Warning**

→ During the month of Ramadan, it is forbidden to eat, drink or smoke in public during daylight hours. Some businesses close or operate on limited hours. However, children are not affected, and some restaurants, especially in international hotels, remain open. Planning ahead and acquainting yourself with local customs will allow you to enjoy your holiday regardless.

🕐 **Time difference**

→ Time zone UTC+04:00

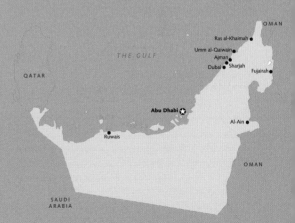

BOOKS FOR THE YOUNG TRAVELLER

› *The Turtle Secret*, by Julia Johnson, is a great story for pre-teens that touches on the wildlife and culture of the Emirates.

› *I Spy From a Beach in Dubai*, by Suzanne Kalloghlian, is an inspirational rhyming picture book for little ones.

CHILDREN'S SOUVENIRS

› Ballet slippers, tiaras and clothes weighed down by sequins to play Scheherazade

› Cuddly toy camels: small, large or huge!

ISRAEL

In Israel your children will have every opportunity to test their knowledge of history in a fun way. But it is not about turning your holiday into just another lesson: beaches on the Mediterranean and Red Sea are great for swimming and the desert offers the possibility of trips not to be missed.

Archaeological sites, blue skies and the sea never far away

CHILDREN WILL LOVE...
Jerusalem, sacred and fun
» A city bus tour of Jerusalem to catch the most important sites.
» The Time Elevator: an interactive experience ideal for sharing the city's past with children. You will find it as moving as the floor and seats!
» Playing Indiana Jones in the 500m-long Hezekiah's Tunnel, carved out an astonishing 3000 years ago.
» The biblical Zoo. Here you will find the animals mentioned in the Bible, even those that are no longer found in Israel today, such as crocodiles.

A walk through the pages of history
» The cable car that climbs up to the top of the cliff and on to the Masada Fortress ruins. The views of the Dead Sea and the surrounding desert are absolutely stunning.
» The remains of Caesarea, where you can see the Roman amphitheatre and the defences built by the Crusaders.
» The caves and galleries of Beit Guvrin and the ruins of Tel Maresha, the largest Hellenistic city in the region.
» The fortified town dominating the port and the underground Crusader town of Akko (Acre).

Natural surprises
» Floating effortlessly, as though by magic, in the Dead Sea.
» Hiking in the Ein Gedi National Park, an oasis in the middle of the desert with lush vegetation and pools for a dip.
» Taking a camel ride in the Judean desert leaving from Kfar Hanokdim, an oasis with resident Bedouins near Masada. Similar excursions are also possible from Eilat.

Family fun
» Diving at Eilat, the famous (and very busy) beach resort on the Red Sea. Head for the Underwater Observatory to study the Red Sea's rich marine life while keeping dry behind huge glass windows.
» Tel Aviv, where they can try the local sport *matkot* (beach tennis) at Gordon Beach and Frishman Beach.
» Mini Israel at Latrun, near Jerusalem. To-scale models of the main historic sites and monuments. Many scenes have moving parts and figures – great fun for children.

BEST TIME TO GO

Israel is a suitable destination any time of year. With children, though, spring and autumn offer the best conditions. In summer the heat can be overwhelming, especially in the south, and the humidity can be a nuisance on the coast. In winter it can be cold on the high ground, and snow sometimes falls on Jerusalem where the temperature settles at around 10°C at this time of year. During Jewish religious festivals, such as Passover, life can become more difficult for visitors: shops close, transport is reduced and the price of accommodation rises.

COST

Israel is not a cheap country and you can expect to pay standard Western prices for most goods and services. Children receive discounts at museums and historic sites. Look out for special internet-only deals for hotels.

HEALTH CHECK

» It is wise to protect the family from insect bites, mainly to avoid the West Nile virus, which is transmitted by mosquito bites and can be present in Israel.

GETTING AROUND

Israel is a small country, easy to travel around by road, particularly as the road system is in a good state of repair. Rapid, comfortable buses serve the whole country, but do not operate on Saturdays (Shabbat, the Jewish day of rest). Collective taxis called *sherut* or 'service taxis' run frequently and have set routes, like buses. It is best to hire a car before leaving your own country, as it is cheaper than hiring one when you arrive.

Mealtimes

Children will really like Israeli cuisine with pita bread dipped in hummus (chickpea purée) or filled with falafels (deep fried balls made from chickpeas), schnitzel (meat in breadcrumbs) or meatballs. Kebabs are always a hit, as are eastern pastries with poppy seeds, honey or dates. The fruit is delicious. Like many young Israelis, your children may appreciate *bamba* (snacks of puffed corn with peanut butter).

! Warning
→ Due to ongoing tensions in and around Israel, check government travel advice prior to booking and departing.

🕐 Time difference
→ Time zone UTC+02:00. Daylight saving time observed in northern hemisphere summer.

BOOKS FOR THE YOUNG TRAVELLER

> Ann Levine's *Running on Eggs* is the story of an Israeli girl and a Palestinian girl who reach across the hostility of their respective communities in friendship.

> Pack an illustrated retelling of classic Bible stories so you can explain the ancient sights.

CHILDREN'S SOUVENIRS

> Hanukkah spinning tops

> Wooden paddles for playing *matkot* (beach tennis)

JORDAN

Moses, the Romans, the Crusaders, Lawrence of Arabia, Indiana Jones! Jordan is a picture book where mythical characters jostle with historic figures. The Jordanians love of children helps make this one of the most enjoyable destinations to visit in the Middle East.

Petra fulfils children's fantasies

CHILDREN WILL LOVE...
Incredible journeys through time
» The Siq, the narrow, 1500m-long passage that serves as the main entrance to Petra, the ancient Nabataean capital, where *Indiana Jones and the Last Crusade* was filmed. You can explore the huge site on a donkey to avoid over-tired children.

» Jerash, one of the most beautiful Roman cities in the Middle East. Children will not want to miss the chariot races and circus games organised every day in the hippodrome.
» Following in the footsteps of Moses at ancient sites in the Jordan Valley, such as Madaba and Mount Nebo: a fun introduction to the stories in the Bible.
» The palaces of the Arab rulers at Qasr Amra and in the eastern desert.
» The 12th-century Crusader fortresses of Karak and Shobak.

Desert sands and green spaces
» The Wadi Rum desert and its red rocks. A night in a Bedouin tent will be an unforgettable experience for everyone.
» Exploring the desert astride a horse or camel, accompanied by a guide or organised through a local agency.
» The Dana Nature Reserve, the most beautiful in the country and one of the few green spaces in Jordan. Parents and kids will have a blast sleeping in an old village house.

Fun swims
» Snorkelling amid the rich underwater colours in the Red Sea.
» Floating without swimming at the Dead Sea. On the shore, the Al-Wadi complex has a pool with a wave machine and water slides.
» The warm waters of Hammamat Ma'in springs, where there is a small family pool.

BEST TIME TO GO

Spring (mid-March to the end of April) and autumn (end of September to mid-October), when the heat is not too intense, are the best seasons for exploring the country with children. In winter, even if it is cool in the north with occasional heavy rain in January and February, you can still swim in the Red Sea and visit Petra without any discomfort. Ramadan, when many businesses open for limited hours, requires planning.

COST

Jordan is not the cheapest country in the area to travel around, but if you spend wisely, good value can be found all over the country. Street snacks such as a felafel or shwarma sandwich are cheap, and so is public transport. The range of accommodation costs are comparable with the USA. One of the biggest sightseeing expenses in Jordan is the entrance fee to Petra (which rises during high season), but it's so worth it! Jerash is not quite so expensive, and most other places are free or cost just a dinar or two.

HEALTH CHECK

» Beware of potentially serious sunburn and heat stroke.
» Make sure you have something with you to treat small cuts from the coral.

Mealtimes

The bread (*khobz* or pita) is delicious and usually on the table at every meal. It goes well with mezze, from neighbouring Lebanon, which allows children to taste a range of dishes. Young carnivores will appreciate shawarma, a sandwich filled with mutton or chicken cooked on the spit, which is fairly common. For a bit of a change, let the children taste *mensaf*, the national dish comprising lamb cooked in milk and served on a bed of rice and pine nuts. Pastries take pride of place at dessert. Outside Amman and nearby towns, hardly any restaurants are open after 8pm.

BOOKS FOR THE YOUNG TRAVELLER
› Pack a biography of Lawrence of Arabia; Alistair MacLean's is a good choice for young readers.
CHILDREN'S SOUVENIRS
› A game of *tawlah* (backgammon)

GETTING AROUND

There is only one internal flight (Amman to Aqaba) and no railway, so roads are the primary way to get from A to B. Public minibuses are a good option and an efficient way to reach Petra and Jerash, but children may find the wait tedious: the bus will only leave once it is full, and that can take time. Tourist buses are a better bet than local buses. For destinations off the beaten track it is best to hire a car (a 4WD is only necessary for the most remote desert locations), which allows you to use the most spectacular routes and reach really isolated sites. Collective taxis are just as good for travelling between towns.

ⓘ Warning

→ Equip children with swimming goggles in the Dead Sea. Avoid swimming in it if anyone has small cuts or sores: the salty water can really hurt.
→ Take plastic sandals for the Red Sea: the scorpion fish has an extremely painful sting and hides just under the sand.
→ Warnings are currently in place advising travellers to avoid areas near the Syrian and Iraqi borders.

🕑 Time difference

→ Time zone UTC+03:00. Daylight saving time observed in northern hemisphere summer.

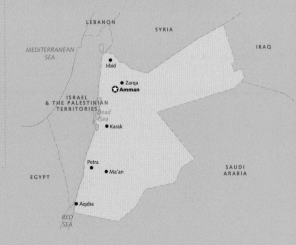

OMAN

A relatively unknown destination, authenticity is Oman's trump card: an unspoilt landscape nestling between the mountains and the sea, an identity firmly anchored in a tradition of openness. The land of Sinbad the Sailor is the ideal destination for the family to discover some genuine jewels of the Arabian Peninsula in perfect safety and comfort.

Swimming holes in the wadis are an Omani highlight

CHILDREN WILL LOVE...
Muscat, the capital of incense
» Old Muscat, with its lime-washed houses and mosques standing in the shadows of the fortresses of Al-Mirani and Al-Jalali. Don't forget the obligatory stop to pose in front of the Sultan's Palace.
» Mutrah souk, bathed in the heady perfume of incense and spices and particularly lively come evening. Stop by the fish market in the same district – equally pungent!
» The Grand Mosque – which is really grand – a breathtaking example of modern architecture.

Traditions that live on
» A sense of reaching the end of the world in the fishing villages at the foot of the steep cliffs of Musandam, a number of which are only accessible by sea.
» A visit to watch dhow (Arab sailboats) under construction at Sur and dreaming about being Sinbad.
» Meeting Bedouin families who live by breeding camels and goats in the Sharqiya (Wahiba) Sands.

Fortress road
» Nakhal Fort, perched majestically on a rocky outcrop overlooking a vast plain of date groves.
» Nizwa Fort and its huge round tower. Watch out for the many traps set for assailants, such as hatches that give way under your feet and openings from which to pour boiling date oil.
» Jabrin Fort, ringed by sturdy ramparts and with splendid decorated ceilings, and the huge Bahla Fort with its crude brick walls and towers. Proof that there are a thousand ways to be a knight or princess!

Natural wonders on land
» A camel ride in the Sharqiya (Wahiba) Sands, sunset in the ochre dunes, then a night spent in a traditional shelter.
» The wadi (valleys) in the Oman Mountains with pools carved into the rock for spontaneous dips. Do not miss the Wadi Bani Khalid, one of the most beautiful.
» Exploring the many grottoes and caverns, such as the Al-Hoota cave, with its wall-to-wall stalactites, stalagmites and karst crystal, all seen from on board a small electric train.

... and at sea
» A cruise on board a dhow, escorted by dolphins, leaving from Muscat. In February and March you can even see whales!
» Snorkelling or an introduction to diving (from eight years) around Muscat – the corals and marine wildlife are dazzling.
» A guided visit to see the turtles in the Ras al-Jinz natural reserve (all year, but mainly June to September).
» Swimming in warm, turquoise waters. The Salalah region has particularly beautiful beaches, with fine white sand.
» Kayaking in the Arabian fjords around the Musandam Peninsula (for bigger children).

BEST TIME TO GO

The best time to visit Oman is between November and mid-March, when daytime temperatures average 25°C. The rest of the year, the heat is a killer throughout most of the country. The monsoon hits the south between mid-June and August. From mid-September, the rain evaporates and any greenery along with it.

COST

Oman is one of the most affordable countries in the Middle East, but that doesn't mean it's cheap. Accommodation is the biggest expense, along with getting around, as you will most likely need to hire a car or take a tour (but petrol isn't costly at all). Eating and sightseeing, however, are quite reasonable. Hotels and restaurants charge a 17% tax.

Mealtimes

Many dishes comprise rice with meat or fish, all flavoured with spices such as cardamom and saffron. Indian cuisine (think tandoori and biryanis) is also widely available. You will also find regional specialities such as meat skewers, mezze and falafels. For really stubborn non-eaters, there are the usual pizzas and burgers. Your children will love the tropical fruits and dates. For drinks, try camel's milk whenever you get the chance, rose flavoured milk or warm ginger milk.

HEALTH CHECK

» Guard against sunburn! Protect children well.

GETTING AROUND

The car is king in the Sultanate of Oman, which has an extensive network of roads and trails. Hiring a car can be a good way to get around. A scrupulous respect of the highway code is expected. Buses operate in major towns. For greater comfort you can fly between Muscat and Salalah. Minibuses and collective taxis are the cheapest form of travel, however they are not always practical with children. Muscat, a bit like Dubai, is not a town that you can explore easily on foot.

ⓘ Warning

⤳ Life slows down considerably during Ramadan. A number of shops and other establishments close their doors.

⤳ Watch out for snakes and scorpions in the desert, and snakes, ray fish and jellyfish in the sea.

🕓 Time difference

⤳ Time zone UTC+04:00

BOOKS FOR THE YOUNG TRAVELLER
> *The Turtle of Oman*, by Naomi Shihab Nye, is a gentle novel for pre-teens about a boy whose family is leaving his beloved Oman.

CHILDREN'S SOUVENIRS
> A thousand and one shining baubles
> Cuddly toy camels
> Incense

TURKEY

With its azure seas and mysterious fairy chimneys, its ancient ruins and exotic bazaars, Turkey is everything any child could wish for. It is an easy destination for a family. You can visit the country for its beaches (perhaps under sail) or mountains, particularly Cappadocia.

Fairy chimneys truly make a magical sight

CHILDREN WILL LOVE...

Fairy-tale İstanbul

» The bazaars, where the smallest trinket seems like a valuable treasure.
» A cruise on the Bosphorus or the Golden Horn.
» The mosques (the Blue Mosque), museums (Aya Sofya), and palaces from the *Arabian Nights* (Topkapı, Dolmabahçe).
» A bike ride or tour in a phaeton (horse and carriage) on Princes' Islands.

Fun in the sea

» Swimming in the Mediterranean, Aegean or Black seas: there's 7000km of coastline to enjoy!
» Family outings in sea kayaks or canoes along the Turquoise Coast, leaving from Kas.
» A day-long cruise around Bodrum, Marmaris, Fethiye or Antalya on board a beautiful *gület* (traditional wooden sailing boat).

Mountain sights

» A flight in a hot-air balloon over the natural fairy chimneys (in particular Göreme) in Cappadocia.
» The spectacular underground cities, including Derinkuyu and Kaymaklı, in Cappadocia.

Ancient ruins

» The monumental sculpted heads on the summit of Mt Nemrut.
» The ruins of the Greco-Roman city of Ephesus, with Hadrian's Temple and elaborate mosaics.
» Monasteries built into the cliffs, such as Sumela in the northeast of the country.
» The tombs carved out of the rock at Fethiye, a miniature version of Petra, in Jordan.

BEST TIME TO GO

Visit in spring (April to May) or autumn (September to October), as the weather will be ideal in İstanbul and on the Aegean and Mediterranean coasts. From mid-May to September it's beach weather. Take care: the east of the country becomes a furnace in summer.

COST

Turkey is no longer a bargain-basement destination, but it still offers good value for money. Costs are lowest in eastern Anatolia, while Cappadocia, Selçuk, Pamukkale and Olympos still offer bargain prices. Prices are highest in İstanbul, İzmir, Ankara and the touristy cities on the Aegean and Mediterranean coasts, where hotels and tours are fairly pricey – Mediterranean diving, however, is good value. Food and drink are reasonably cheap, and a lot of historical sites are free.

HEALTH CHECK

»   Turkish medical services vary. The best care, provided in private hospitals in Ankara and İstanbul, is expensive. Outside the major towns, small cuts and grazes are treated by *sağlik ocaği* (chemists).

GETTING AROUND

For travel between the towns and villages, *dolmus* (a sort of minibus) are practical and friendly. There is an extensive network of comfortable and reasonably priced buses. For long distances, there is the train – a relaxing way to take in the superb landscapes – or domestic flights, which are offered by a number of carriers. Hiring a car is a good option, as the roads are in good condition, but watch out for a cavalier disregard for road rules.

Mealtimes

Children will love tasting the different mezze, hot and cold, with helpings of vegetables (puréed, in salads or as fillings), meat or seafood. Dishes include meat prepared in many different ways, often as kebabs (grilled on a skewer) or köfte (meatballs). Fish is usually grilled. Pide, a sort of Turkish pizza, is unbeatable and comes garnished with cheese, egg or minced meat. The sweet-toothed will enjoy the baklavas, *lokum* (Turkish delight) and *dondurma* (ice cream).

❗ Warning

↠ It is inadvisable to travel in the areas bordering Syria and Iraq.

🕐 Time difference

↠ Time zone UTC+02:00. Turkey observes daylight saving time in the northern hemisphere summer.

BOOKS FOR THE YOUNG TRAVELLER

› *The Stone of Destiny: Tales from Turkey*, by Elspeth Tavaci, is a rich collection aimed at pre-teens.

› *The Trojan War*, retold by Olivia E Coolidge, is a great interpretation for school children.

CHILDREN'S SOUVENIRS

› For older children, a game of *okey* or *tavla* (backgammon), two traditional Turkish board games

› Puppets or *kukla*, stars of traditional Turkish theatre

› A blue evil-eye good-luck charm, mirrors and other accessories

INDEX

ACKNOWLEDGEMENTS

Managing Director, Publishing: Piers Pickard
Associate Publisher: Robin Barton
Managing Editor: Bridget Blair
Editors: Lauren O'Connell, Ross Taylor, Simon Williamson
Layout design: Laura Jane
Cover design: Daniel Di Paolo
Image research: Barbara Di Castro, Rebecca Skinner
Image pre-press: Ryan Evans

Thanks to: Joe Bindloss, Jo Cooke, Laura Crawford, Megan Eaves, Helen Elfer, Gemma Graham, Alex Howard, Kate Morgan, MaSovaida Morgan, Karyn Noble, Lorna Parkes, Matt Phillips, Sarah Reid, James Smart, Anna Tyler, Branislava Vladisavjevic, Tasmin Waby, Dora Whitaker, Clifton Wilkinson.

Text & maps: © Lonely Planet 2015
Photographs: © Getty Images: p4 Image Source; p6 Echo; p8 Tyler Stableford; p10 mother image; p17, p212 PhotoAlto/Thierry Foulon; p18 D.R. Hutchinson; p19, p32 Chris Cheadle; p21 Ed Freeman; p23 Thomas Barwick; p24 Apeloga; p26 Uwe Krejci; p28 JGI/Jamie Grill; p29 Kav Dadfar / Design Pics; p31 Witold Skrypczak; p34 Michele Westmorland; p36, p42, p44, p204 Laurence Monneret; p38 Ryan McVay; p40 Will Gray; p44 Pete Atkinson; p44, p150, p198 David Wall Photo; p45 picturegarden; p45 Brian Lawrence; p45, p132, p148 Danita Delimont; p46 Peter Wilson; p46 Frank Deim; p46 Hedda Gjerpen; p47 Nancy Brown; p47 Kelly Cheng Travel Photography; p48 Nils-Johan Norenlind; p50 Ramiro Olaciregui; p52 amriphoto; p54 Imgorthand; p56 Beauty; p58 Wayne Walton; p60 Maya Karkalicheva; p62 Photo by cuellar; p64 Lumi Images/Dario Secen; p66 Richard Nebesky; p68 Westend61; p70 Thinkstock; p72 Cultura Travel/Philip Lee Harvey; p74, p156 Shaun Egan; p76 Karl Johaentges; p78, p172 Karan Kapoor; p80 Deejpilot; p82 An Lumatic image; p84 Laurence Monneret; p86, p130, p134, p196 Philip and Karen Smith; p88 Holger Leue; p90 Luis Davilla; p92 Alan Copson; p94 Richard Wareham; p96 no_limit_pictures; p98 Henryk T. Kaiser; p100 Trish Punch; p102 Stefan Cioata; p104 Ken Scicluna; p106 Adina Tovy; p108 littleluis; p110 caracterdesign; p112 Jan Greune; p114, p188 Ingolf Pompe; p116 HUGHES Hervé / hemis.fr; p118 Alfred Pasieka; p120 Rafael Campillo; p122 Viviane Ponti; p124 David Nunuk; p126 Michele Falzone; p128 Mike Tauber; p136 Design Pics / Keith Levit; p138 Angus Oborn; p140 Ralf Nau; p142 Walter Bibikow; p144 Oliver Strewe; p146 John White Photos; p152 Ingram Publishing; p154 Robert Churchill; p158 MATTES René / hemis.fr; p160 Poras Chaudhary; p162 Vicki Couchman; p164 Edmunds Dana; p166 Tatsuya Matsunaga; p168 Anders Blomqvist; p170 Poncho; p174 Timothy Allen; p176 Jane Sweeney; p178, p182 Jodie Griggs; p180 Imagebook; p184 Bartosz Hadyniak; p186 Olivier Cirendini; p190 John Warburton-Lee; p192 Harry Hook; p194 Clarissa Leahy; p200 Christian Aslund; p202 Mike Timo; p206 Ariadne Van Zandbergen; p208 Stefan Randholm; p210 Yellow Street Photos; p214 Adam Kuylenstierna / EyeEm; p216 Danijela Pavlovic Markovic; p218 Tom Lau; p220 Thomas Stankiewicz.

TRAVEL WITH CHILDREN

6th Edition - July 2015

Published by Lonely Planet Publications Pty Ltd
ABN 36 005 607 983

LONELY PLANET OFFICES

AUSTRALIA Locked Bag 1, Footscray, Victoria 3011

USA 150 Linden St, Oakland, CA 94607

UK 240 Blackfriars, London, SE1 8NW

ISBN 978 1 74360 789 3

Printed in China

10 9 8 7 6 5 4 3 2 1

MIX
Paper from
responsible sources
FSC™ C021741

Paper in this book is certified
against the Forest Stewardship
Council™ standards. FSC™ promotes
environmentally responsible, socially
beneficial and economically viable
management of the world's forests.

31901056494257